ART IN MOTION

Riding the Paris Metro

ART IN MOTION

Riding the Paris Metro

Anaël Pigeat

PHOTOGRAPHS BY
Philippe Garcia

ABRAMS / NEW YORK

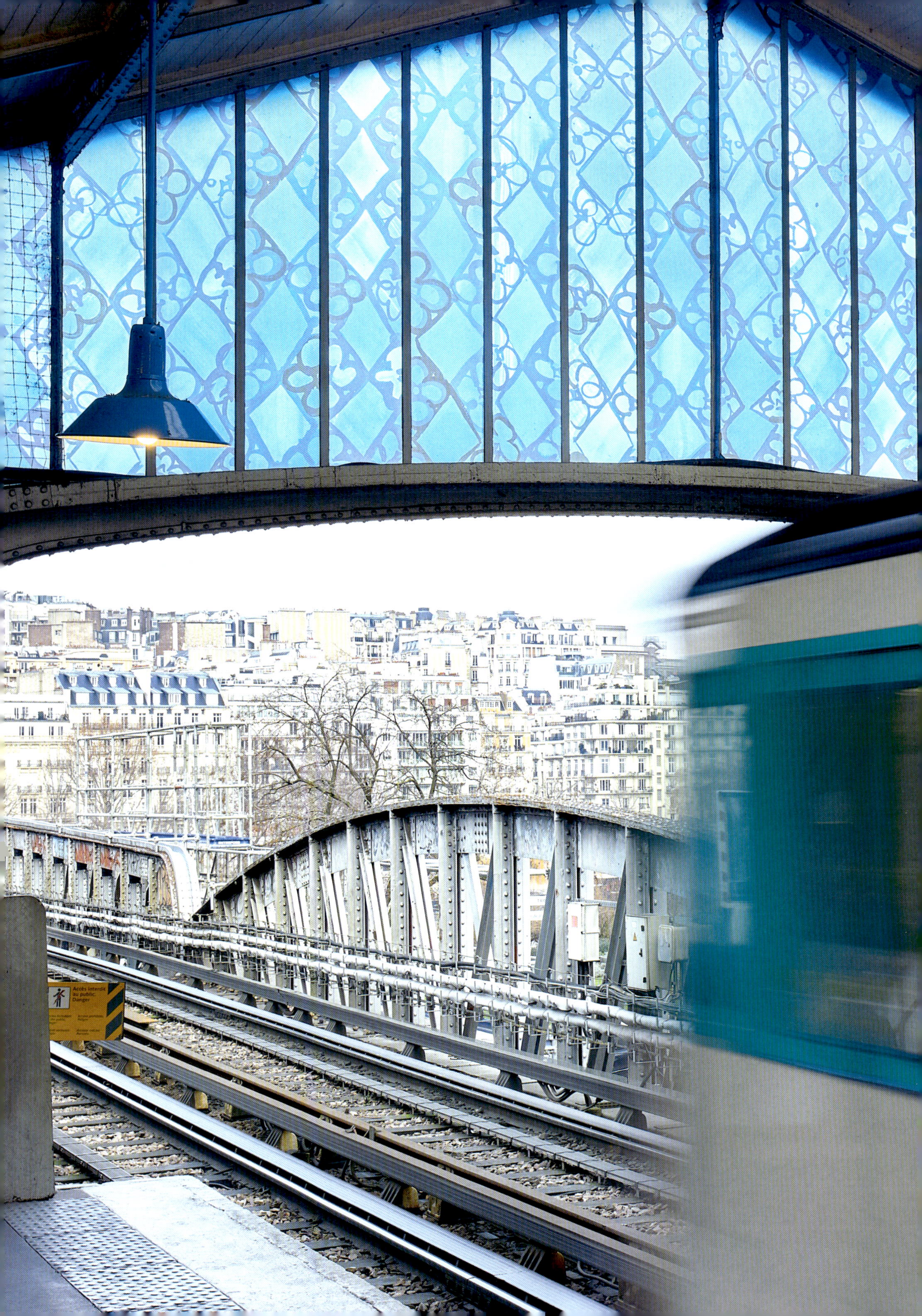
Accès interdit
au public
Danger

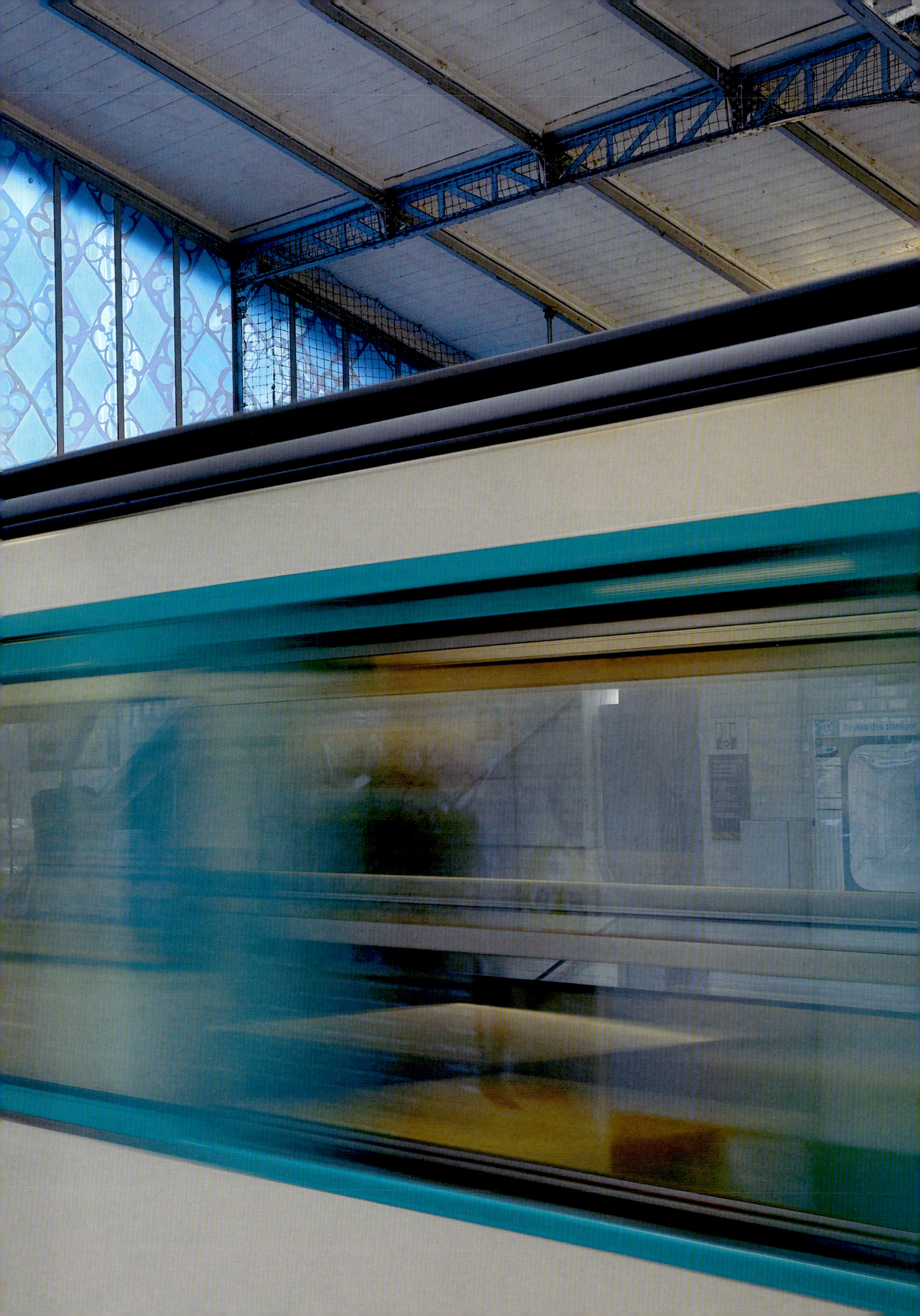

CONTENTS

ART FOR ALL, THE AMBITION FROM THE VERY BEGINNING

In 1900 the Compagnie du Chemin de Fer Métropolitain de Paris (CMP) entrusted the architect Hector Guimard, the best-known French representative of art nouveau, with the design of its station entrances. This was a fundamental act—and a mission statement. From the very beginning, the company has associated public transportation with art that is free, accessible to all, surprising, moving, and ambitious.

Art has long accompanied the modern saga of public transportation in Paris, and this unique cultural approach continues to this day.

For over a century, the Paris transportation network has been home to works by French and international artists that have enriched the journeys of commuters and tourists alike. A number of Paris metro stations are enlivened by such works: Arts et Métiers contains a fabulous submarine interior; the ceramic tiles at Concorde spell out the French text of the 1789 Declaration of the Rights of Man and of the Citizen; a stained-glass window featuring a Russian hen illuminates Madeleine; the red lips of a huge mosaic mouth adorn a corridor in Saint-Lazare; and an entirely new take on the station entrance, decorated with Murano glass beads, rises above Palais-Royal–Musée du Louvre, in front of the Comédie-Française theater.

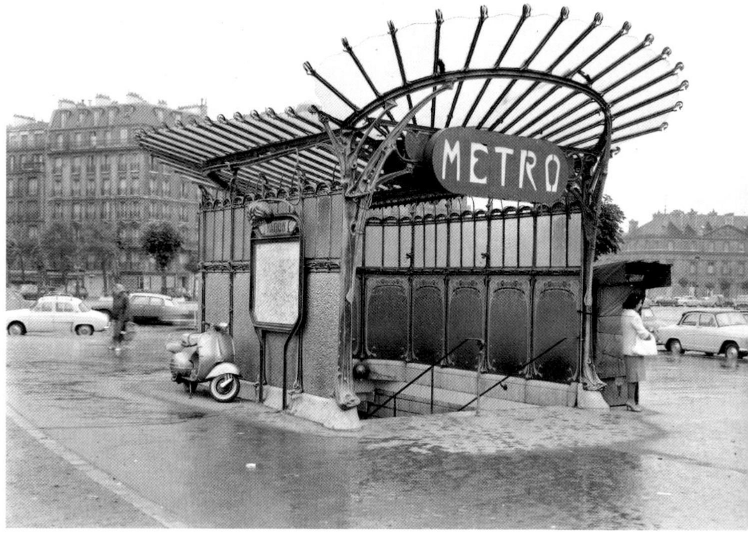

Art has always celebrated, and continues to celebrate, **the grandeur and modernity of public transportation.**

ART TO CONNECT US WITH TIME, THE ENVIRONMENT AND OTHER PEOPLE

The RATP transports and connects thousands of people every day. It is acutely aware of how necessary these connections and exchanges between territories and their inhabitants are.

And we know that art also has the extraordinary capacity to create links to both time and history. Art can bring millions of passengers in all their diversity together and has the power to break down barriers during journeys.

ART TO ENRICH DAILY COMMUTES

Being the main urban transportation operator of an area as emblematic as the Paris region means shouldering a great responsibility. While service quality is our priority, we are also concerned with enriching the passenger experience by creating positive moments.

Each work of art tells a story. Whether it is inspired by a station, commemorates a past event, interacts with the city, is part of a wider international exchange, or immerses us in an imaginary world, the artwork can engender more positive perceptions of travel.

Meeting this objective requires powerful works that go beyond the simply decorative approach. The works we commission and install are meaningful. They can immediately open eyes and minds, even though they may comprise several levels of interpretation.

Location also determines the artistic approach. The chosen space must enhance the work and vice versa, thus creating a holistic experience. The objective remains the same: obtaining a perfect alliance between artwork and architecture to increase the power of both.

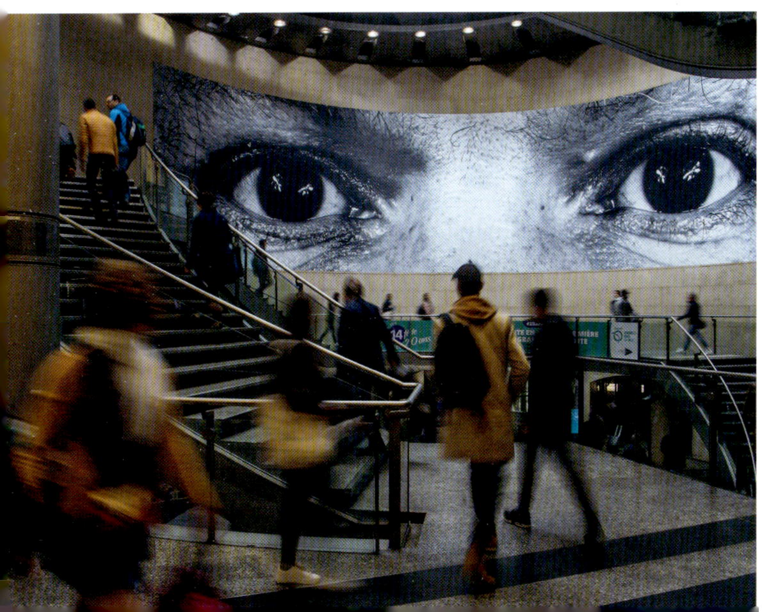

A work of art has the power **to transform passenger experiences for the better by combining efficient travel** and opportunities for discovery.

ART TO HELP US SERVE THE GENERAL INTEREST

In a way, the RATP with its millions of passengers is the most popular museum in Paris. With this comes responsibility—and the commitment inherent in our public service mission.

But how do we appeal to millions of people who might not share the same cultural references? This balancing act requires experience. For over twenty years, the RATP has been bringing poetry to life on the Paris transit network. From major works to poems written by the winners of competitions open to the public, poetry is now an essential part of the network, as are design, music, photography, and immersive installations. All these artistic genres have become part of the RATP heritage.

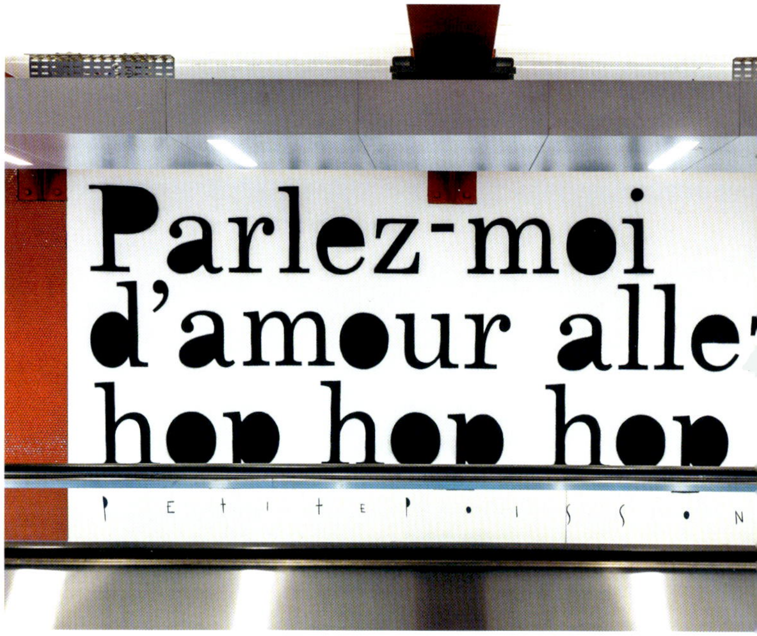

> Our aim is not to please everybody immediately but to provide **opportunities to discover and access art.** Besides, Guimard did not meet with universal approval back in the day.

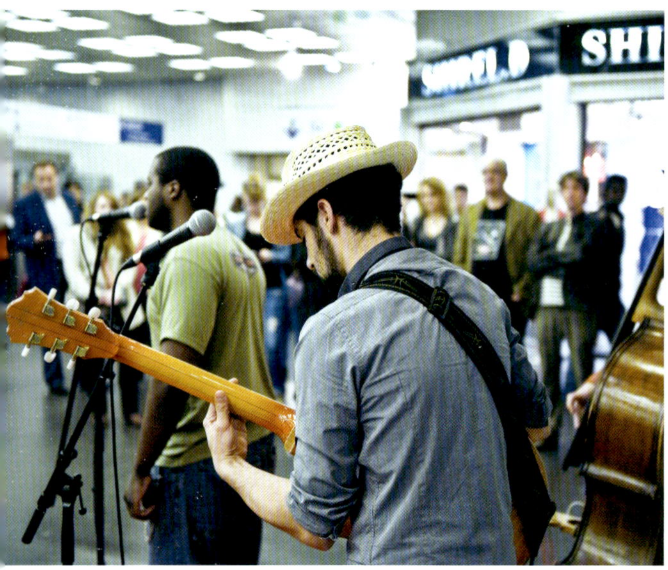

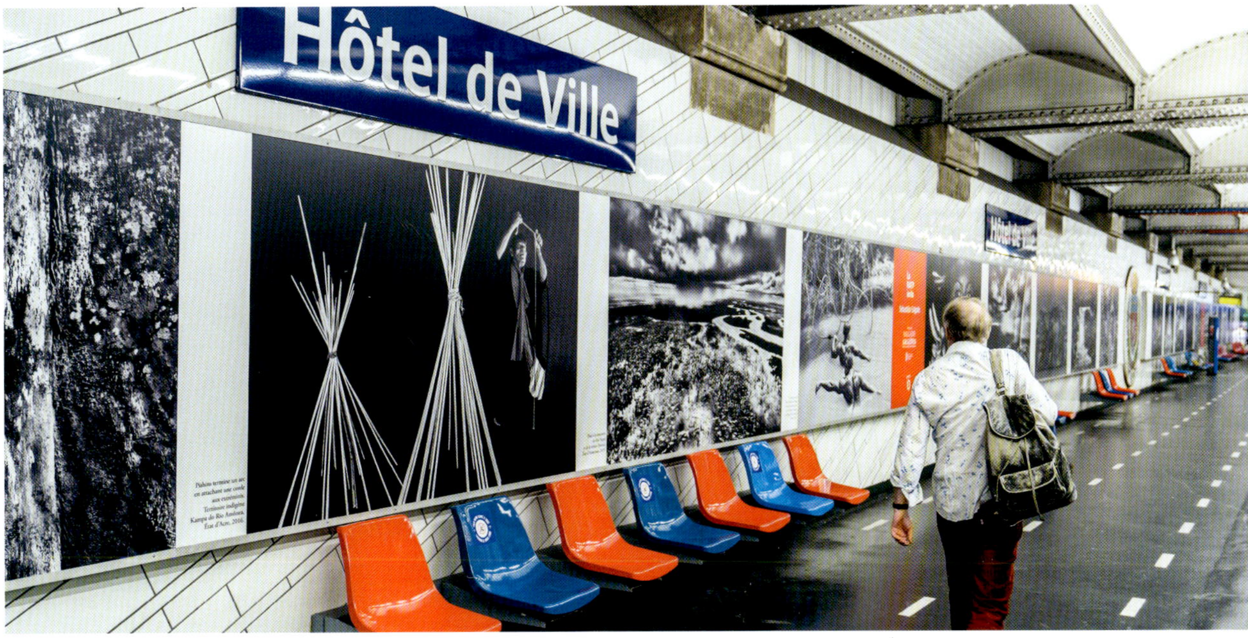

ART TO REALIZE OUR AMBITION TO CONTRIBUTE TO A BETTER CITY

Our primary mission is the provision of expert urban mobility services that respect the environment. It would be incomplete without the artistic dimension that makes us one of the main cultural actors in the city. For us, this role involves acting as a conduit for culture, promoting the wonderful cultural institutions of Paris and its region, and providing cultural programming that reveals new talent and offers unique exhibition spaces to established artists.

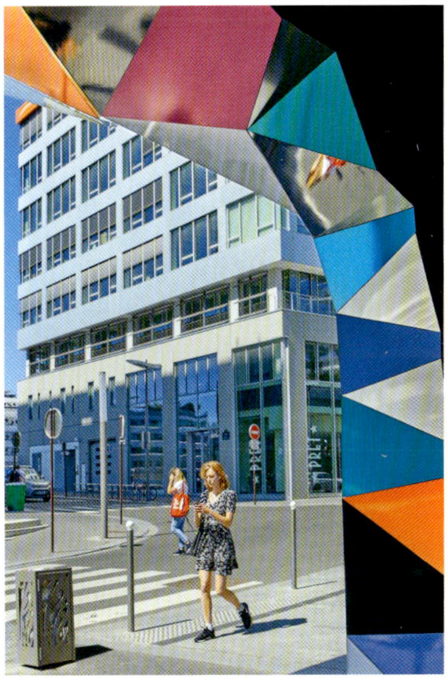

Dedicating everyday to better city living is the ambition we have set for ourselves.

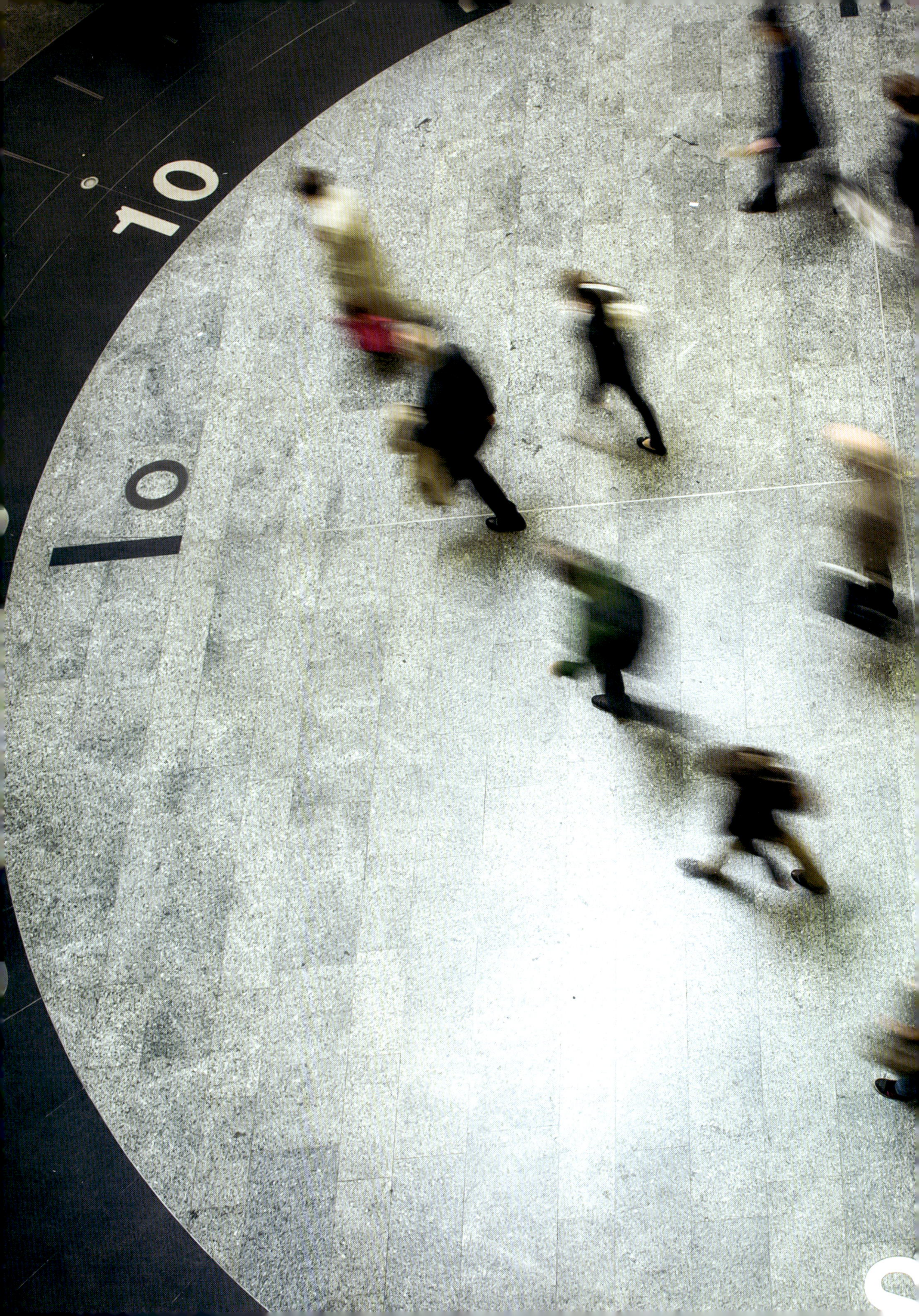

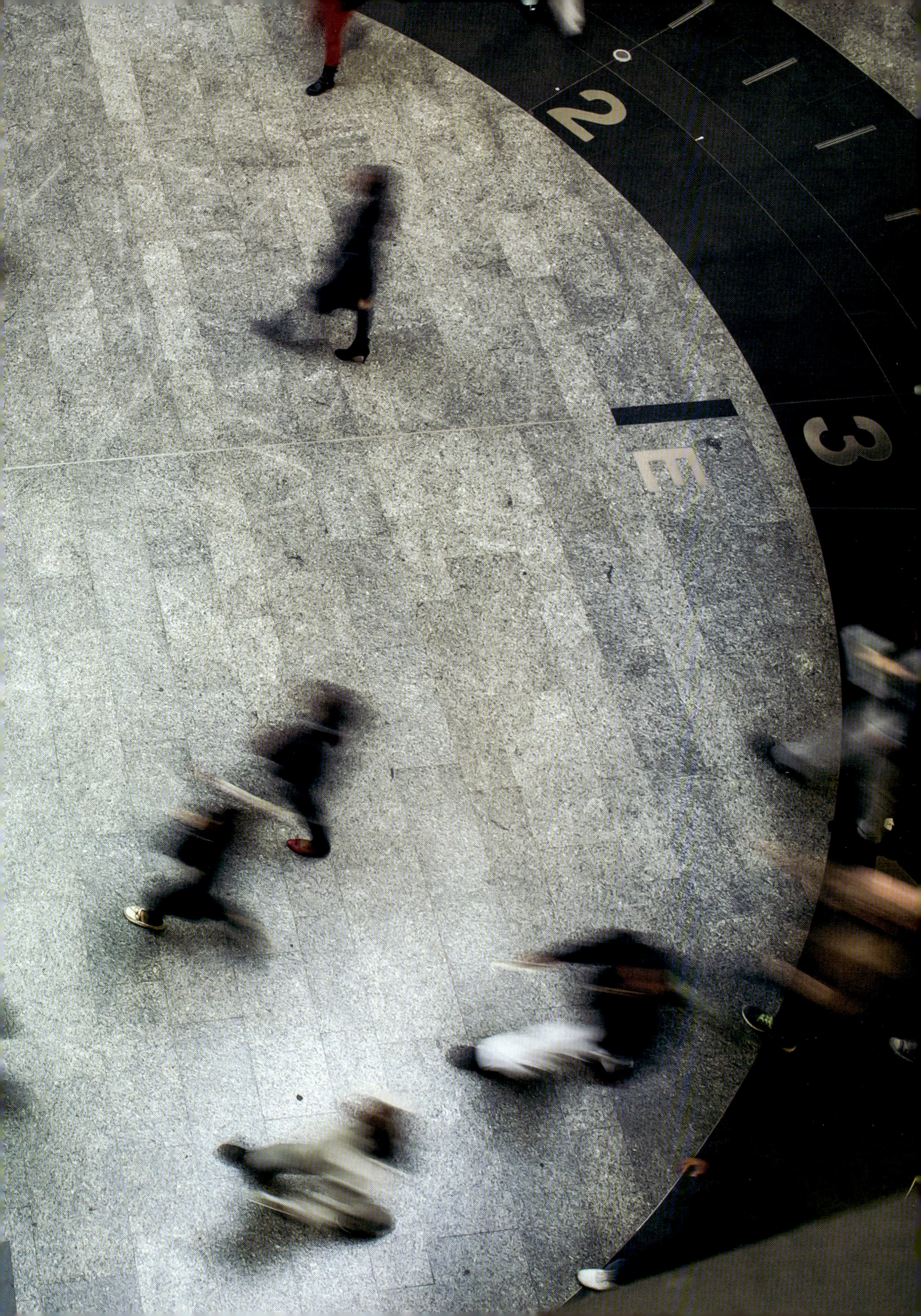
2
E
3

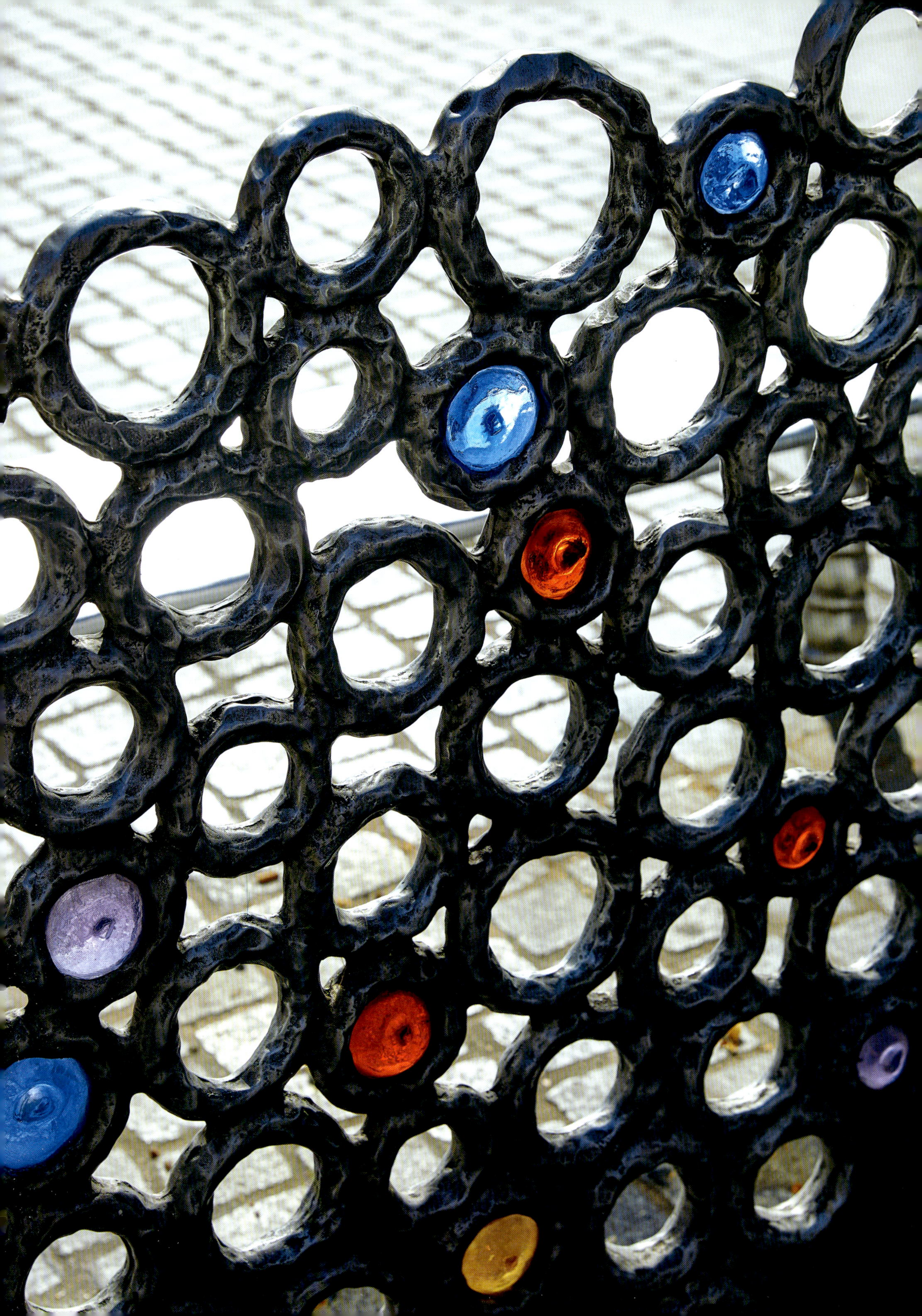

EMBLEMATIC ENTRANCES

HECTOR GUIMARD / Metro Entrances

WITH THEIR DELICATE ORGANIC SHAPES, THE METRO STATION ENTRANCES DESIGNED BY HECTOR GUIMARD HAVE LONG BEEN PART OF THE CITY'S IDENTITY. THEY HAVE LOST NONE OF THEIR POWER AND CONTINUE TO SERVE AS SOURCES OF INSPIRATION FOR THE METRO OF TOMORROW.

A DESIGN COMPETITION

In 1899, when the first metro lines were being built, a competition for the design of the entrances was launched. None of the candidates proved satisfactory, so Hector Guimard was chosen for the job without having to compete. Ten years previously, he had attracted a great deal of attention with his electricity pavilion for the Universal Exposition and his buildings in the western neighborhoods of Paris, designed after a trip to Brussels where he had discovered the work of Victor Horta. Guimard's metro entrances have become emblems of Paris around the world as they embody the atmosphere of joy and artistic boldness that reigned over the city at the turn of the twentieth century.

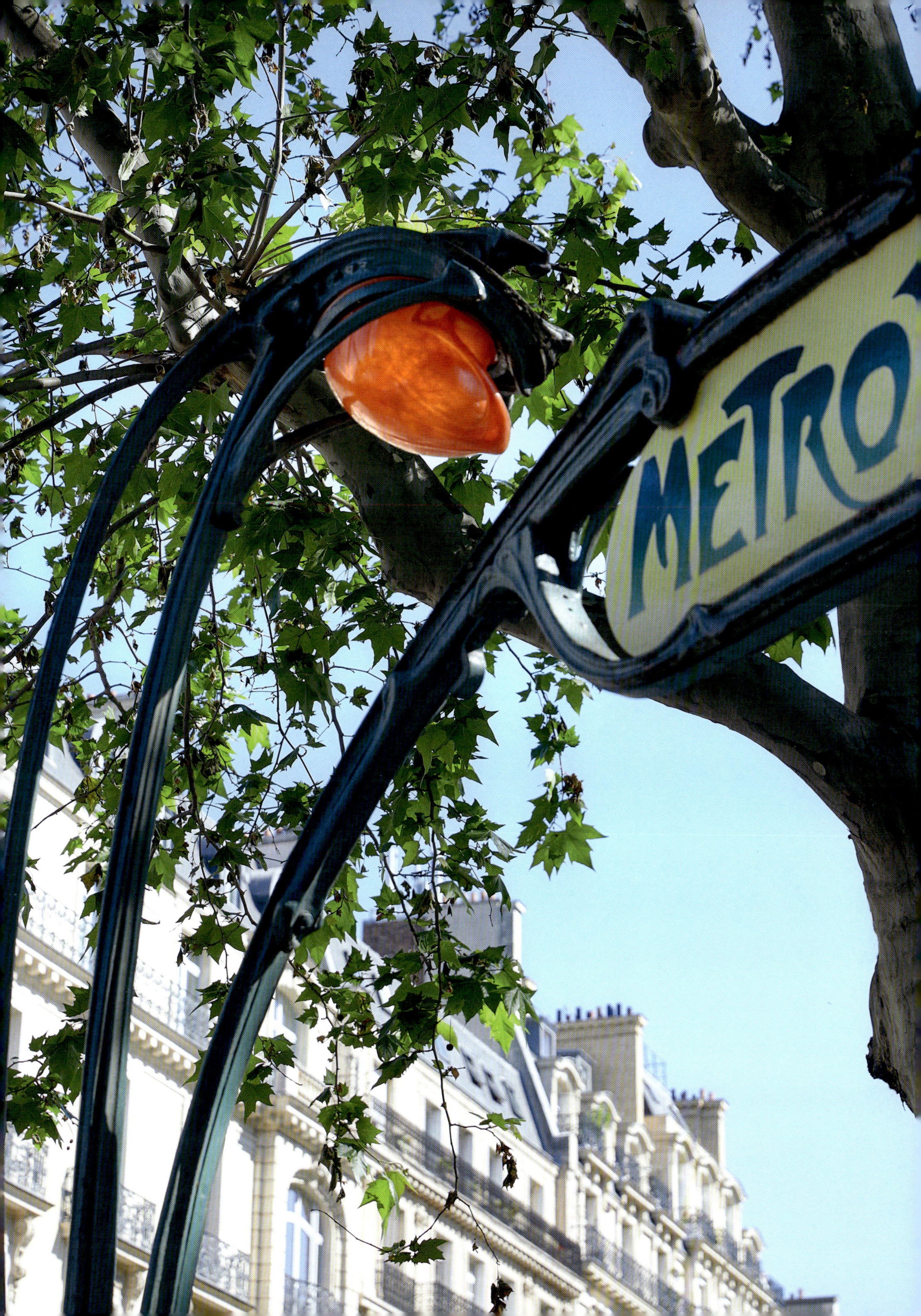
METRO

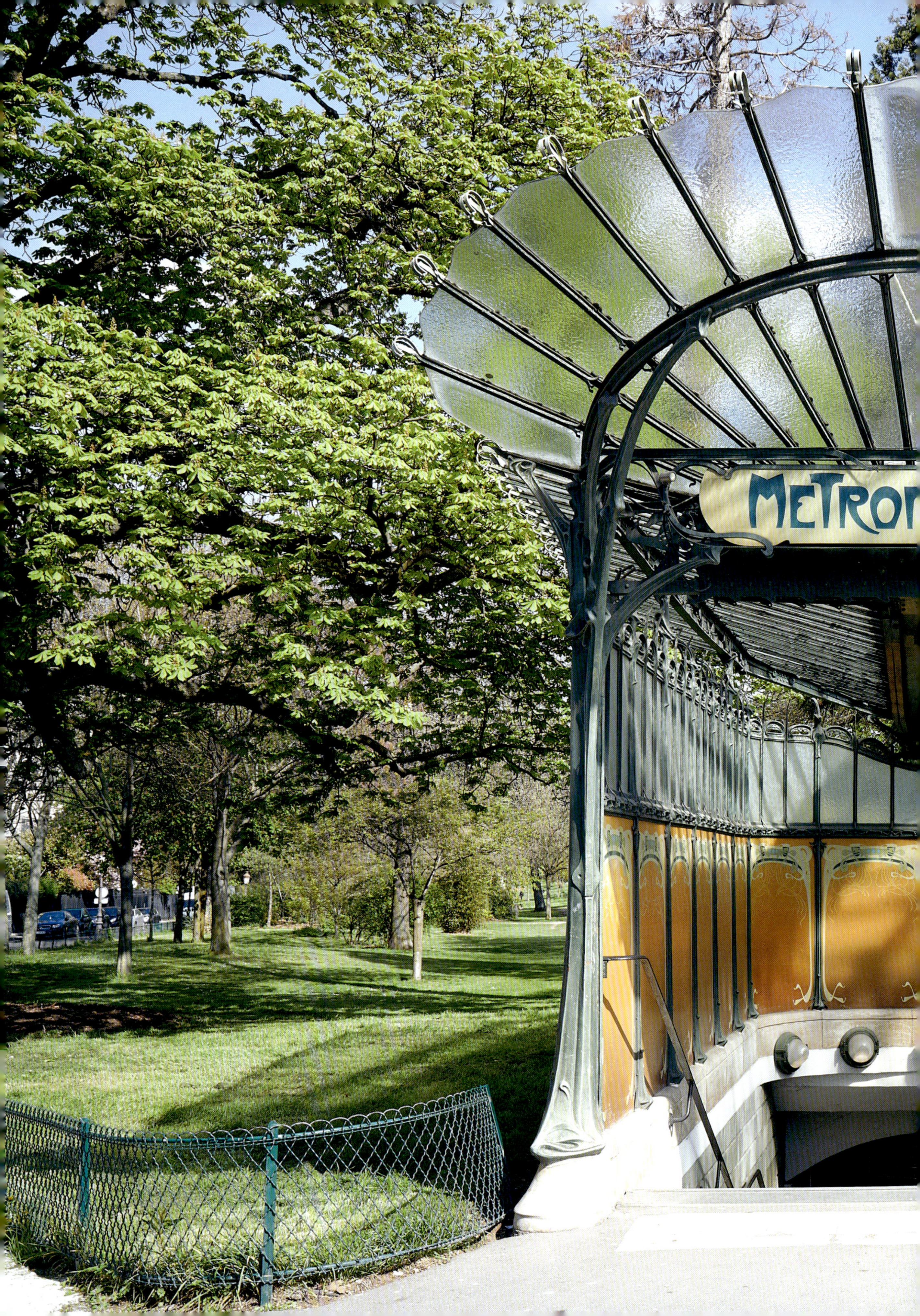
METRO

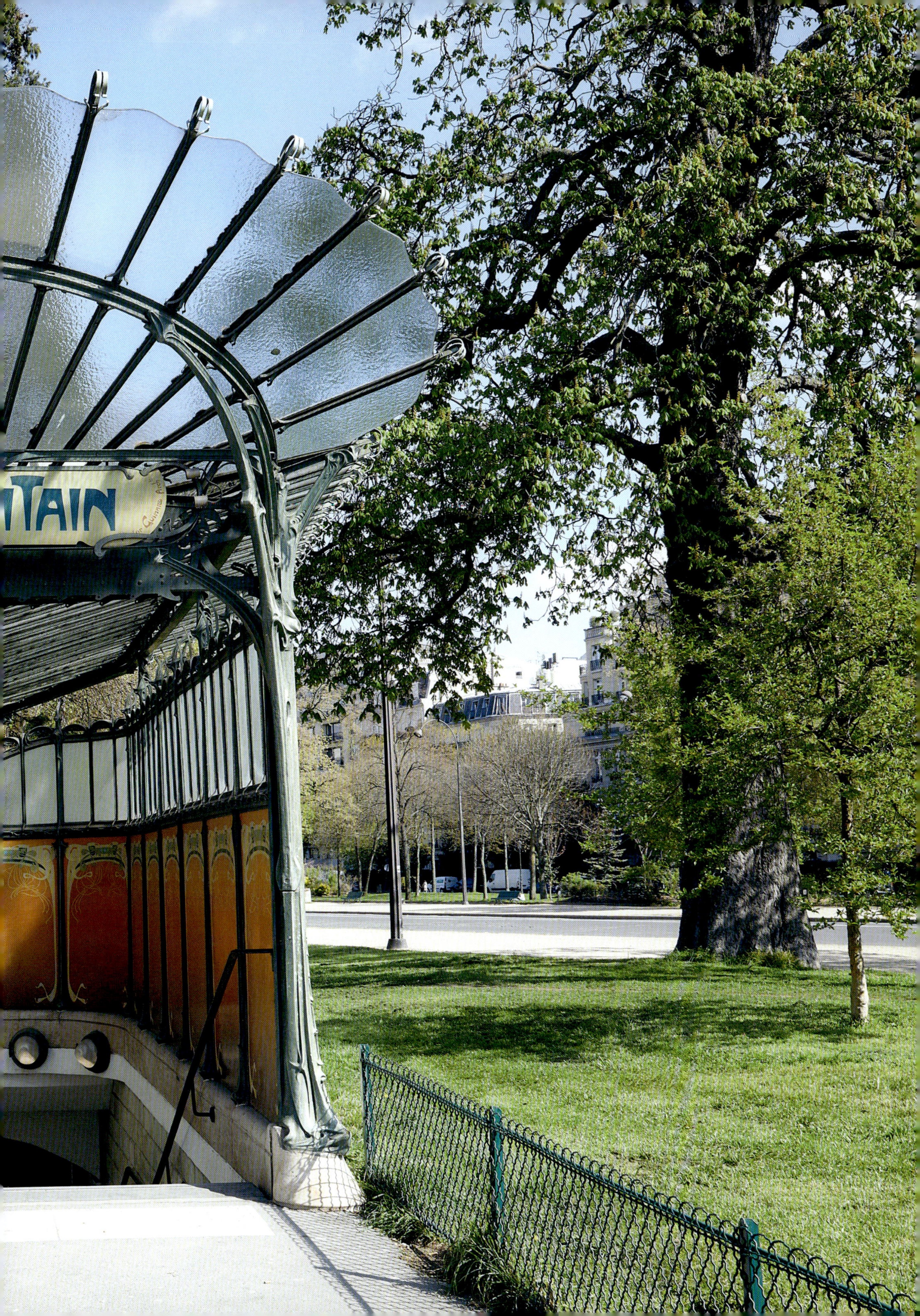
TAIN

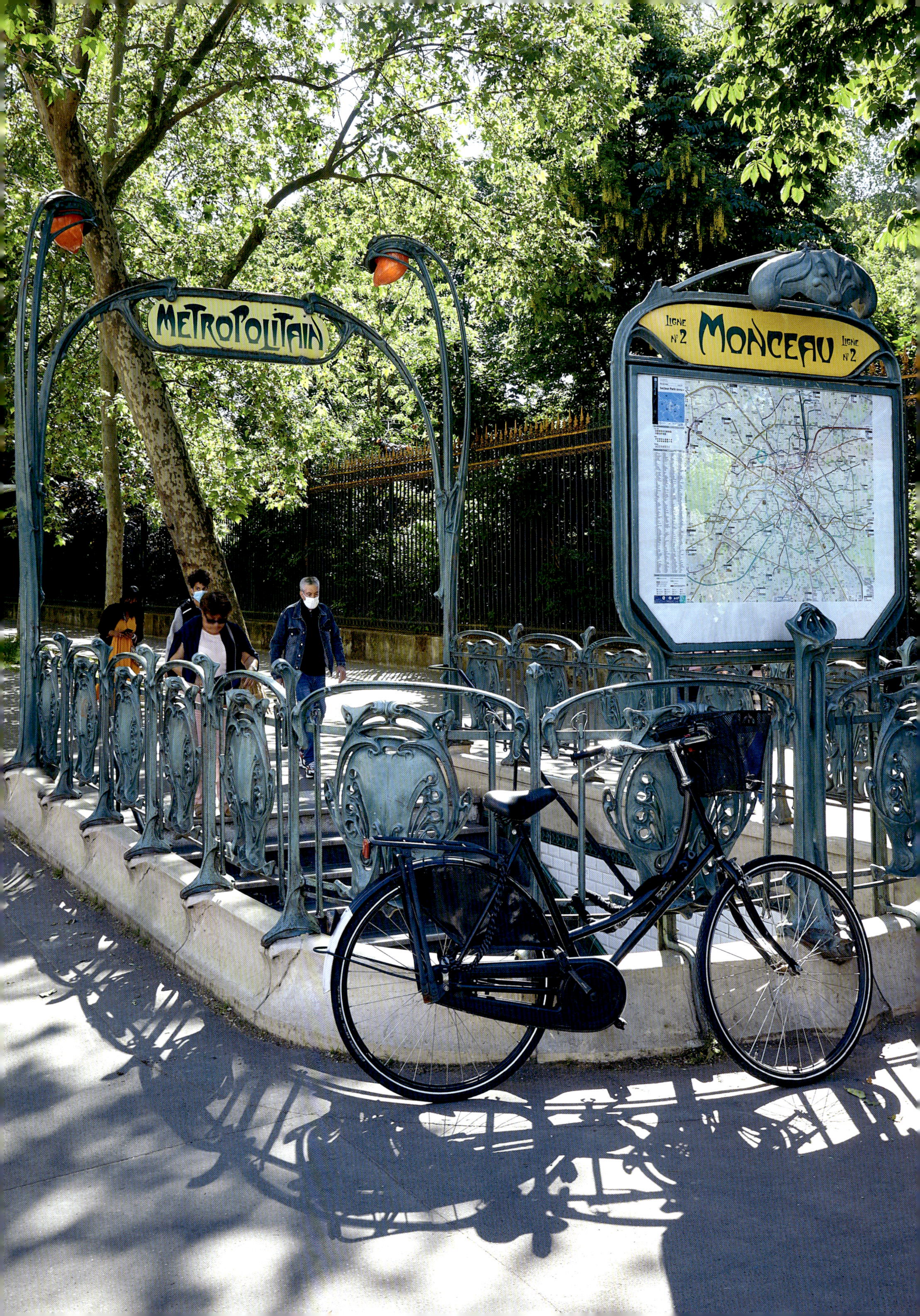

METROPOLITAIN
LIGNE Nº2
MONCEAU
LIGNE Nº2

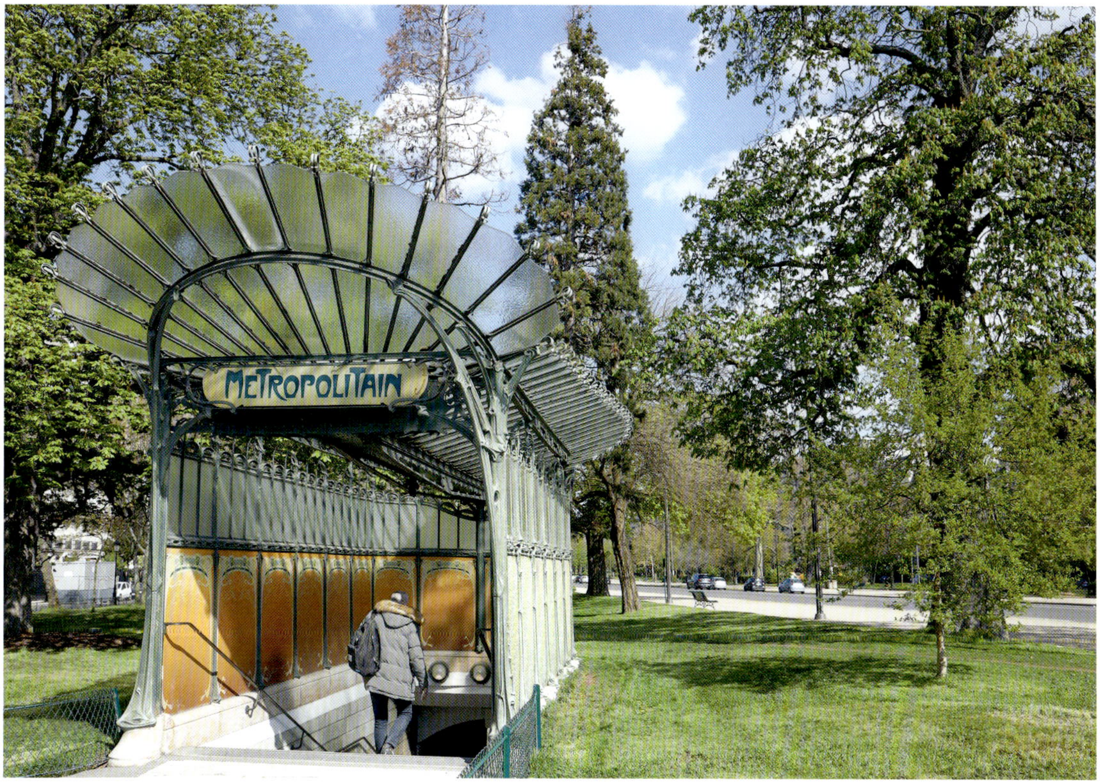

ENTRANCES AND STRUCTURES: VARIATIONS ON A THEME

These structures are reminiscent of lily of the valley, beetles, and dragonflies. As their style is characterized by sinuous, botanical, and dynamic lines, they are the embodiment of art nouveau. During the Belle Époque, the Guimard metro stations featured a combination of forms inspired by nature, Gothic architecture, and Japanese art. Guimard designed two types of entrance and several structures for each of them: closed, openwork, straight, or curved. Most of them are uncovered: cast-iron decorated with floral motifs and the letter M for "Métropolitain" surrounds three sides of the stairs leading to the platforms. Guimard also designed several versions of the structures overhanging these entrances. The largest take the shape of "pagodas," with a double-sloping glass roofs supported by cast-iron pillars and extended by a canopy. The more modest ones take the shape of "dragonflies". Simple entrances are framed by two streetlights decorated with orange glass globes that look like lily-of-the-valley sprigs. Their posts hold up a panel supporting the word "Métropolitain," in a characteristic script of curves and counter-curves. The principle was to adapt to all sites using elements that were independent of each other and of varying sizes. Molded cast iron was used because of its lightness and because it cost less than wrought iron.

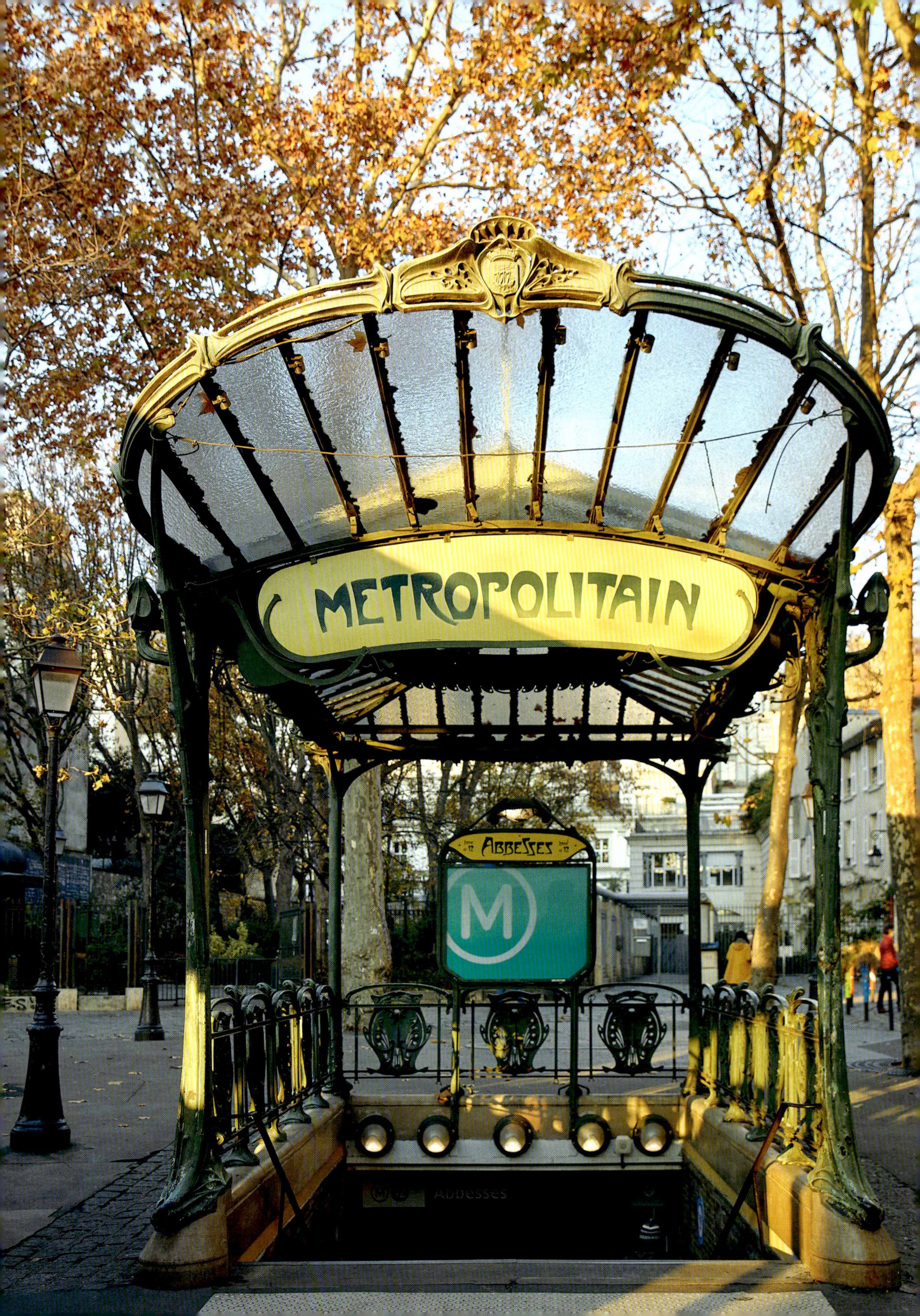
METROPOLITAIN
ABBESSES
M

FUTURE HERITAGE

Hector Guimard, who had failed—oh, the irony—to win the Prix de Rome in architecture after studying at the École des Beaux-Arts and did not get a professional qualification, became a star of the artistic life of the period. But in Haussmannian Paris, the stations were thought to be unsuitable. A flurry of critical remarks soon followed. Journalists wrote of "monsters' mouths" and "apocalyptic aediculae," while detractors of art nouveau spoke of "noodle style" and bad taste. The collaboration between Hector Guimard and the Compagnie du Chemin de Fer Métropolitain de Paris (CMP) came to an end in 1903. Thirty years later, Salvador Dalí was inspired by Guimard's soft forms, as were many artists after him. However, some of the entrance structures were destroyed before they could be protected by being listed as historical monuments in 1978.

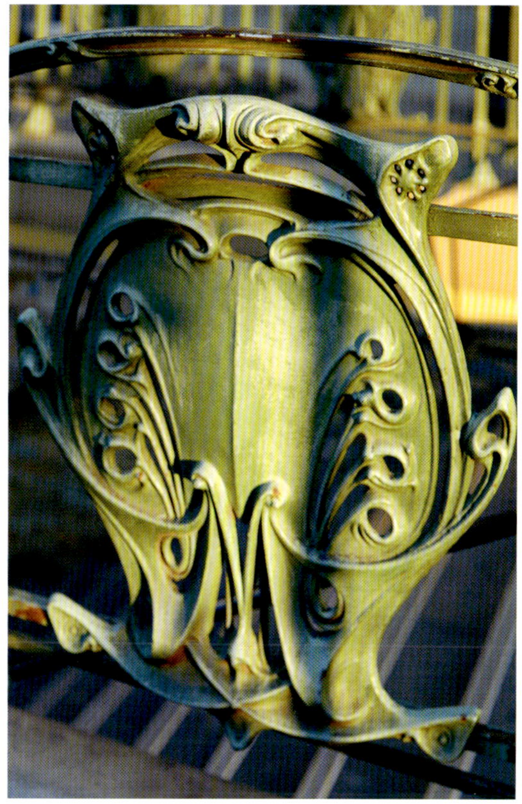

Today, 88 of the initial 167 entrances have survived (86 of them are listed on the Inventaire Supplémentaire des Monuments Historiques). An entrance has been set up in front of the Maison de la RATP, near Gare de Lyon. Several Guimard entrances adorn metro stations in other countries—they are replicas made using the original molds, except in Montreal—owing to cultural exchanges that led to the installation of works by artists from the countries concerned in the Paris metro.

—

Metro Entrances

Comblanchien stone, enameled lava stone, cast iron, and glass
Varying dimensions

AMID THE COMÉDIE-FRANÇAISE, THE PALAIS-ROYAL, AND THE CAFÉ LE NEMOURS IS A WONDROUS VISION: ARABESQUES OF BLUE, YELLOW, AND RED BUBBLES BECKONING YOU TO HOP JOYFULLY INTO THE METRO.

JEAN-MICHEL OTHONIEL

/ *Le Kiosque des noctambules*

The story of *Le Kiosque des noctambules* (The Nightwalkers' Kiosk) began shortly before the year 2000 with the preparations for the metro centennial and new millennium celebrations. Jean-Michel Othoniel was selected from a shortlist of twenty or so famous artists. This choice was greeted enthusiastically, even by neighboring institutions such as the Comédie-Française theater, the Louvre, and the Conseil d'État (Council of State). At the time, Othoniel was thirty-five years old and in residence at the Villa Médicis, the headquarters of the Académie de France in Rome. "Before designing the new metro entrance," he says, "I asked myself what my memories of the Paris metro were as I was so far from home." The entrance has become another landmark and photo opportunity, a postcard recognized by tourists from around the globe and Parisians alike. The memory that came back to Othoniel was that of the metro entrances designed by Hector Guimard in 1900, their decorative leafy forms evoking an idyllic natural world. He wanted to pay tribute to all of this.

A TASTE FOR ALCHEMY

Jean-Michel Othoniel is best-known internationally for his glass-bead sculptures and for his recent election to the Académie des Beaux-Arts, the French fine-arts academy. Born in Saint-Étienne in 1964, his vocation has always been artistic. His early works were in wax and sulfur, materials that mutate and change—Othoniel had a taste for alchemical transmutations. A few years later, he investigated the properties of molten glass, developing a passion for the shapes and colors he could give the material.

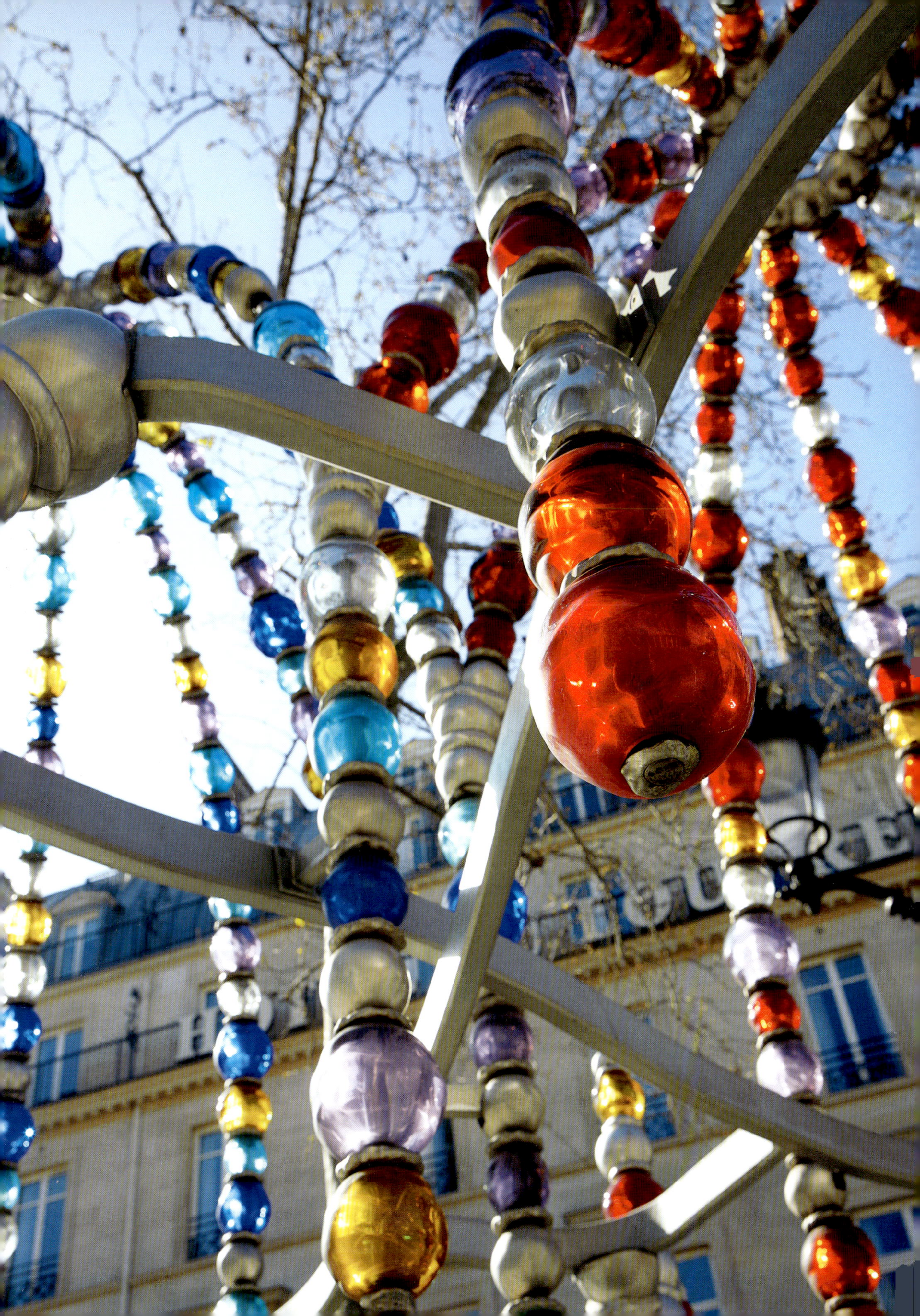

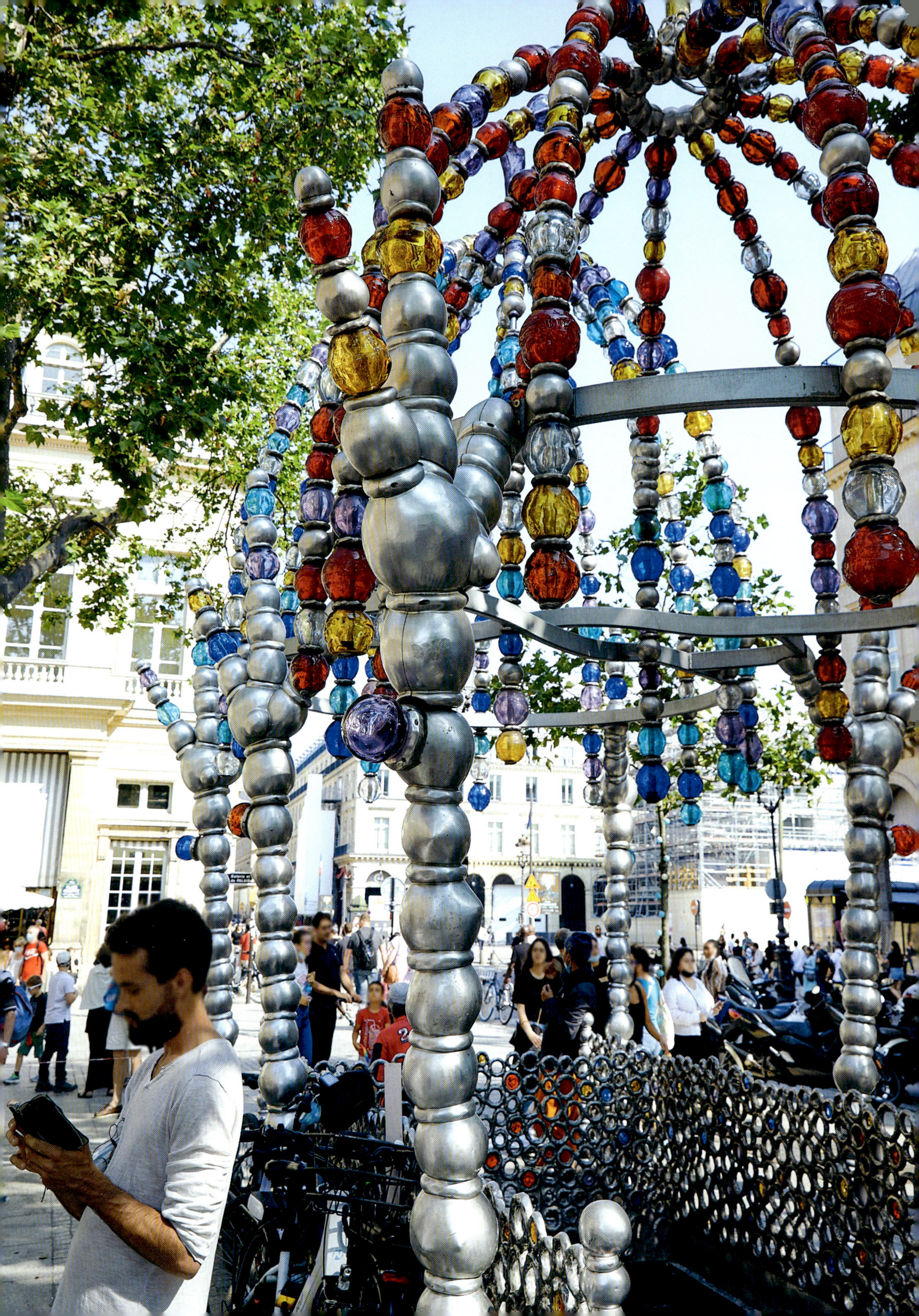

"For me, the RATP commission for the Palais-Royal–Musée du Louvre metro station was an opportunity to further my experimentation with the material and develop my way of working in public spaces," he says. "I was assisted by the Centre International de Recherche sur le Verre et les Arts Plastiques [CIRVA] and the glass workshops of Murano, as well as by members of the RATP heritage team, who were all behind me. They really were the first ambassadors for the metro entrance. It made me a popular artist, an artist whose works are aimed at the widest audience. The commission was a lucky break that left its mark on all my work."

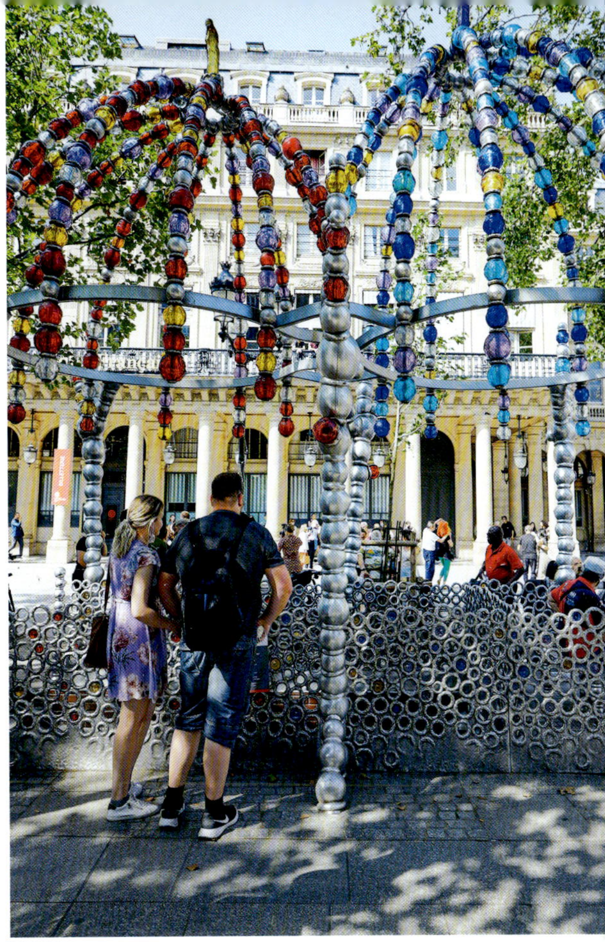

INSPIRED BY VENICE

Jean-Michel Othoniel may have designed *Le Kiosque des noctambules* in Rome, but the metro entrance is largely inspired by Venice. It looks like a festive barge floating on the surface of Place Colette. "I drew inspiration," he says, "from four-poster beds, the look of the Temple of Mercury, and above all the Festa del Redentore [Feast of the Redeemer], held in Venice every July to celebrate the end of the great plague of 1575, when regattas of gondolas decorated with garlands and balloons are organized all over the city canals." With its references to utopian Italian gardens, *Le Kiosque des noctambules* is also an open invitation to take part in the re-enchantment of the Parisian square.

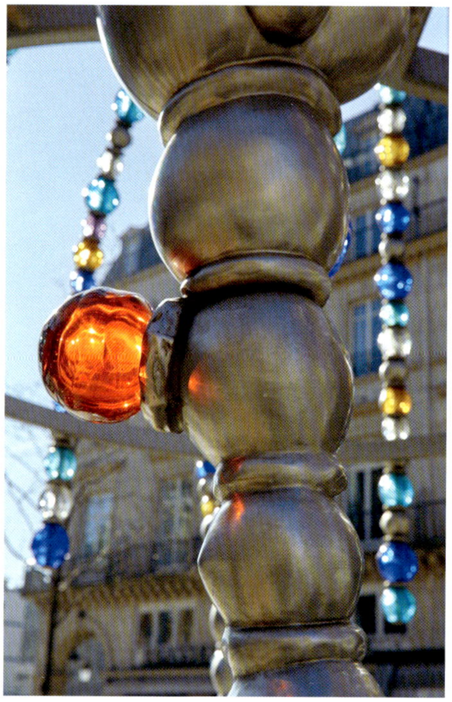

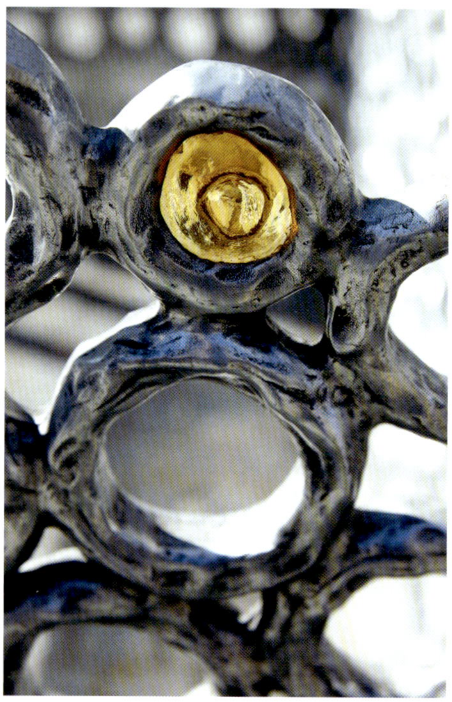

BEHIND THE SCENES

Jean-Michel Othoniel did not work alone. He was supported, he says, by specialists in an extraordinary variety of fields, who were supervised by the architect Geoffroy Aurousseau, the bronze foundry Gire Bronze, and the Ateliers de Chaudronnerie et de Mécanique in Conflans-Sainte-Honorine, outside Paris. The specialists included the glassblowers who produced over a thousand cabochons—each one different—in seven different colors, the architects who designed the structure of the cast aluminum kiosk, the urban planners with whom Othoniel discussed the proportions of the work, and even a lacemaker from Bayeux who made the chain mail for the figures topping the structure. Under the two cupolas symbolizing day and night, stairs lead down to the metro. As in a grotto decorated with ceramics, oculi display pieces of glass like treasures. Later, the City of Paris entrusted Othoniel with the layout of Place Colette, which he designed *à l'italienne*. An intimate piazza at heart of the capital, it is a place to dream and to celebrate. After all, a metro entrance is simply a place of transition, a threshold between one world and another—a concept dear to Othoniel. *Le Kiosque des noctambules* is a bearer of hope, a romantic folly, and the embodiment of a world of wonder in the very heart of Paris.

***Le Kiosque des noctambules*, 2000**

Murano glass, aluminum, ceramic tiles
5.6 x 6 x 2 m

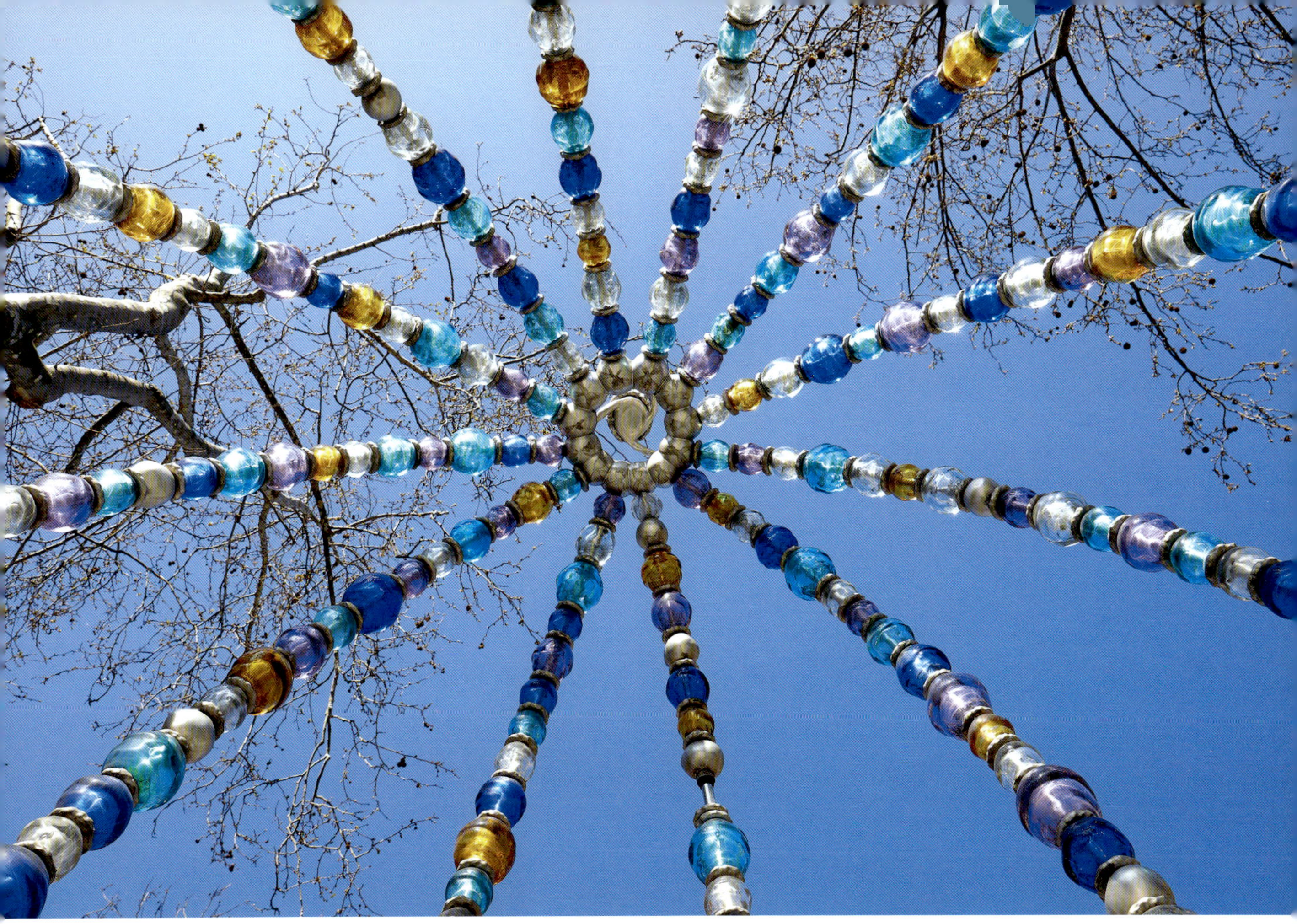

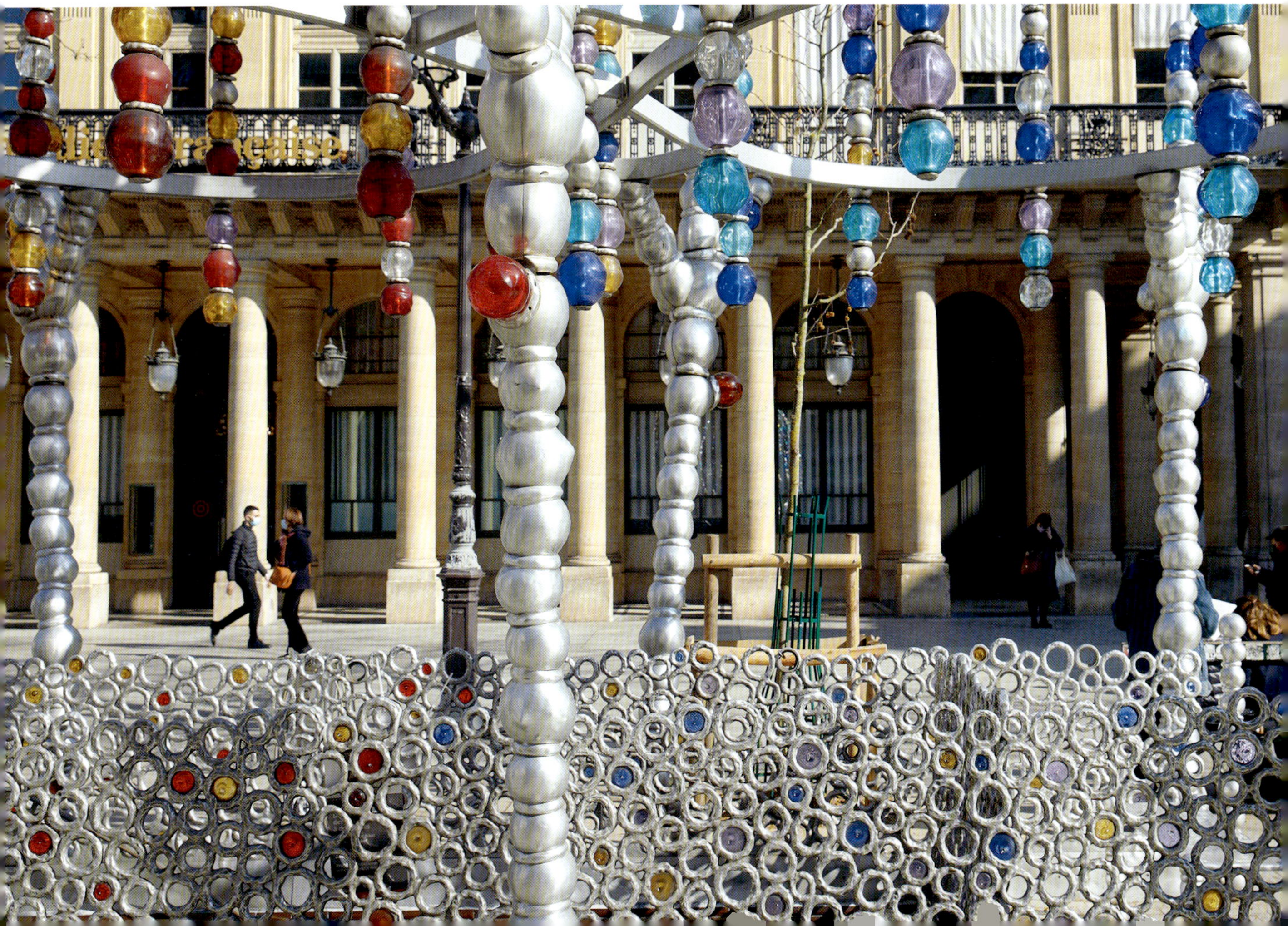

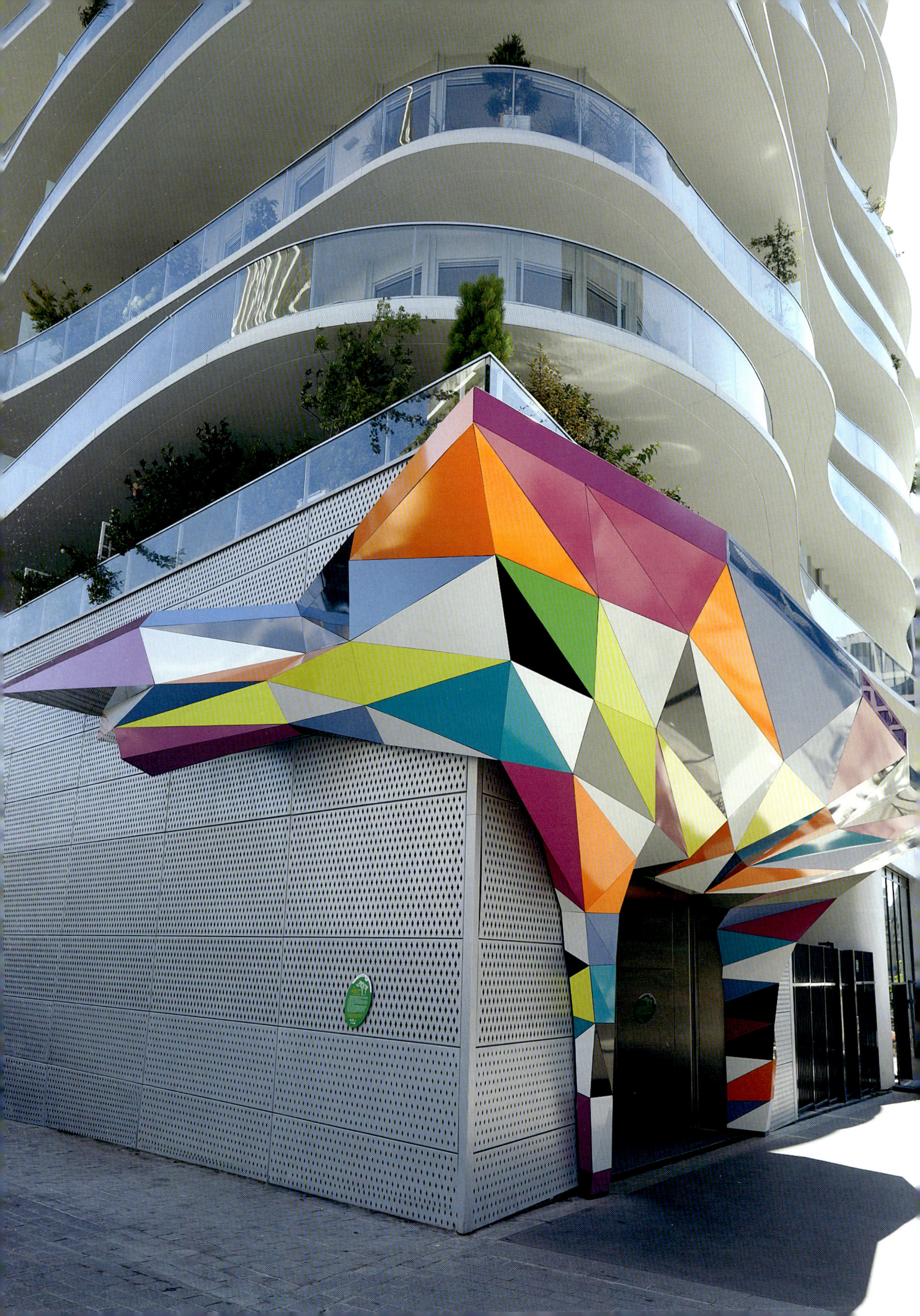

TOBIAS
REHBERGER

/ Je ne suis jamais allé nulle part

COLORFUL TRIANGLES FORM A VAULT AT THE FOOT OF A BUILDING AND AN OVERHANG ON THE FACADE OVERLOOKING PARC MARTIN LUTHER KING. LIKE A LIGHTHOUSE, THE NEW ENTRANCE TO PONT CARDINET METRO STATION DESIGNED BY TOBIAS REHBERGER CAN BE SEEN FROM AFAR.

Tobias Rehberger's work *Je ne suis jamais allé nulle part* (I've Never Been Anywhere), an RATP-Emerige group coproduction, was completed in the spring of 2021. It was proudly inaugurated a few steps from the Batignolles neighborhood and the brand-new courthouse, the Tribunal de Paris. Its painted aluminum panels, which flank the metro entrance, were produced by a metalwork firm based near Marseille. A team of four Tour de France journeymen pre-assembled them on a metal structure in a workshop, then sent them to Paris.

The work is, of course, meant to be a joyful tribute to Hector Guimard's metro entrances, as well as an apartment building designed by Beijing-based MAD Architects.

A WORK TO MAKE PEOPLE SMILE

The winner of the Golden Lion at the 2009 Venice Biennale, Tobias Rehberger (b. 1966) is a major figure on the German art scene. He explores the boundaries between art, design, and architecture. Whether meant for exhibition rooms or public spaces, his works are always conceived as part of a context. "Hector Guimard has designed stations that look like flowers and dragon's teeth. The idea is a hole that swallows visitors and digests them." And even though Rehberger's creations have always had a playful dimension that does not exclude depth, he designs them as sculptures: "Sometimes, a work of art is functional. We could make sculptures that we could swim in."

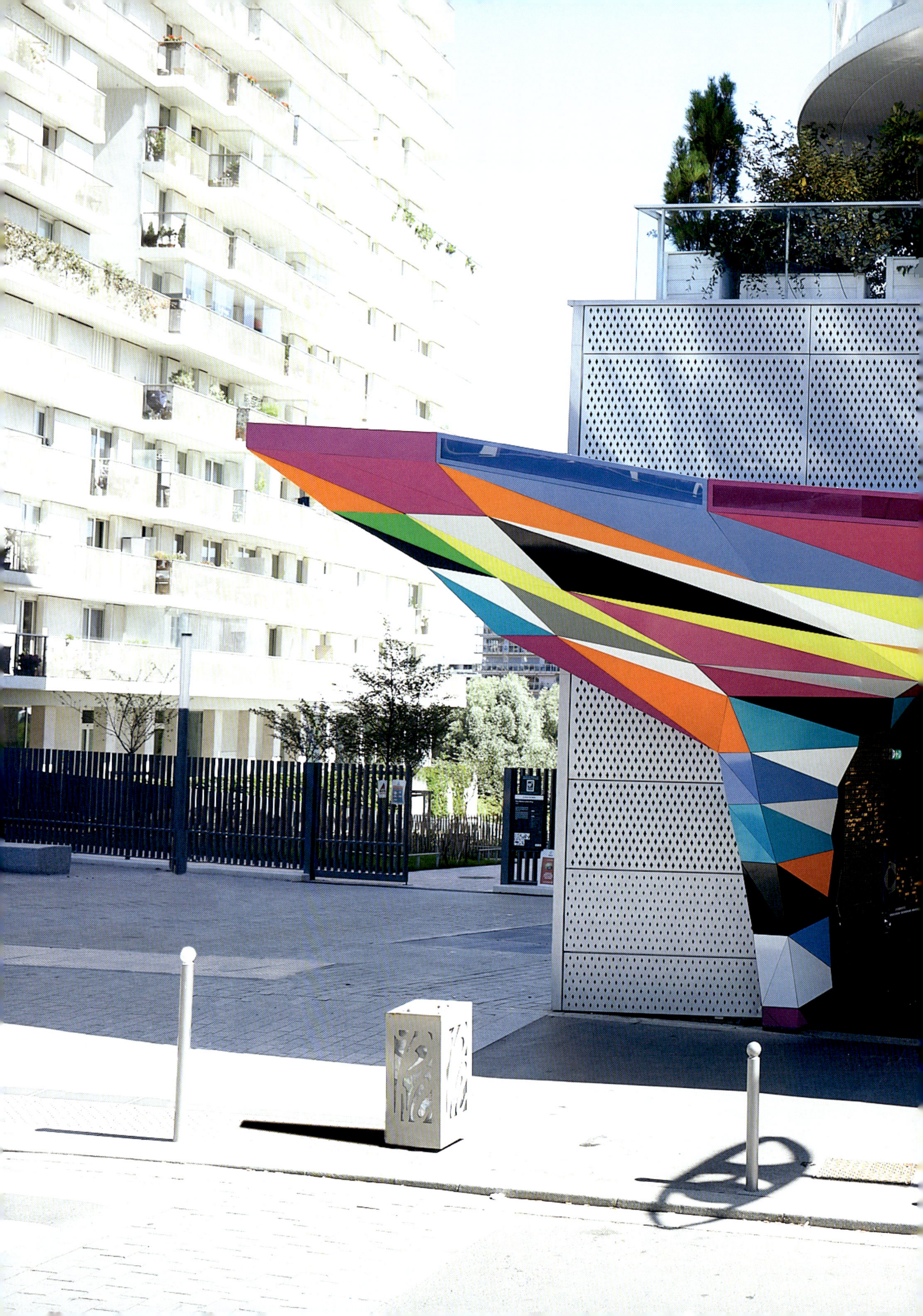

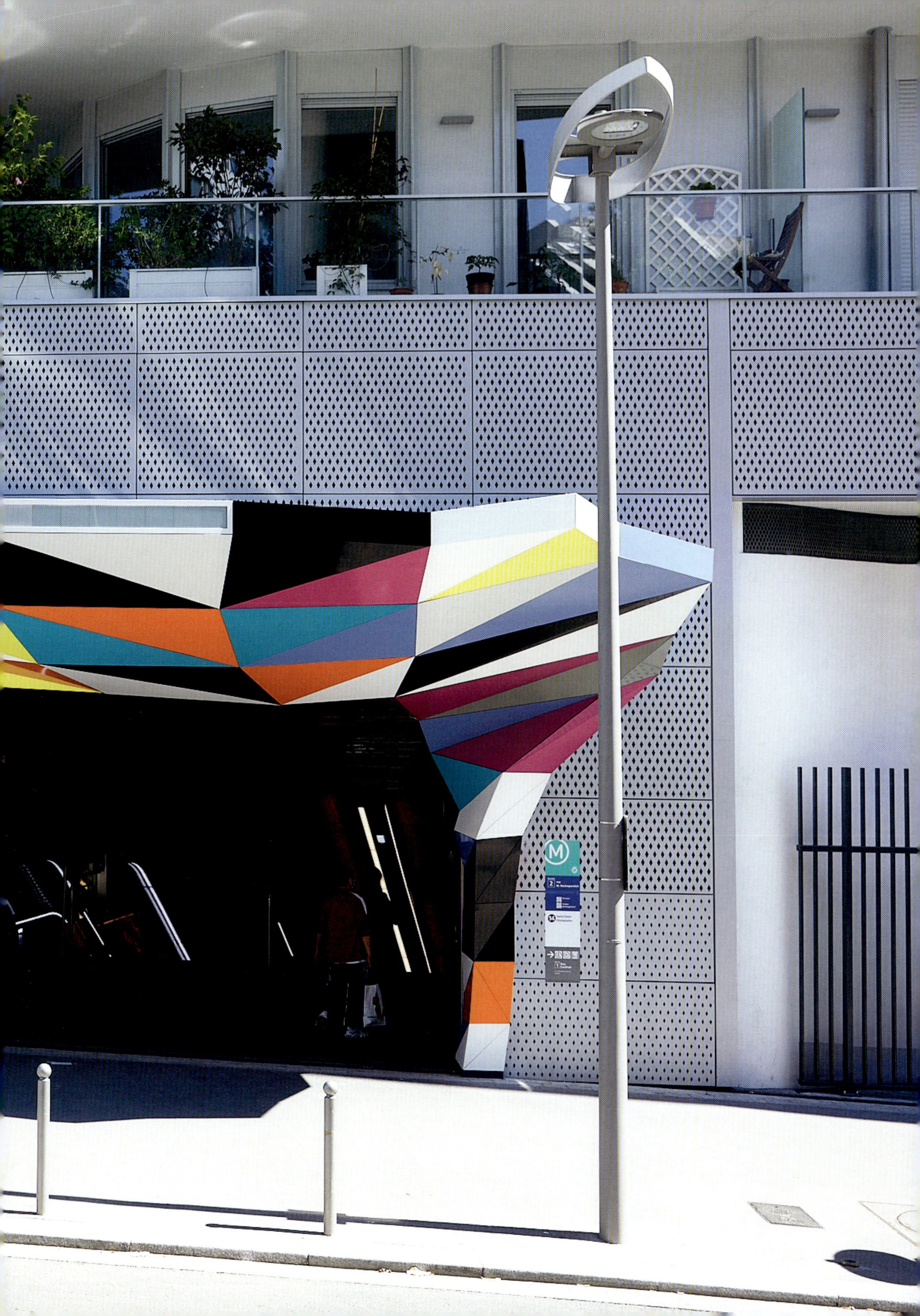

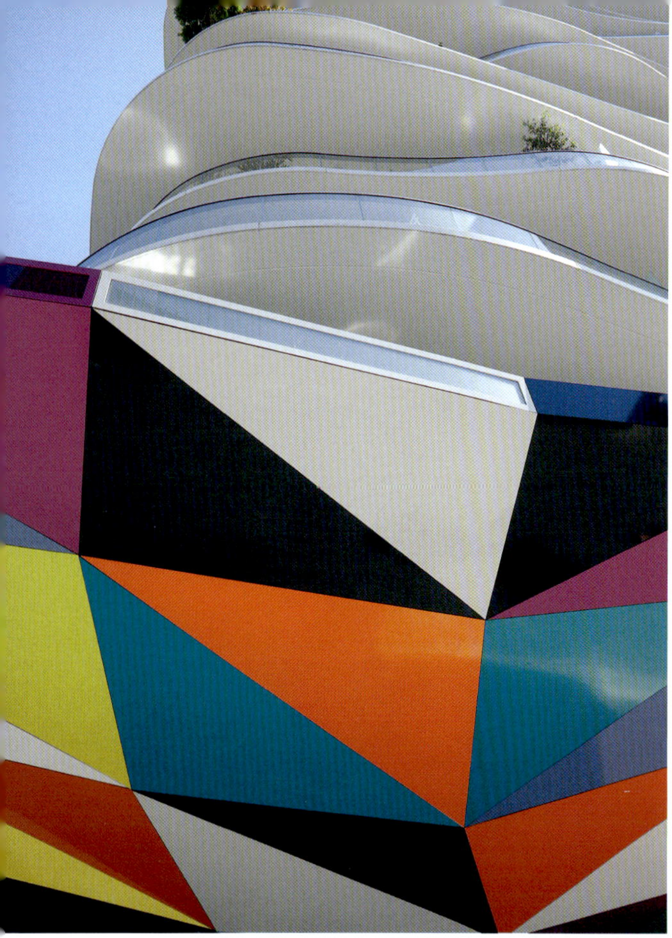

He defines himself as an artist and makes not looking like a designer a point of honor. Rehberger is firmly rooted in the present. Unlike artists who sometimes want to make a timeless gesture, he seeks to bear witness to a moment. "When you build something," he says, "especially a metro station, you have to demonstrate that it contains a contemporary element. The metro is not just about transportation. There's the question of time, too. And you can imagine entering one station during one era and coming out of another station in another. That's the type of game I wanted to offer here."

A REAL CLOCK

Pont Cardinet metro station also tells the time. "It works a little like those watches that only have hands, no numbers: there are three different areas, which are progressively colored to the rhythm of the minutes and seconds. In a way, it is a reminiscence about a functional dimension," he adds. Often monumental, his installations always stimulate our senses. A museum setting is never enough for him, he needs to create interactions with his visitors. Here, he was fascinated by the contrasts of his colored plates with the very white surrounding buildings. "I created a real oddity. To install a work, the context of a metro entrance is very particular. It's not the same thing as an office tower in Shanghai, a forest, or a river." He wanted to make the Pont Cardinet metro station arch a place to inspire the imagination. Looks like he succeeded.

***Je ne suis jamais allé nulle part*, 2021**

Painted aluminum

Nearly 6 m high

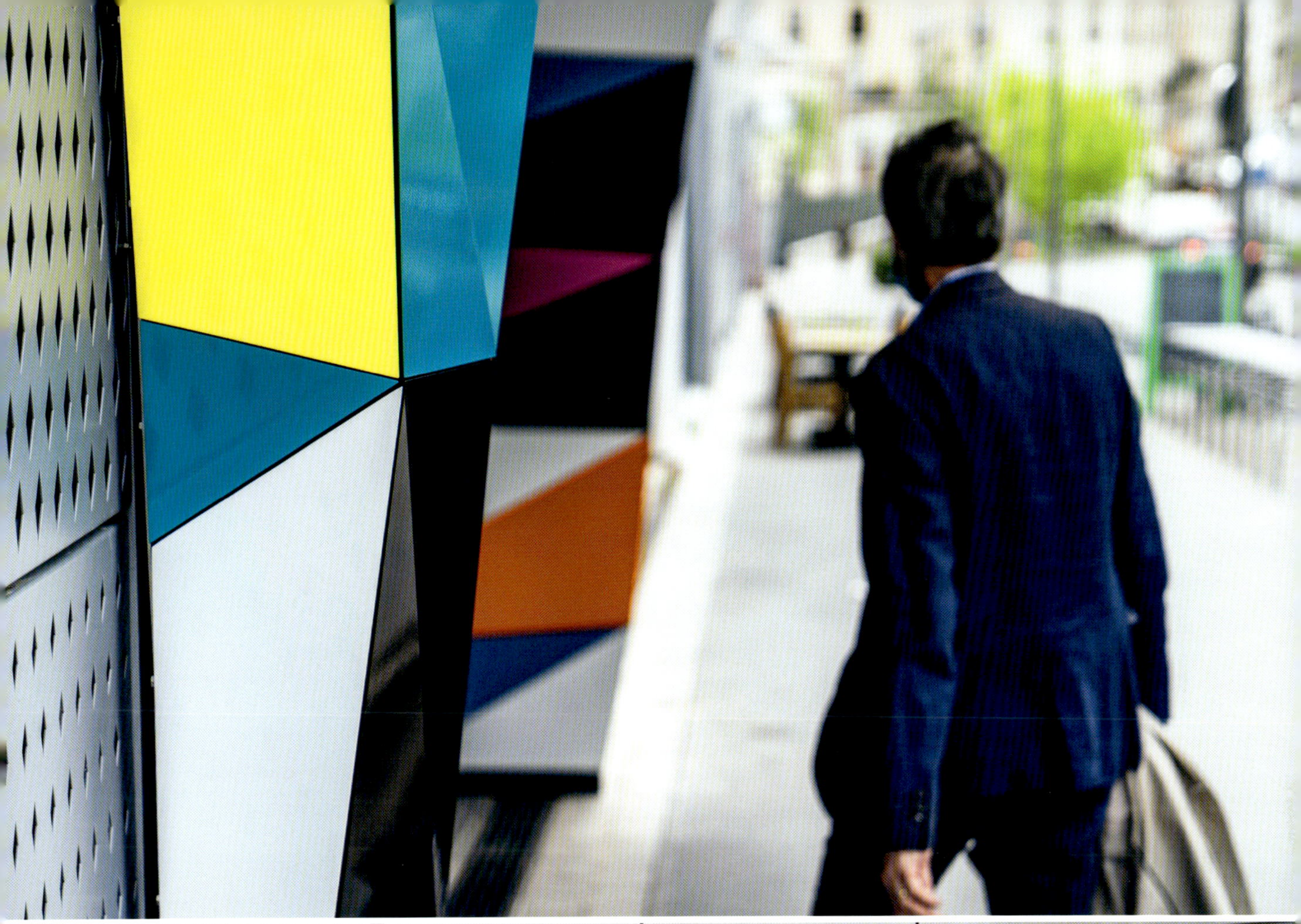

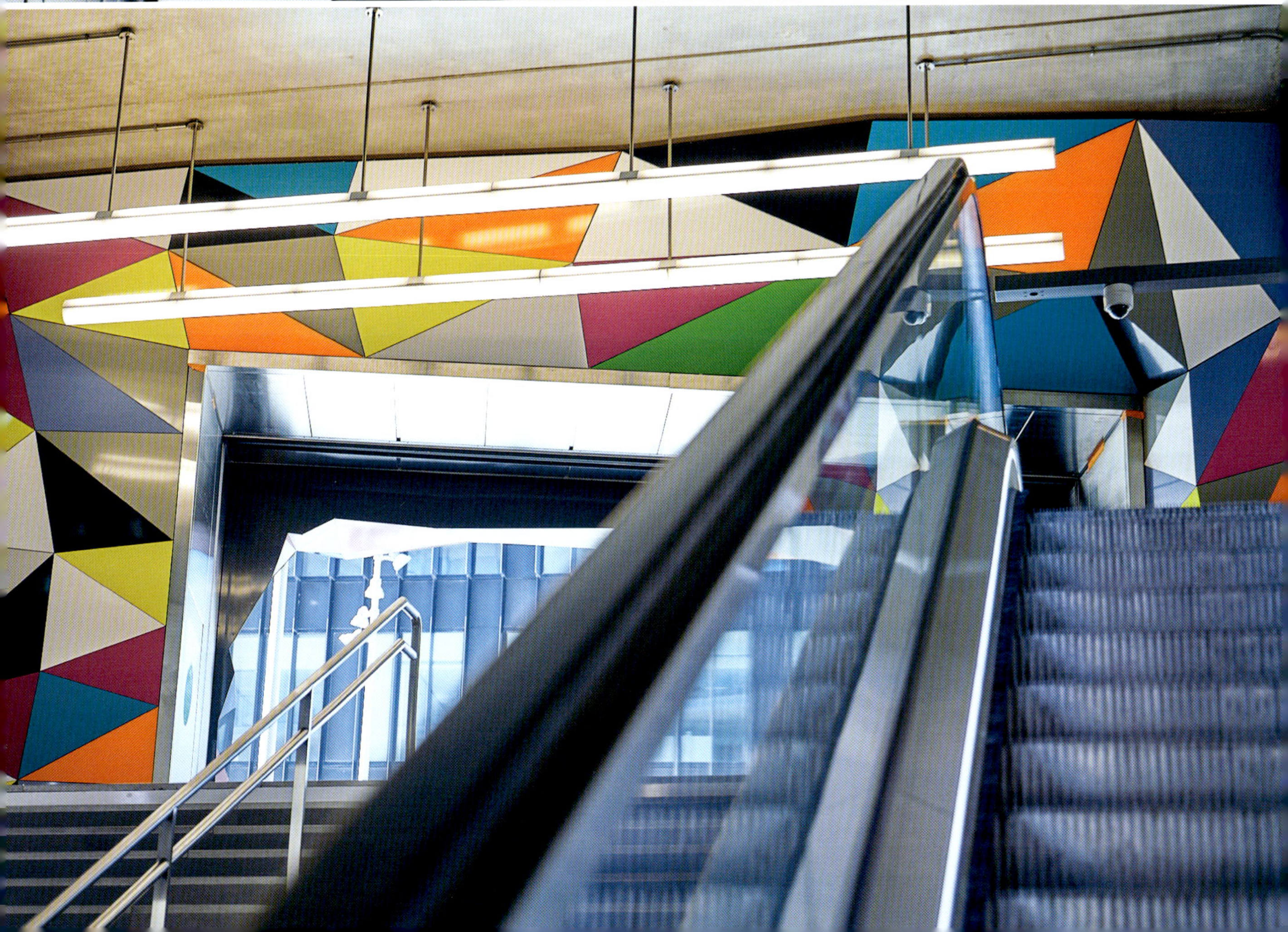

BEN LANGLANDS NIKKI BELL / *Call & Response*

THE BRITISH DUO LANGLANDS & BELL HAVE DESIGNED TWO HARMONIOUS NEW ENTRANCES FOR PORTE DE VINCENNES METRO STATION.

MIRROR, MIRROR

Ben Langlands and Nikki Bell installed *Call & Response* on Cours de Vincennes in 2012. That was the year when line 1, one of the busiest, was fully automated. Inaugurated in December 2012, the work put the finishing touch on the further extension of tramway line T3 to Porte de Vincennes. It comprises two metro entrances located on Cours de Vincennes. Langlands & Bell follow in the footsteps of Hector Guimard, whose early twentieth-century entrances were revolutionary. The duo's entrances mirror the columns of the Barrière du Trône, a tollbooth designed by the architect Claude-Nicolas Ledoux in the eighteenth century and built on the far end of Cours de Vincennes, east of Place de la Nation. They make direct reference to the bases of Ledoux's columns. They transformed the entire area surrounding them—new metro entrances always represent an important contribution to the fabric of a city and its planning.

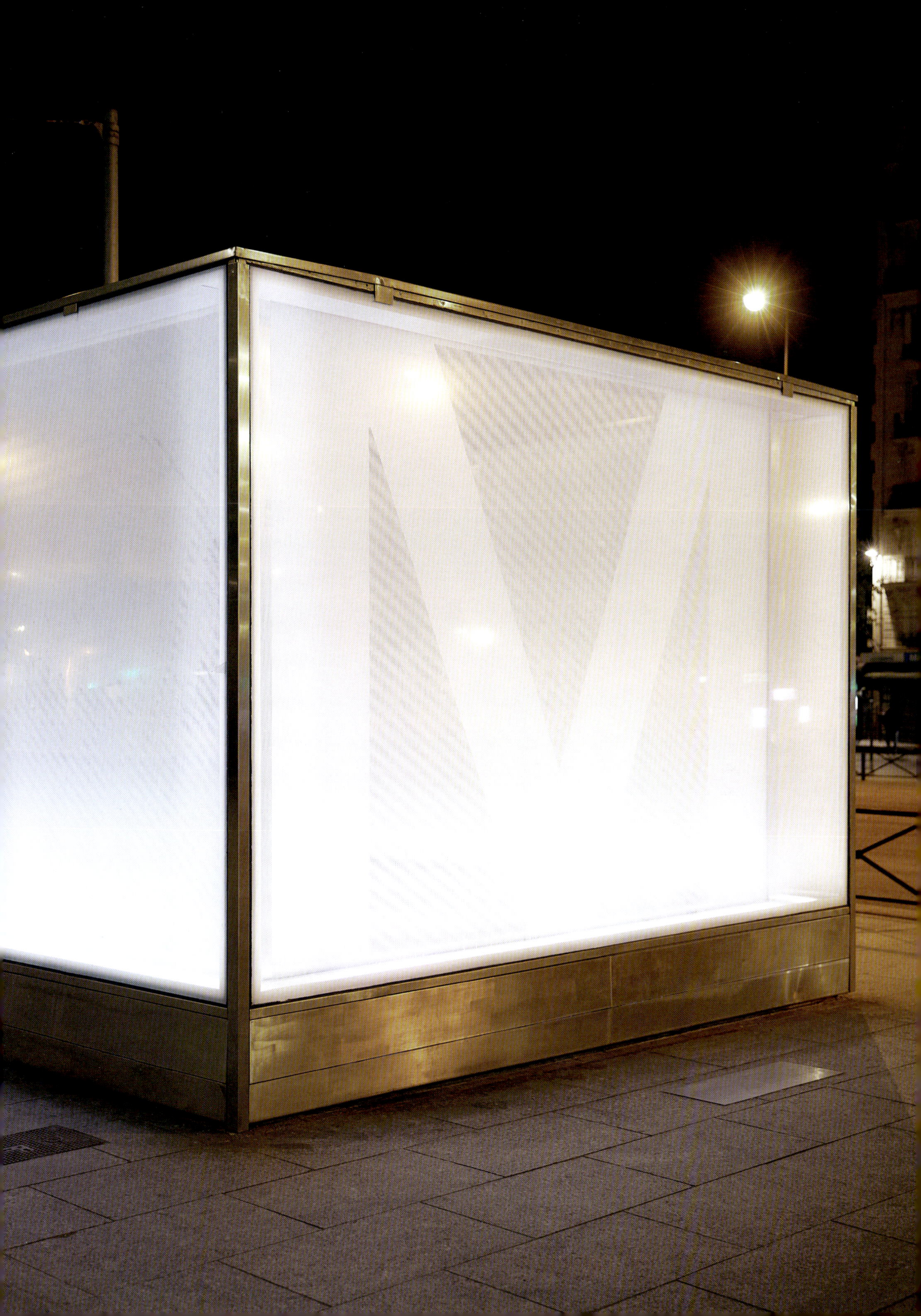

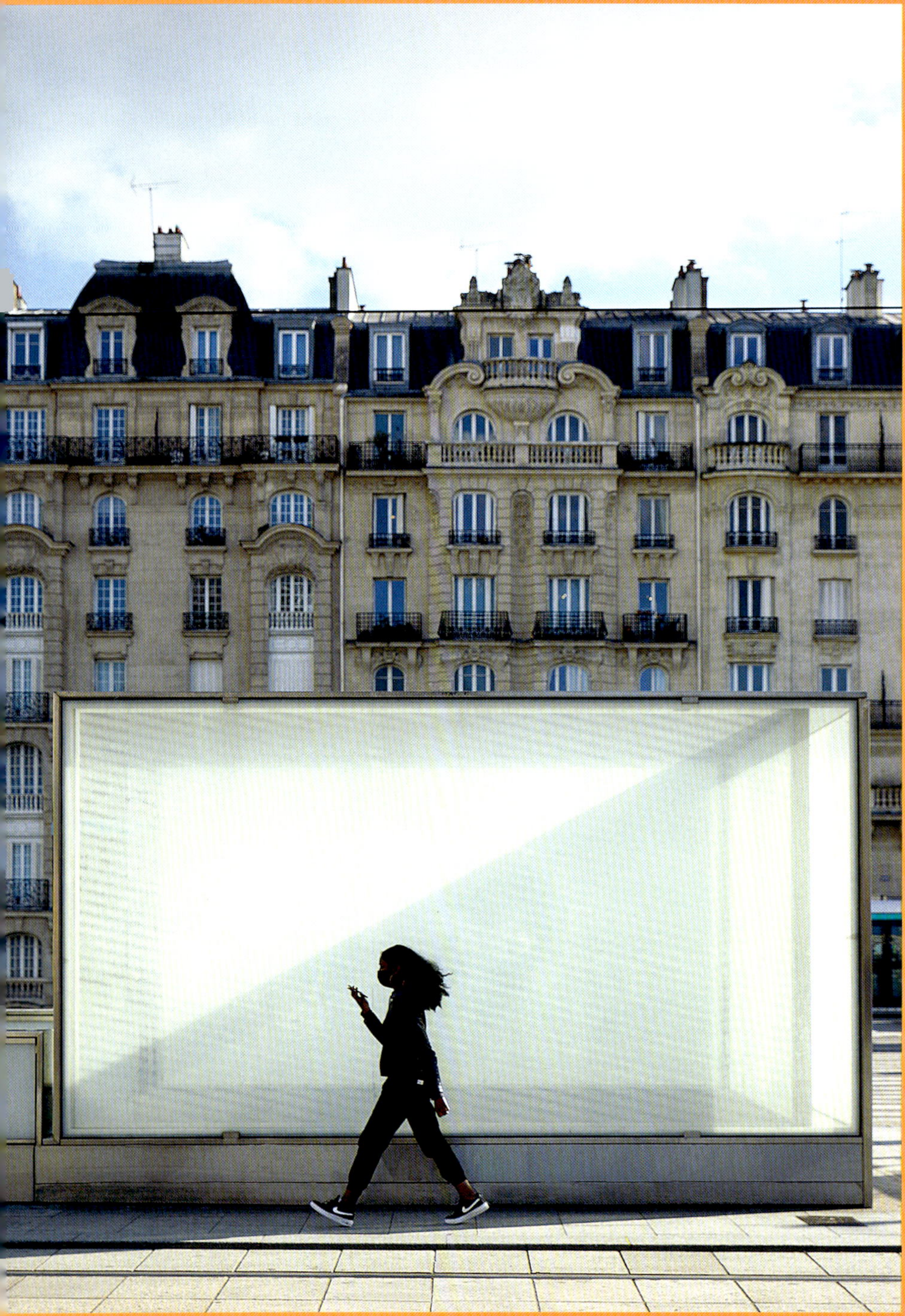

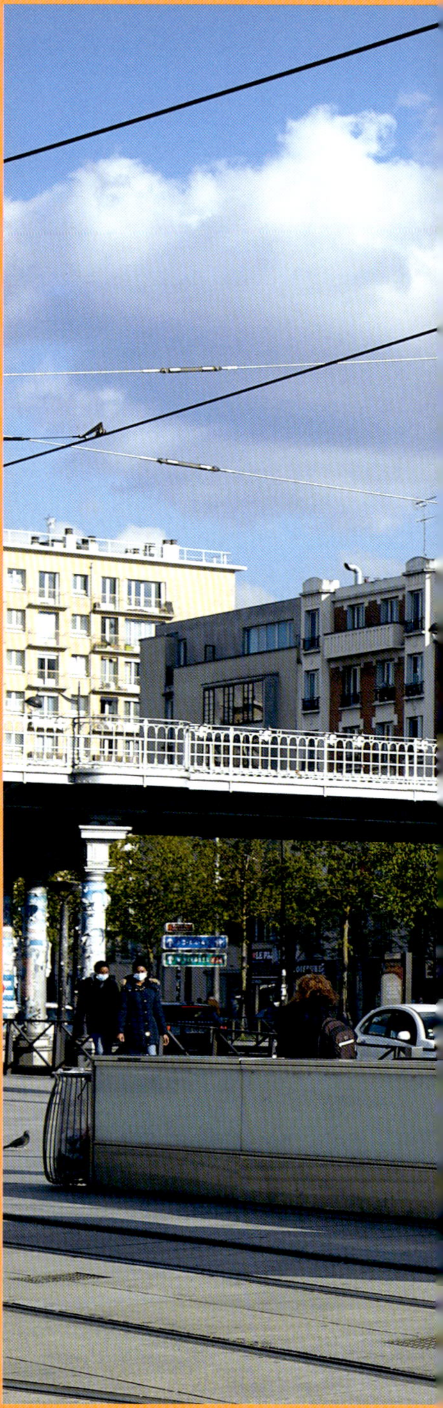

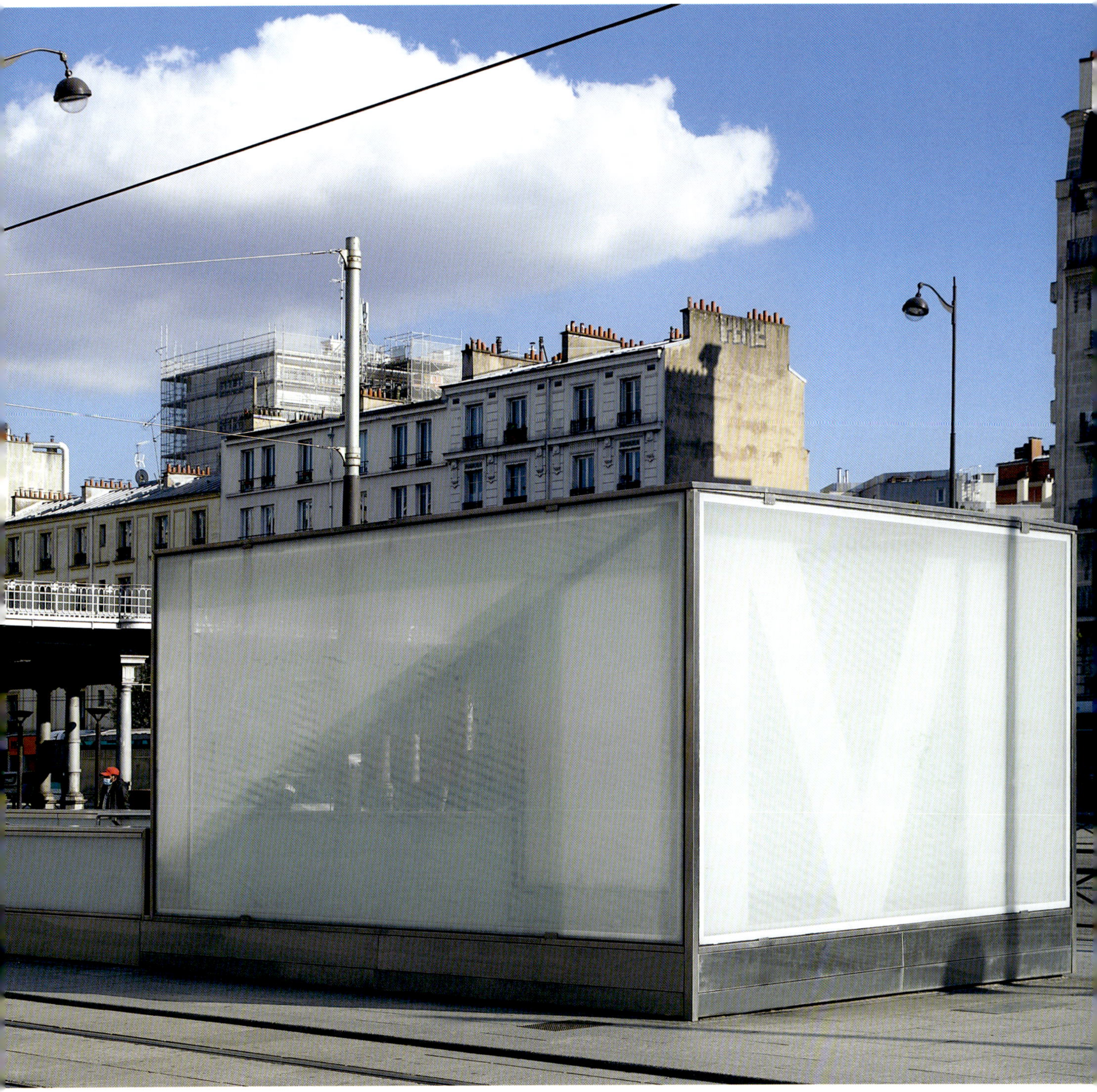

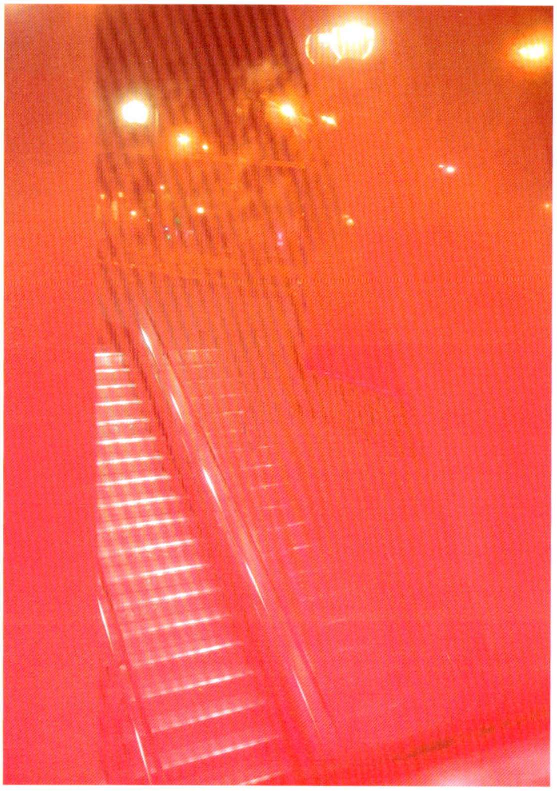
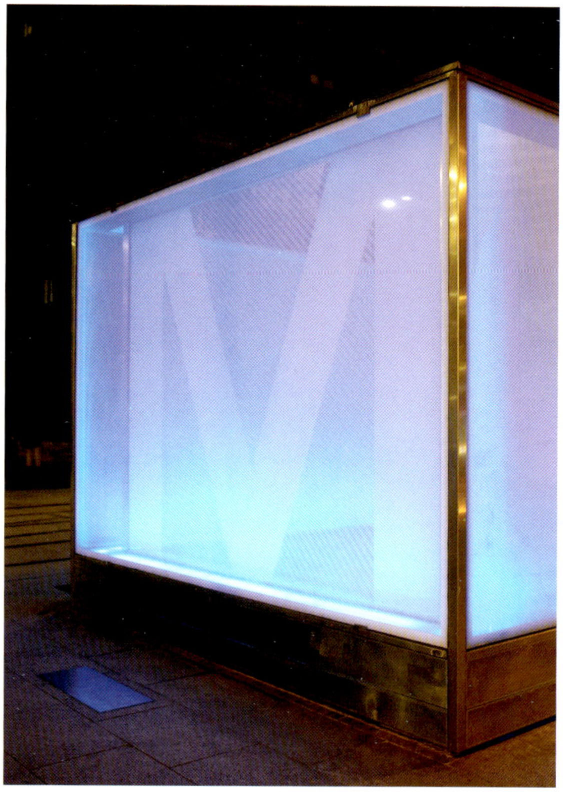
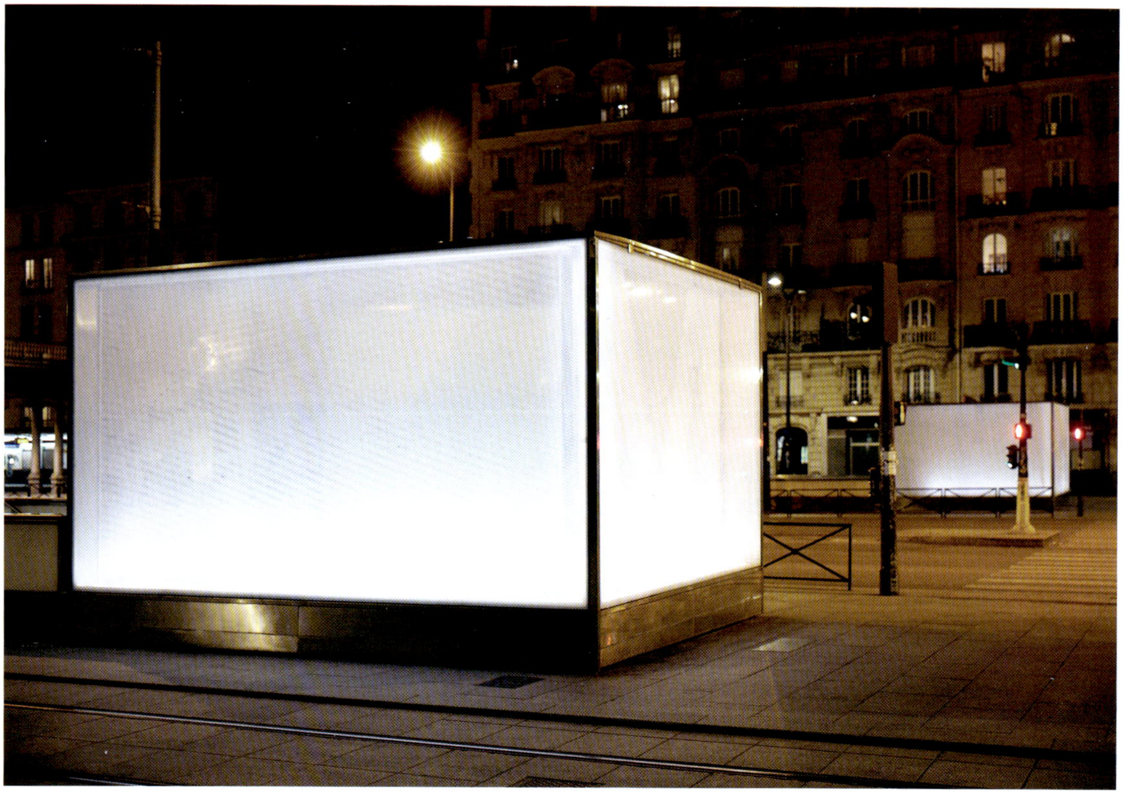

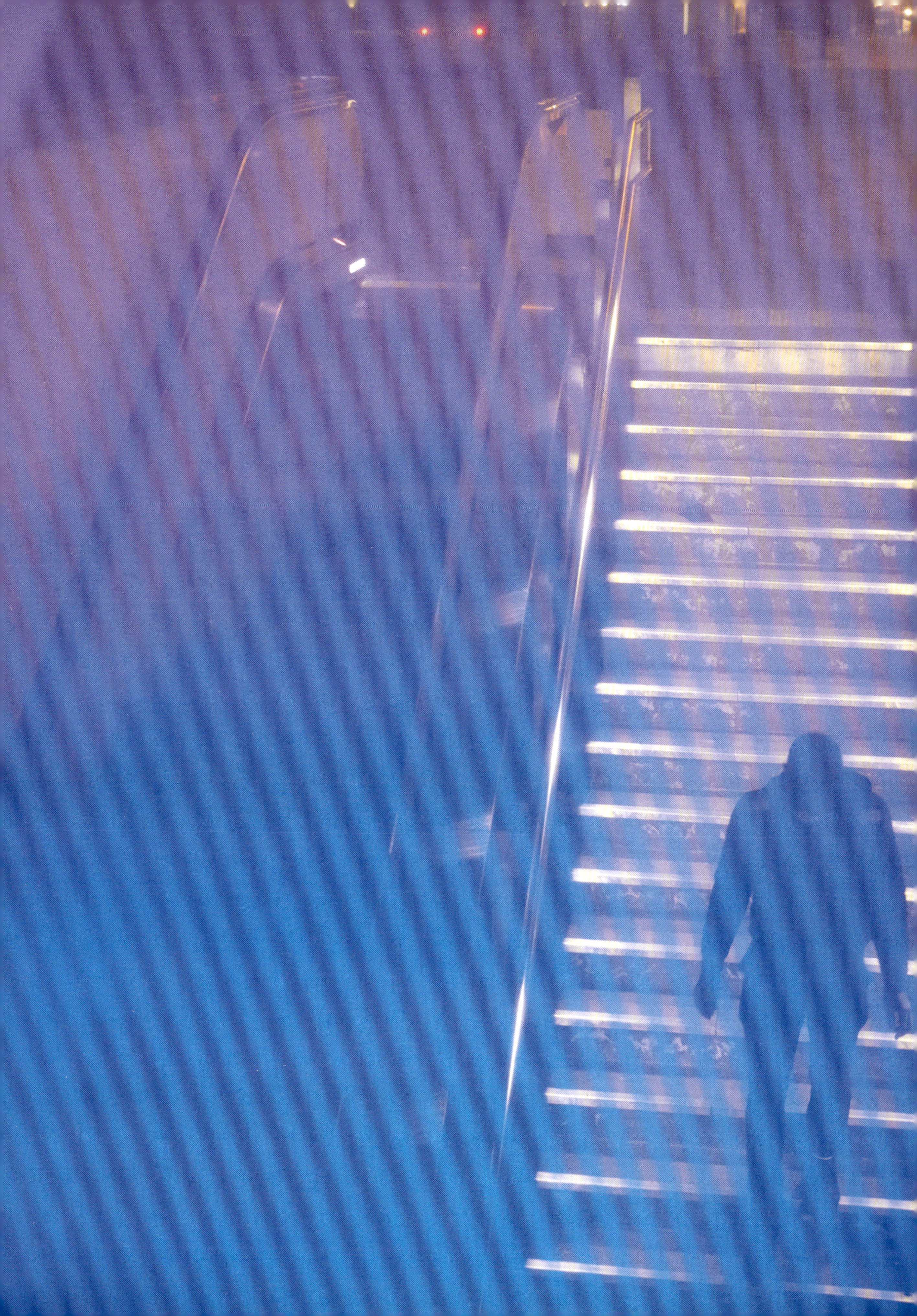

IMMERSIVE

From a distance, two familiar white Ms can be seen on either side of Cours de Vincennes: the traditional metro monogram is recognizable, but its geometric lines seem to have been given a face-lift. At each entrance, three glass panels framed in stainless steel form three sides of a cube placed on the surface of the sidewalk. A halo of warm light bathes each of the metro entrances. By day, there is a moiré effect; by night, a sophisticated system of LEDs produces a gentle light. They are like two headlights whose colors change from pink to blue. Immersive, the work is spectacular but not flashy. It is also useful: the change from one color to another, at regular intervals, signals the arrivals and departures of the streetcars.

A UTOPIAN MESSAGE

Ben Langlands and Nikki Bell are mainly concerned with the individual and political relations between human beings. Their method involves questioning the way we inhabit the world and interact with the space around us. Their tools are varied: film, video, digital projects, and architectural constructions.
The artists, born in 1955 and 1959 respectively, formed a duo in London in 1978 when they were both studying fine art at Middlesex Polytechnic. In recent years, they have often intervened in public spaces, notably at Paddington station and Heathrow airport.
And their work in the Paris metro inspired later ones: in 2016 Transport for London (TFL) invited them to pay tribute to Franck Pick, the visionary of the legendary Underground, affectionately known as the Tube. They designed a monument for Piccadilly Circus station. It is a work in the same vein as *Call & Response*; Langlands & Bell had already affirmed in Paris that art and artists can really improve our everyday environments.

Call & Response, 2012
Fritted Optiwhite glass, stainless steel, intelligent LEDs, and associated electronics
5 × 5 × 5 m

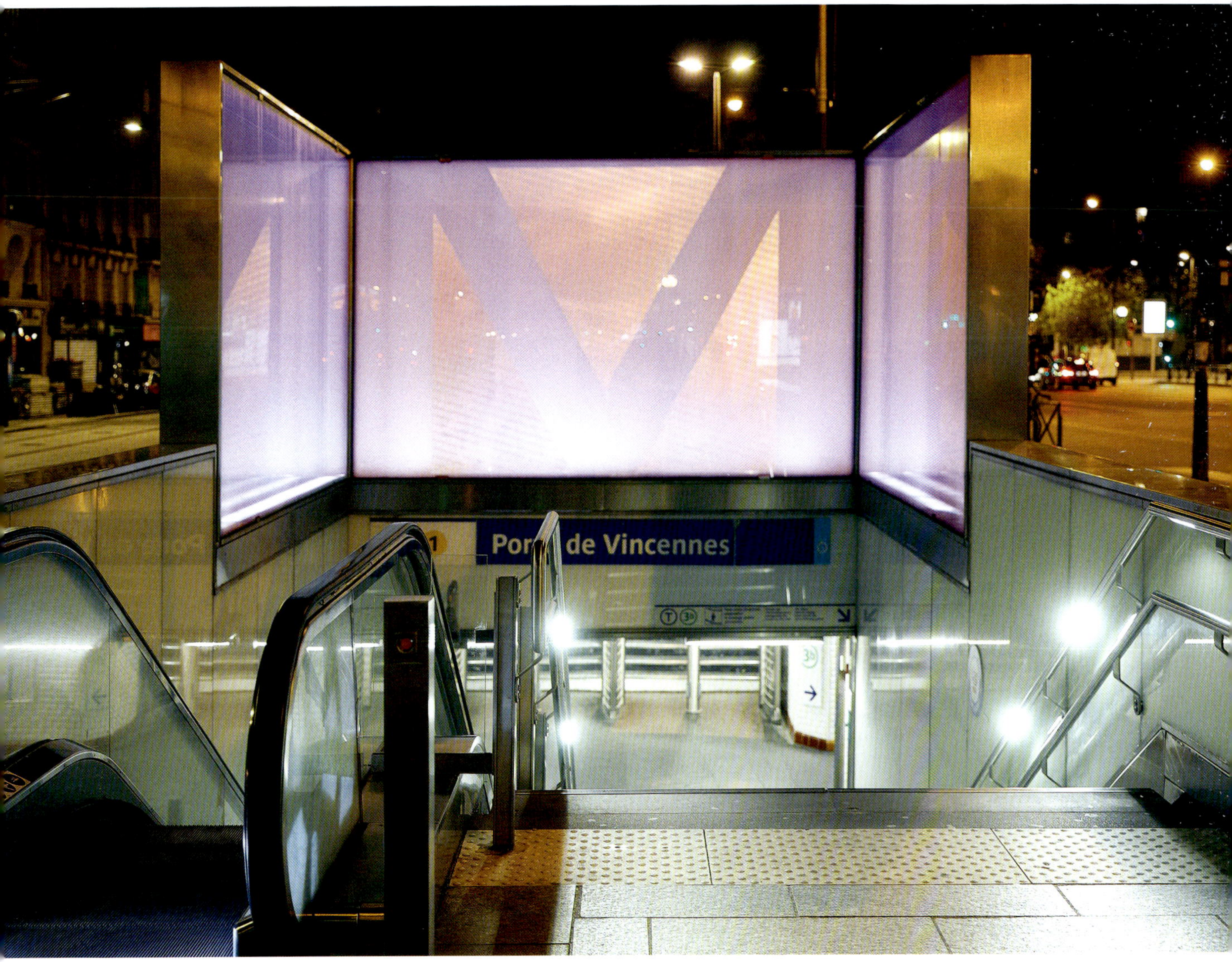
de Vincennes

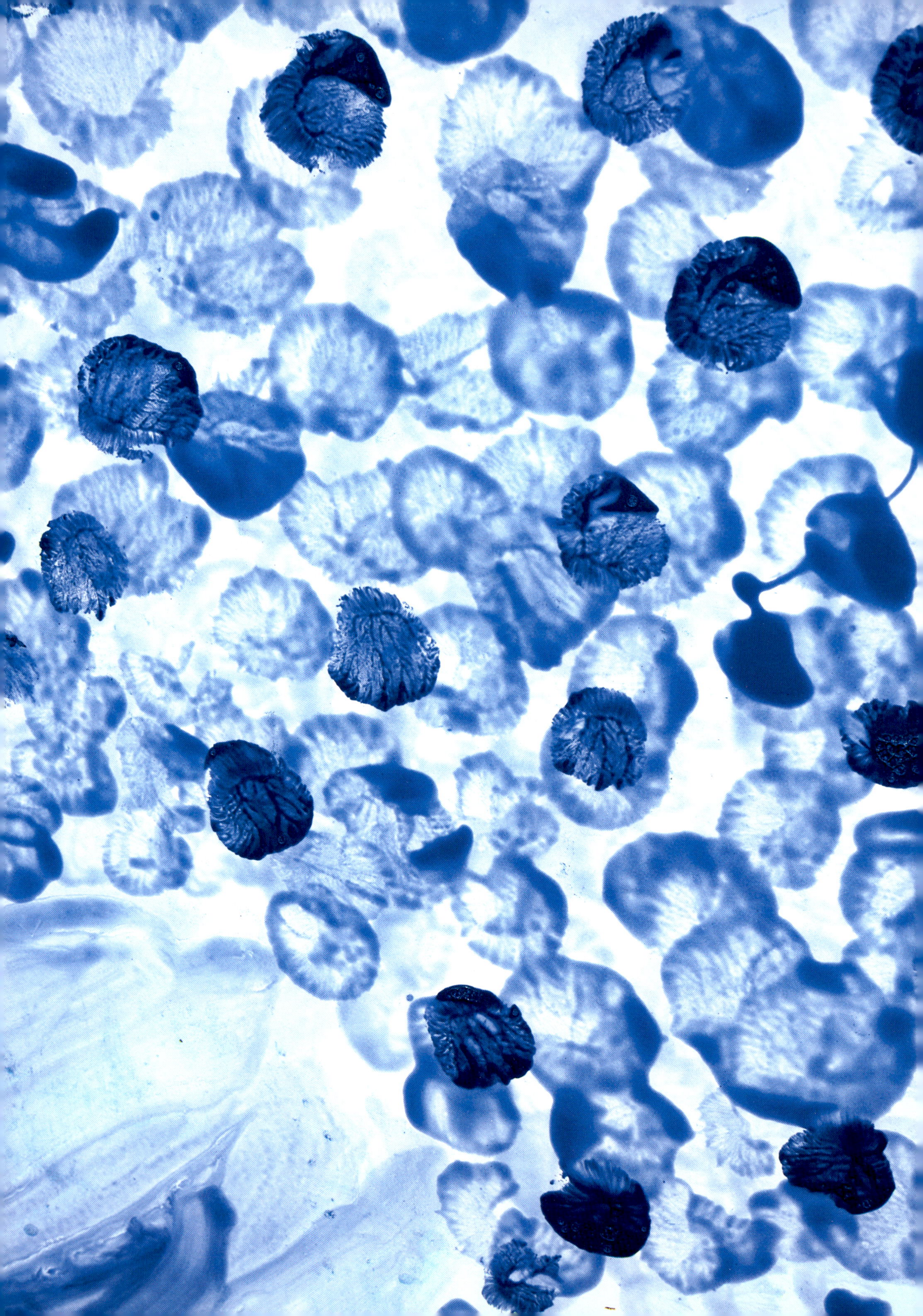

URBAN DIALOGUES

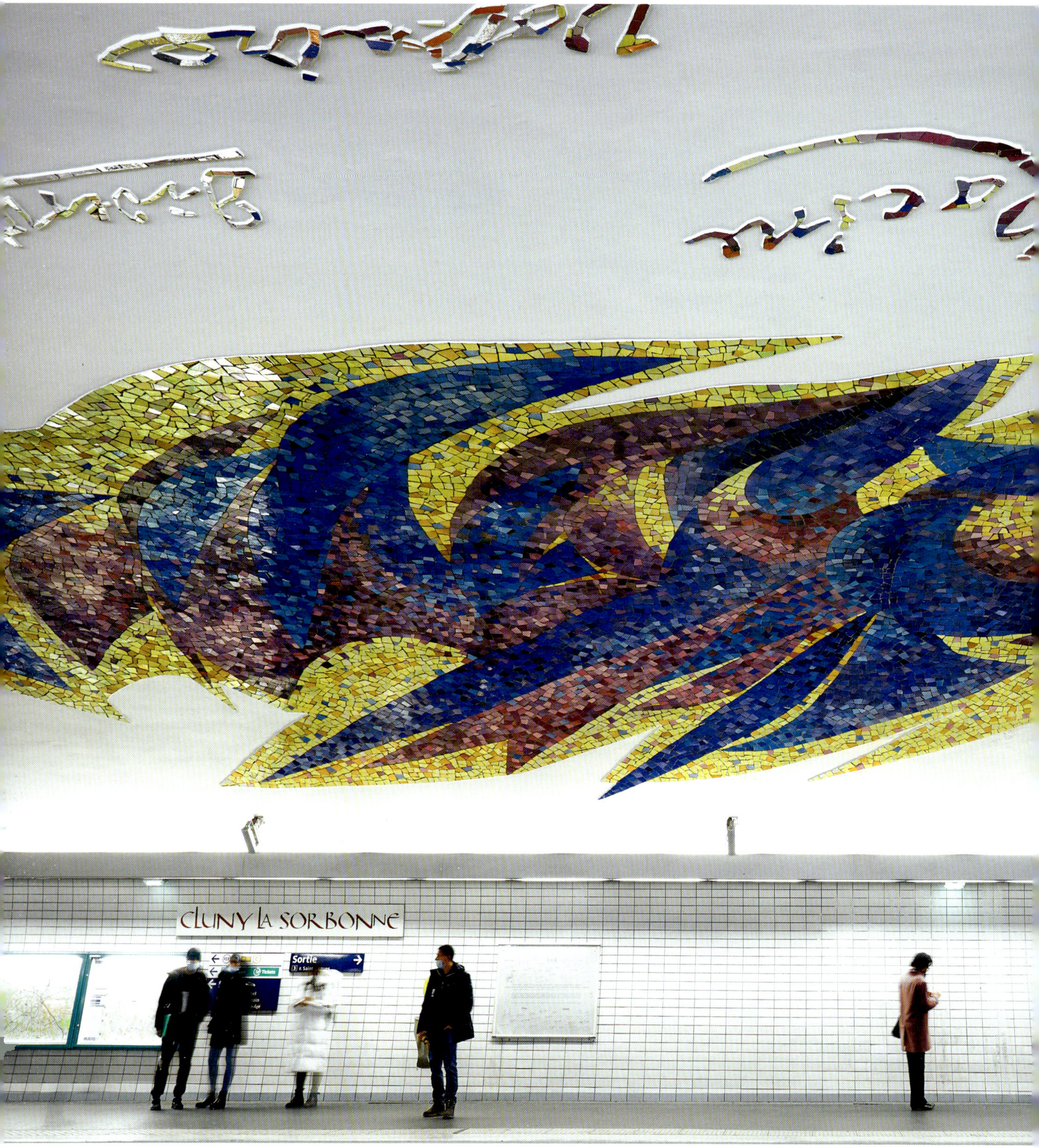
CLUNY LA SORBONNE
Sortie

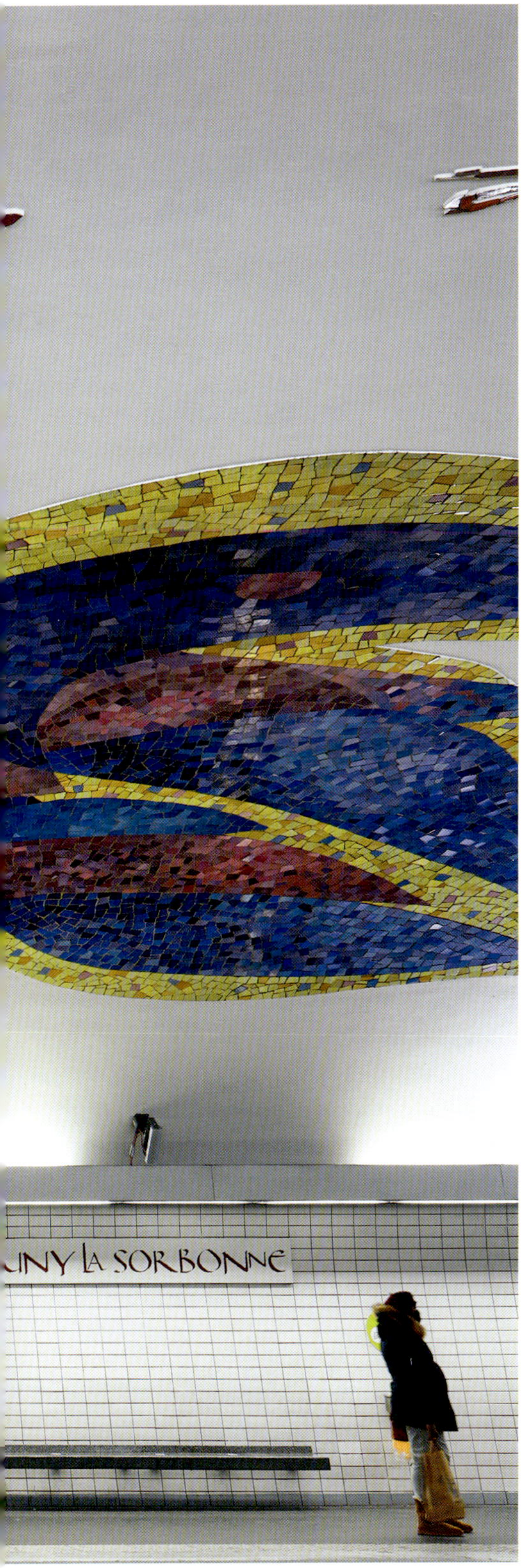

FROM THE METRO TRAINS, YOU CAN SEE THE NAME OF THE STATION, CLUNY–LA SORBONNE, IN A TYPEFACE IMITATING A HANDWRITTEN SCRIPT THAT CAN BE FOUND NOWHERE ELSE ON THE NETWORK. BUT IT'S NOT UNTIL YOU STEP OUT ONTO THE PLATFORM THAT YOU SEE THAT THE ENTIRE VAULT HAS BEEN ILLUMINATED BY JEAN BAZAINE'S MONUMENTAL MOSAIC, *AILES ET FLAMMES* (WINGS AND FLAMES).

JEAN BAZAINE

/ *Ailes et Flammes*

AN AVANT-GARDE FIGURE

Jean Bazaine began to explore abstract painting in the early 1940s. His name is usually associated with the second school of Paris, along with artists such as Alfred Manessier, Édouard Pignon, and Charles Lapicque. Unlike most of his fellow artists, however, Bazaine chose a form of abstraction that was not entirely intellectual. It reflected the energies of the planet and the presence of the elements, perhaps because for most of his life he divided his time between his studios in Clamart, outside Paris, and Saint-Guénolé on the rocky, windswept coast of Finistère, Brittany.

Bazaine, who was born in 1904 and died in 2001, was the descendant of an English portraitist to Queen Victoria. He trained in Paris in the 1920s, first at the Académie Julian, then the École des Beaux-Arts, the Sorbonne, where he attended Henri-Focillon's art-history classes, the studio of the sculptor Paul Landowski, and, most importantly, the Louvre, where he regularly went to paint. He chose to pursue painting. He became friends with Georges Braque and Jacques Villon, established himself on the Parisian art scene, and had his work shown in the world's most prestigious museums.

He also produced a great many theatrical costumes and lithographs to accompany the texts of his writer friends, including Jean Tardieu, Raymond Queneau, and Marcel Arland. Monumental works also make up a large proportion of his oeuvre. He designed mosaics for the ocean liner *France* and the UNESCO and Radio France headquarters in Paris, as well as the new stained-glass windows for the church of Paris and the cathedral of Saint-Dié-des-Vosges in northeastern France.

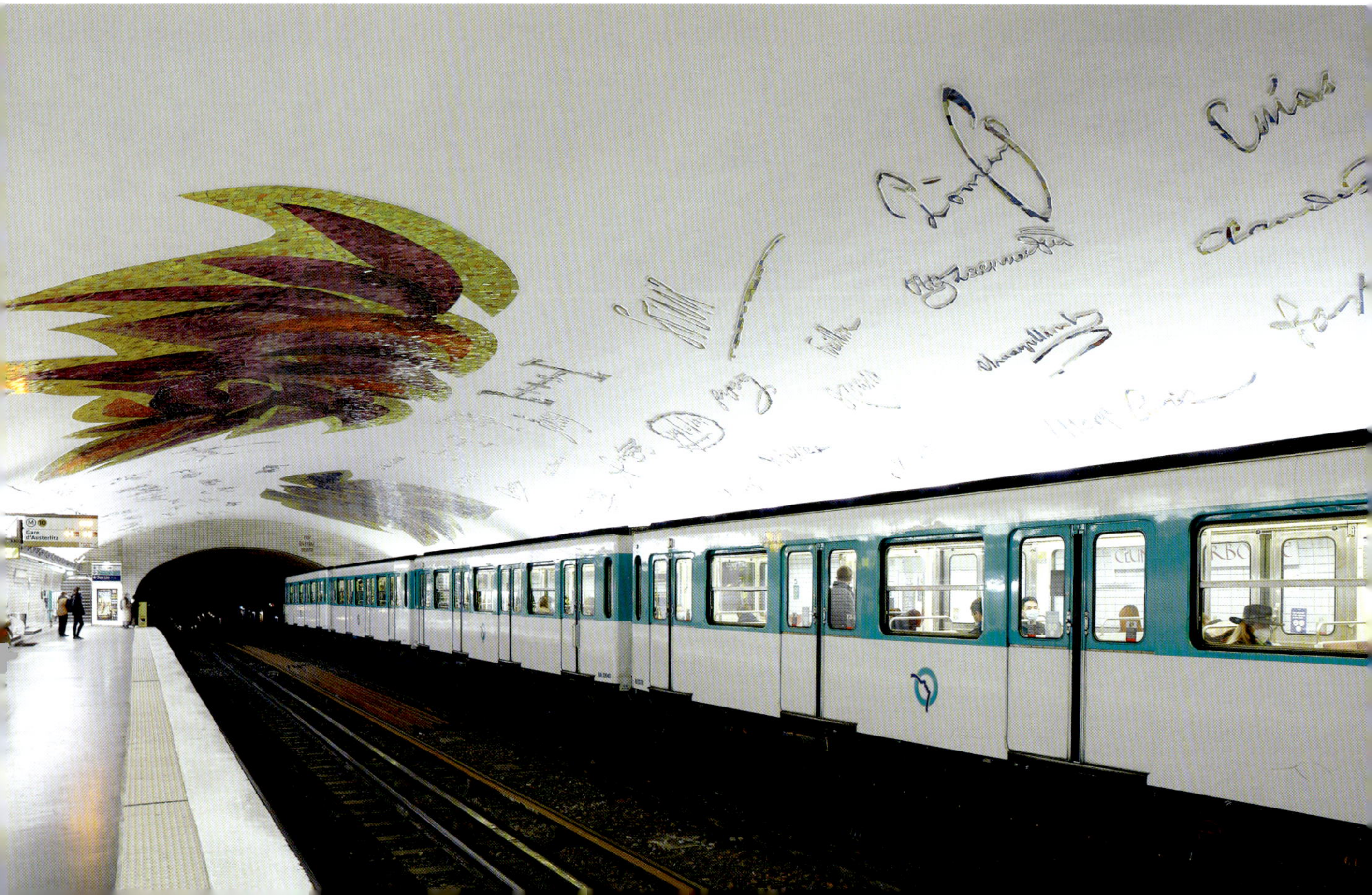

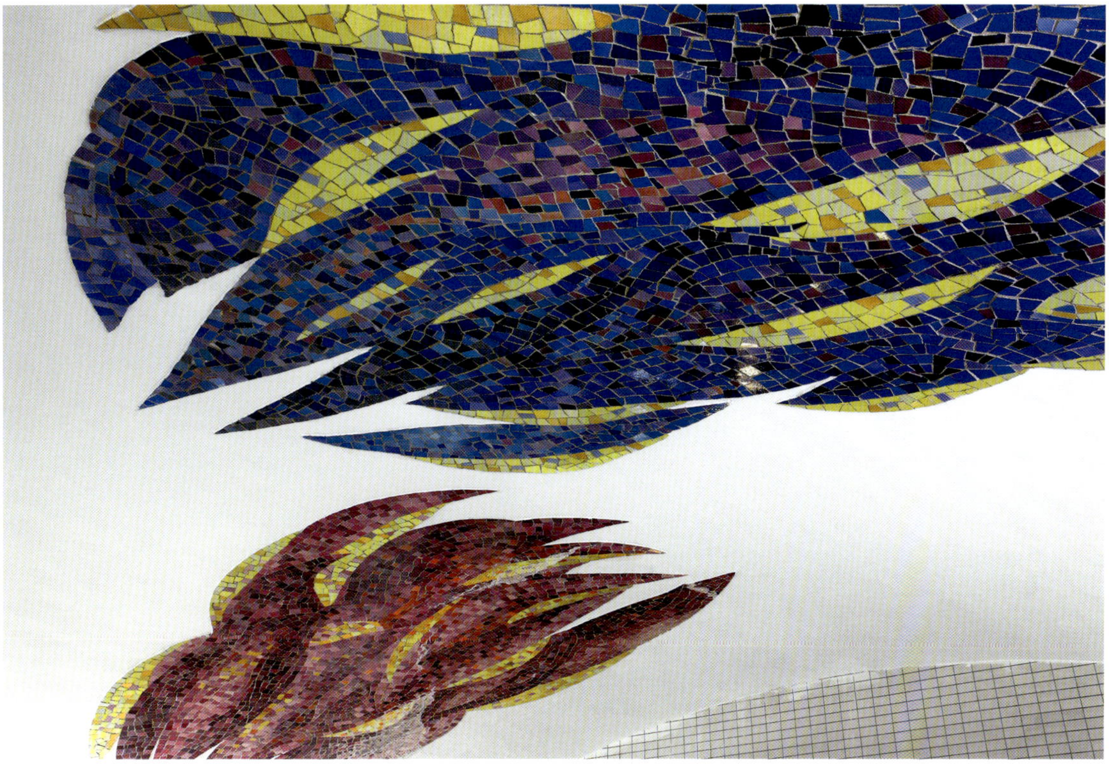

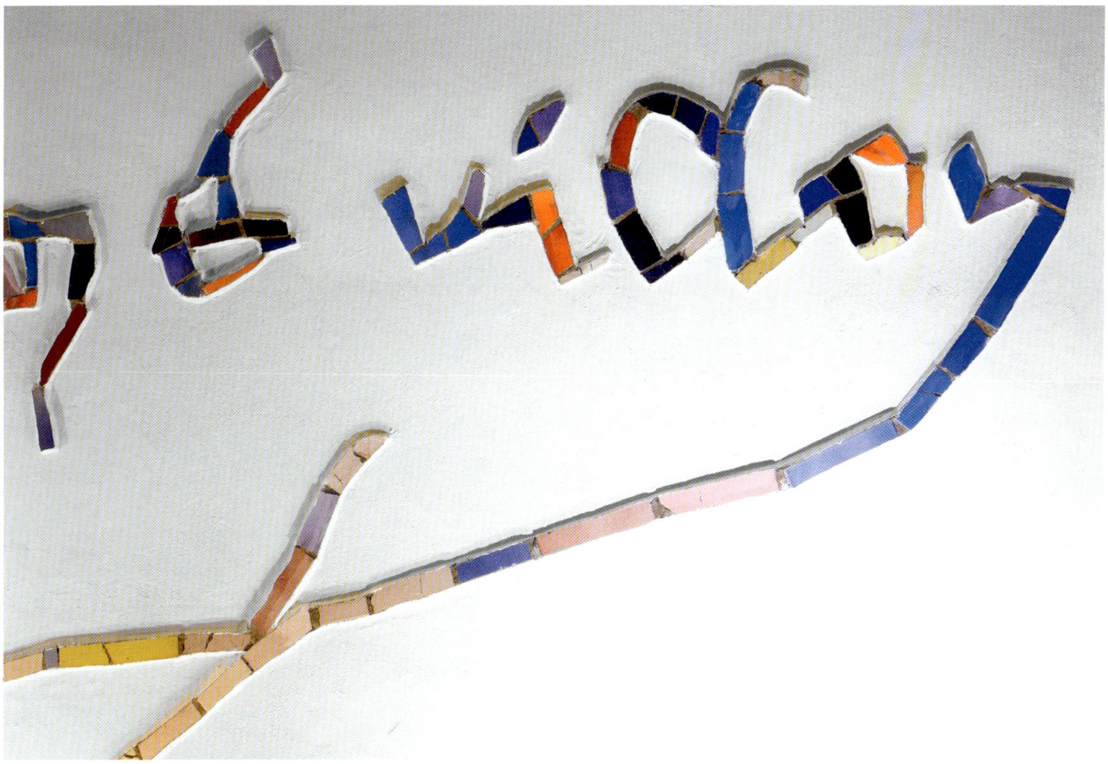

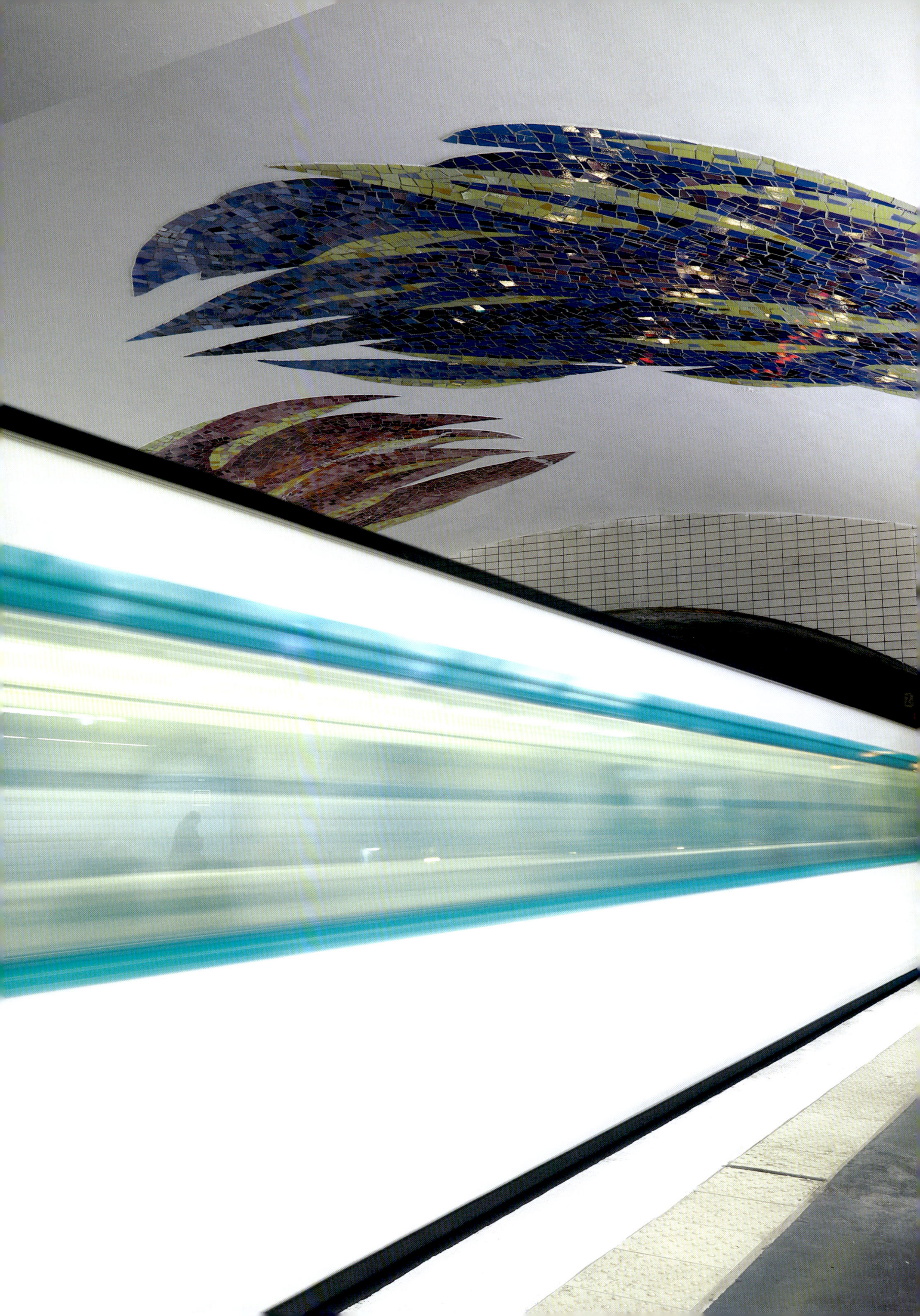

A SINGULAR TRADITION

The metro station for which Jean Bazaine created *Ailes et Flammes* is an amazing place. Opened in 1930 as Cluny station, it was closed in 1939 because of the reduction in service during the Occupation; it was a ghost station for forty-nine years. In 1984 the RATP had corridor built between the RER B and C lines at Saint-Michel–Notre-Dame metro station. The ghost station was reopened as Cluny–La Sorbonne.
Jack Lang, the then minister of culture, entrusted its decoration to Bazaine. The commission was confirmed by François Léotard, who succeeded the minister in 1986. Inspired by the new station name, Bazaine decided to pay tribute to the great minds who inspired the Latin Quarter: the mosaic comprises two immense birds with outspread wings, one mainly blue, the other red, symbolizing the spirit, and fifty-four signatures of statesmen and figures renowned in the arts, letters, and sciences, including Héloïse and Abélard, Philippe-Auguste, François I, Montaigne, Henri IV, Pascal, Racine, Danton, and Courbet.

The station itself is an architectural feat: its semicircular, surbased arch measures 75 meters long, 18 meters wide, and 8 meters high, with no central support. Bazaine chose enameled lava stone from Volvic in central France for his work—60,000 tesserae in 100 colors—because it is very resistant and well-suited to the site. The preparation of the work in a neighboring station under the Jardin du Luxembourg took six months. Perched on top of a ladder so he could have an overall view of the work on the floor, he guided the team of mosaicists overseen by Gino Silvestri da Belun. Then the panels were transported and applied to the station arch, which continues to feel both protective and magnificently spacious.

***Ailes et Flammes*, 1988**
Enameled lava stone
75 × 18 m, 8 m high
400 m^2

FRANÇOISE SCHEIN

/ Concorde

AT FIRST GLANCE, THIS LOOKS LIKE A JUMBLE OF LETTERS. LET YOUR EYES ADJUST. WORDS AND SENTENCES WILL BEGIN TO FORM. IF YOU READ FRENCH, YOU WILL REALIZE THAT THE CERAMIC TILES COVERING THIS PART OF CONCORDE METRO STATION CONTAIN THE TEXT OF THE 1789 DECLARATION OF THE RIGHTS OF MAN AND OF THE CITIZEN.

THE FACTORY BEHIND THE WORK

The story began in New York during the late 1980s. Françoise Schein, who had been living there for about ten years (she is now based in Paris), was working on the cartography of cities: "I had been thinking about disseminating the text from the French Revolution that changed the world on the main thoroughfares of Paris. First, I made drawings that weren't meant for the metro. Then I decided to show my small models to the RATP. I went from office to office, talking to the technical team and the president of the RATP at the time, Christian Blanc. The project was accepted, and it evolved. I just wanted to work on a corridor, and they offered me a whole station—and not just any station."

For Schein, the opportunity to work on Concorde metro station was providential: "It evokes entire history of France and the Revolution. For me, as I had worked in human rights, having that particular word, *'concorde* [concord],' was wonderful." Little by little, she discovered the inner working of the Paris transportation network. She visited the Beauvais factory where the white ceramic tiles still used in many metro stations were made. "I got into my car and went to the factory to ask if they could make square tiles measuring 15 × 15 centimeters so that I could put a single letter on each one. They said yes." The text was reproduced one-and-a-half times over the surface of the vault. Françoise Schein herself had made freehand drawings on a huge sheets of tracing paper. Finally, engineers calculated the installation of the tiles down to the nearest millimeter: "It was somewhere between IT and artistry. A year of preparation was followed by a year of construction."

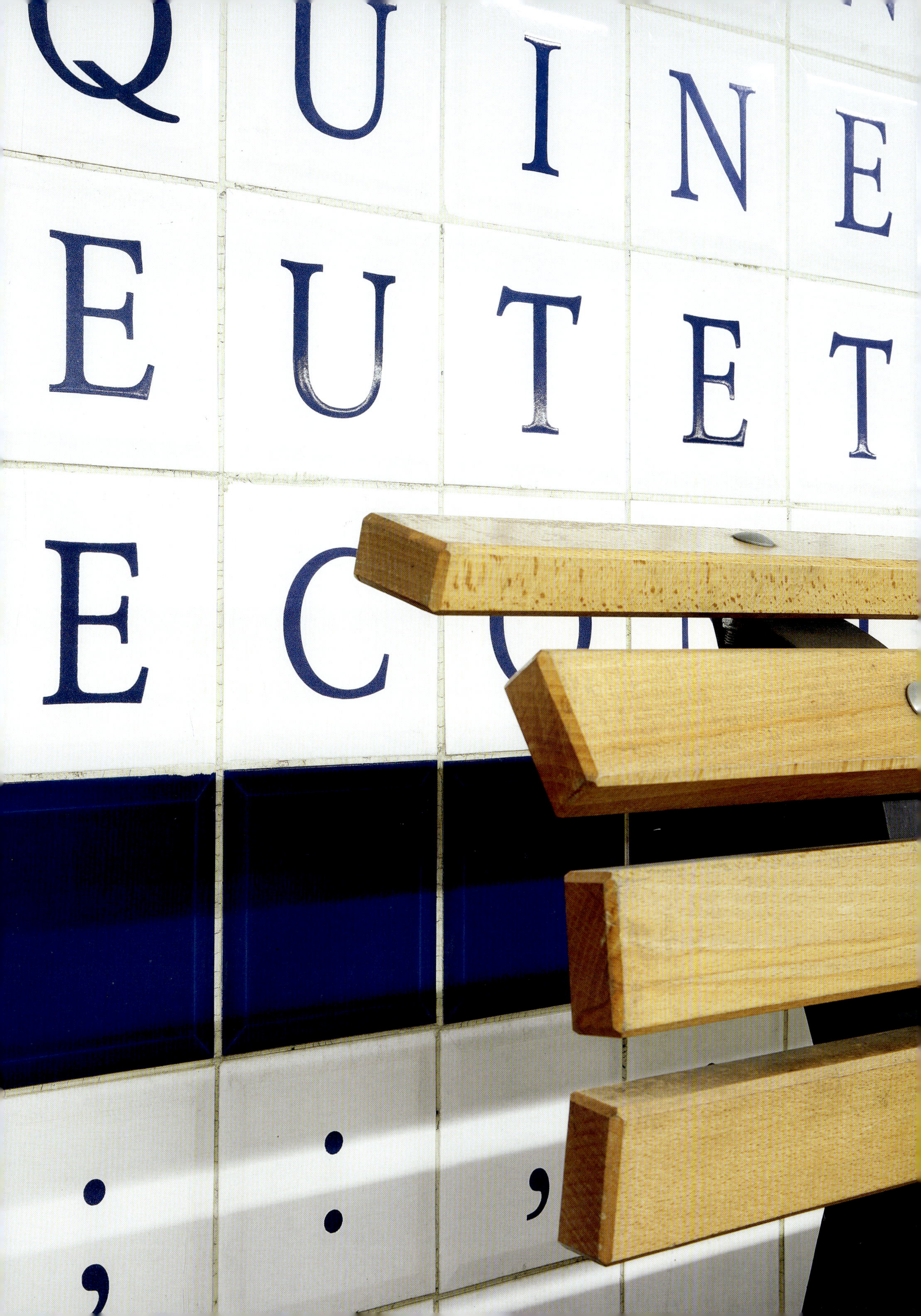
QUINE
EUTET
EC

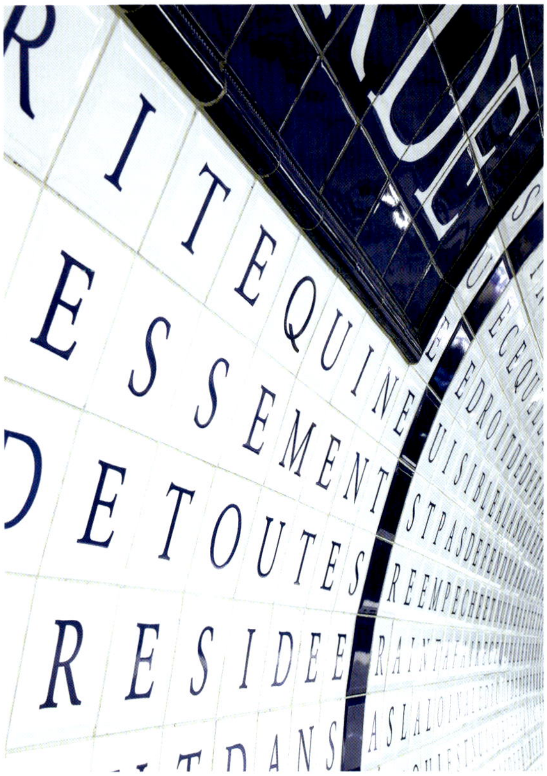

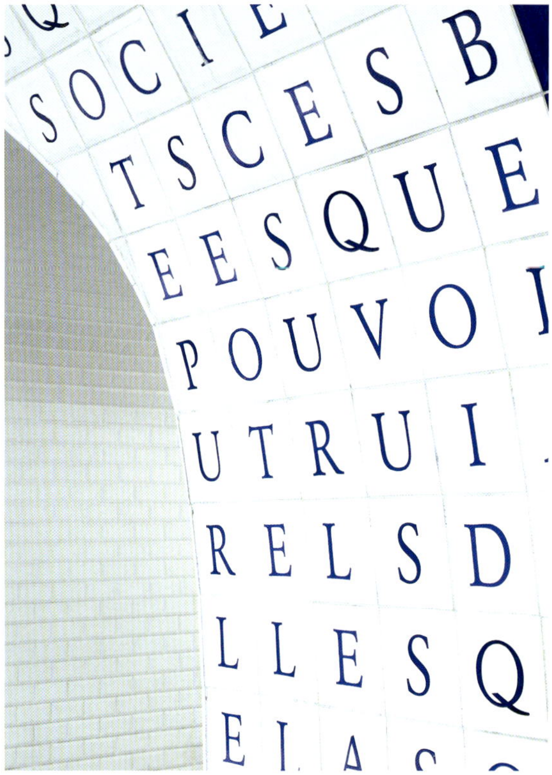

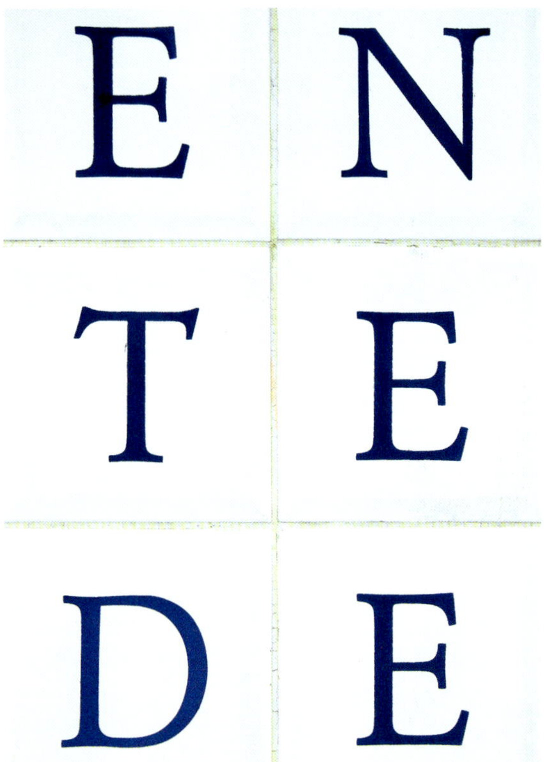
EN
TE
DE

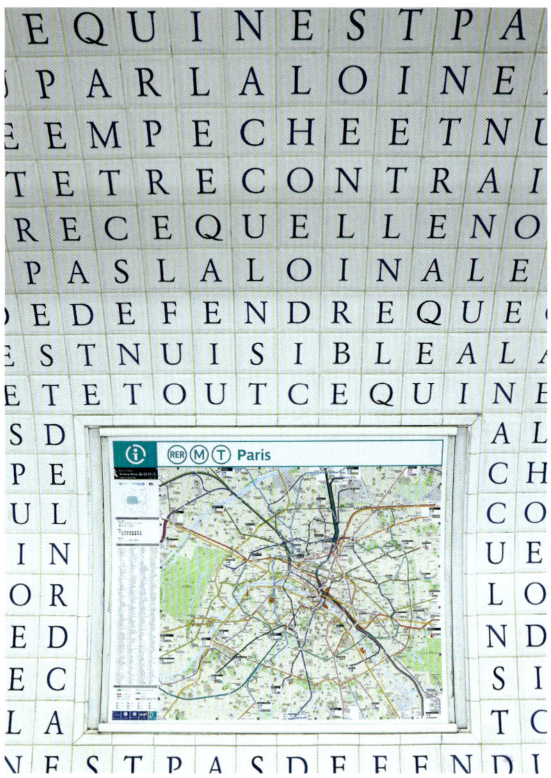
EQUINESTPA
PARLALOINE
EMPECHEETN
TETRECONTRAI
RECEQUELLENO
PASLALOINALE
EDEFENDREQUE
STNUISIBLEAL
ETETOUTCEQUINE
Paris

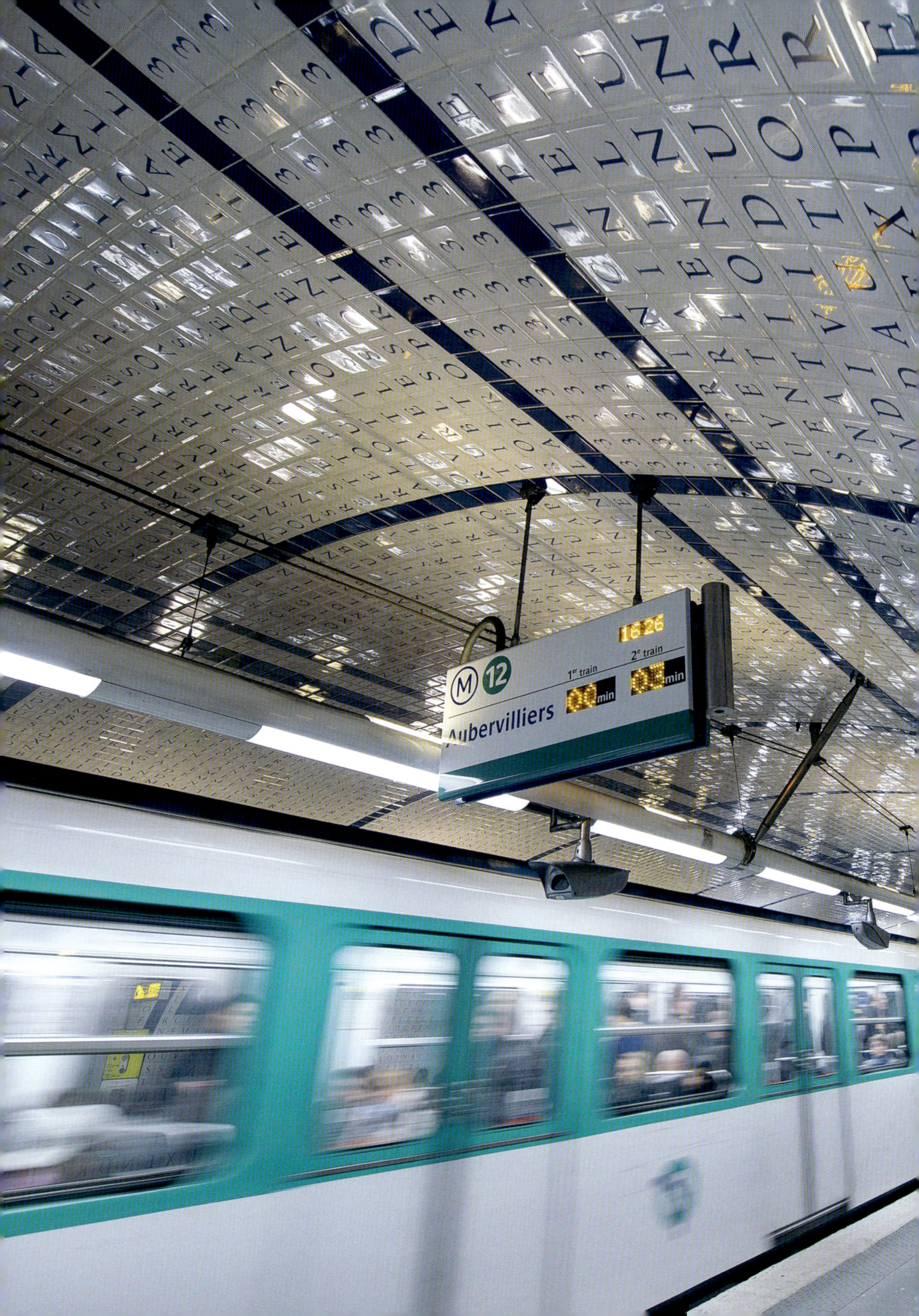
M 12
Aubervilliers
1er train
2e train
min
min

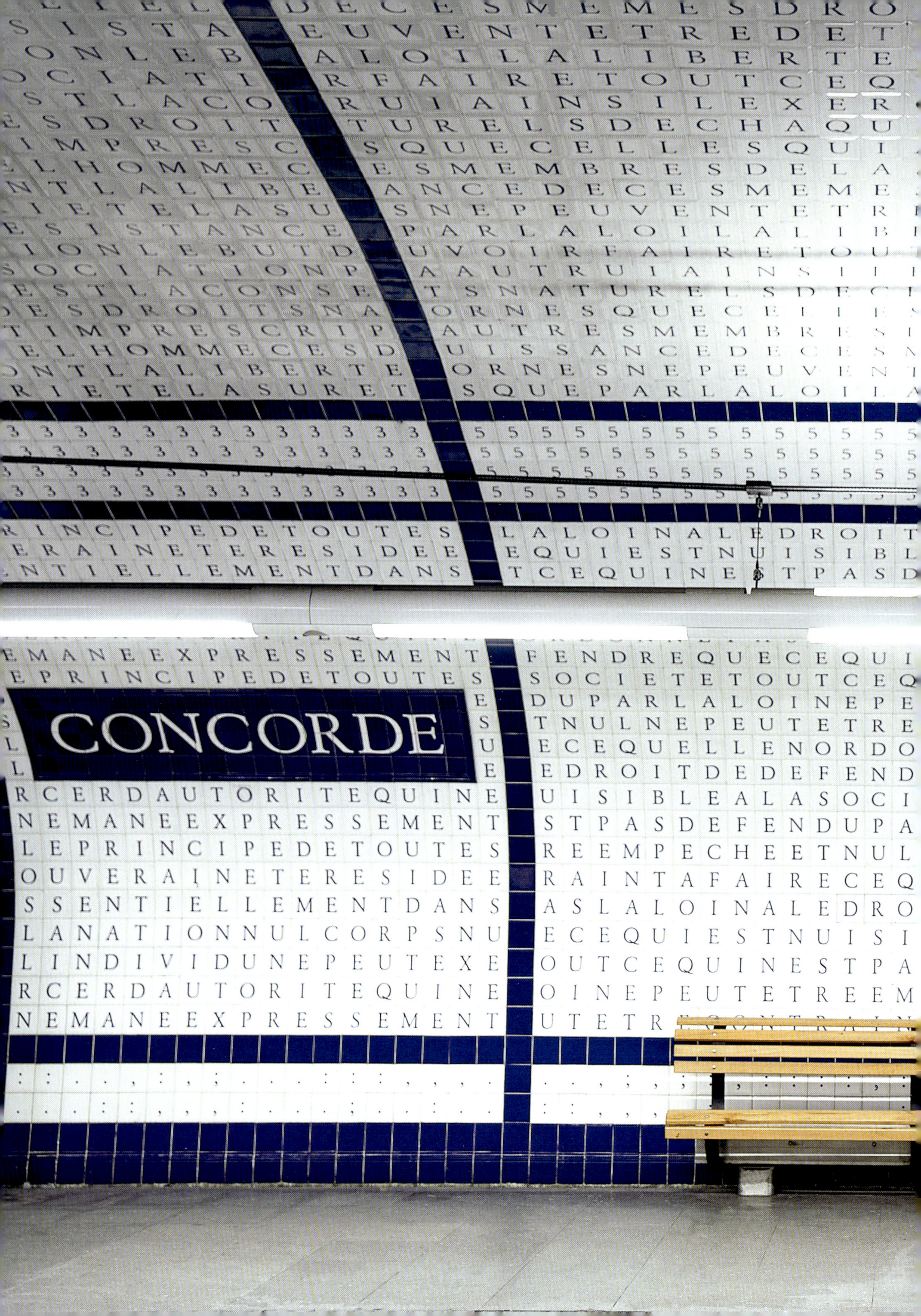
CONCORDE

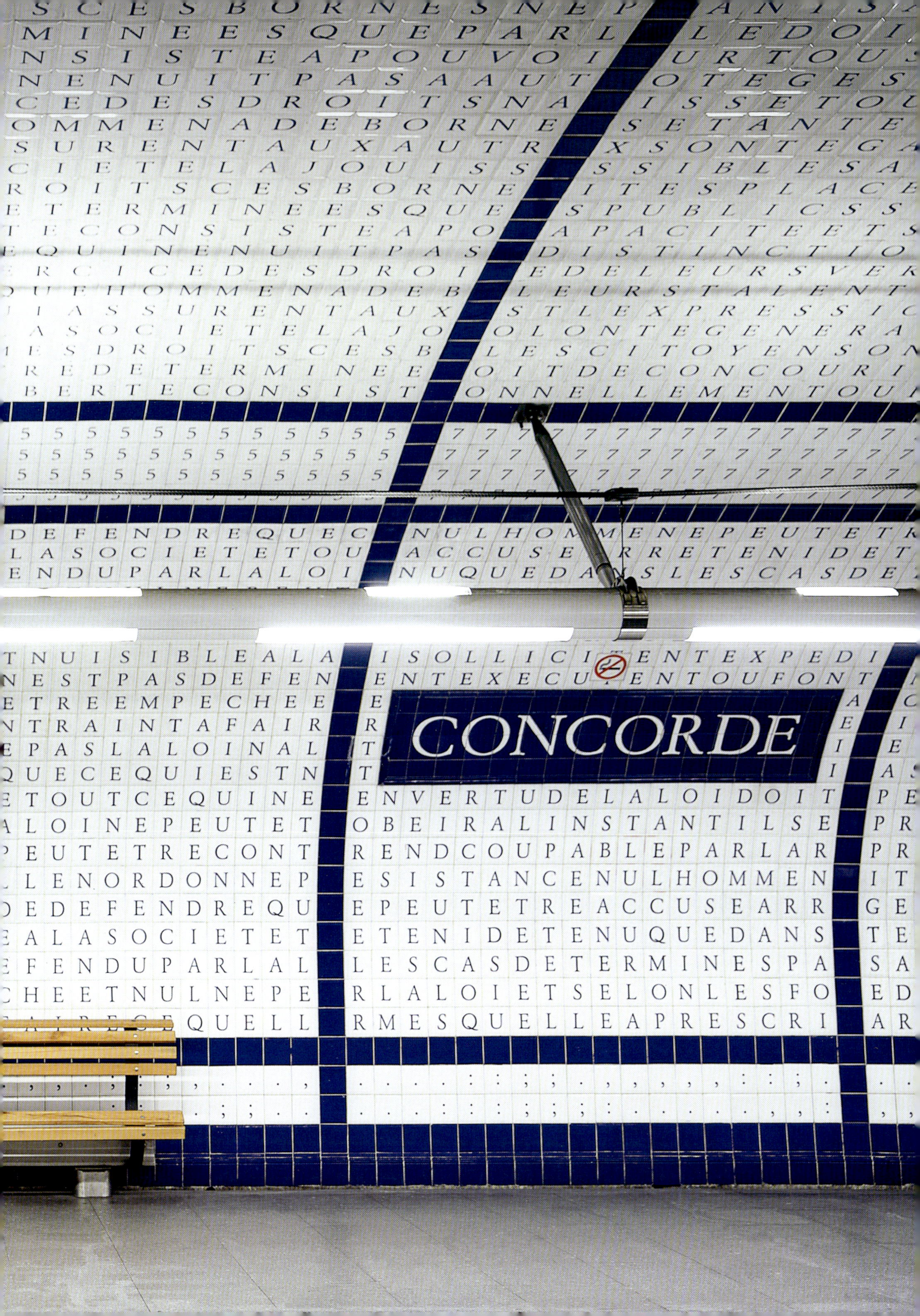
CONCORDE

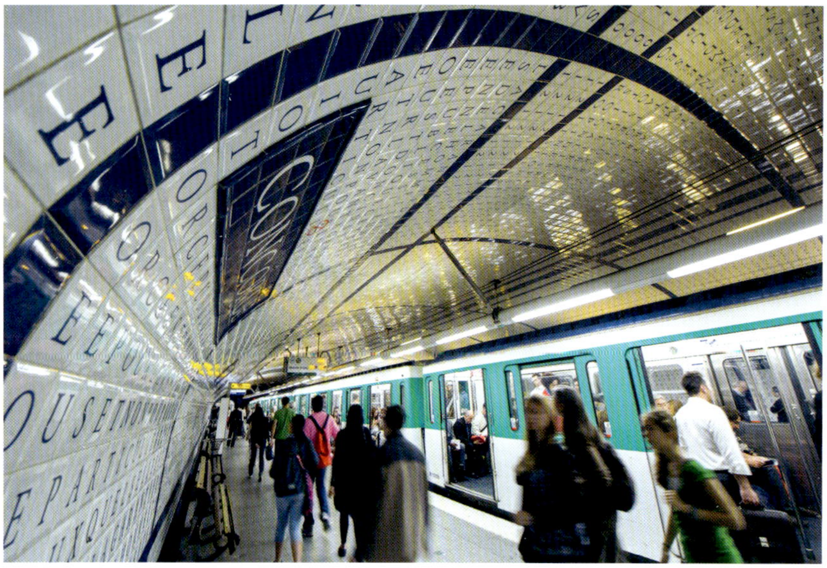

A TEXT TO DECIPHER

The year 1989 saw both the bicentennial of the French Revolution and the fall of the Berlin Wall. Françoise Schein describes her work as being "rooted like a tree." It interacts with geography, past, and present underneath Place de la Concorde, where history looms large. It also has a strong humanist dimension: "I am a great romantic. This work speaks to travelers," she says, "and I wanted its content to deeply affect everybody." She chose to use the Garamond typeface, which dates from the sixteenth century, and blue letters instead of black because she thinks they represent the formal perfection of French design. An architect and urban planner by training, she wanted to make "a text map" that was as difficult to decipher as a geographical one. That's why she decided to remove the spaces between the words and focus the text on itself. "I wanted people to read it slowly like children because that is how democracy is learned."

THE MATRIX FOR A SERIES OF STATIONS

One of the particularities of this work is its international dimension: it was the matrix for a series of other creations that Françoise Schein was later invited to transcribe in seven other cities around the world. Thanks to Concorde metro station in Paris, the cities of Brussels, Lisbon, Berlin, Stockholm, São Paulo, Rio de Janeiro, and Brasília all have stations celebrating the Rights of Man.

***Concorde*, 1989–91**
49,000 ceramic tiles, each measuring
15 × 15 cm
1,000 m^2

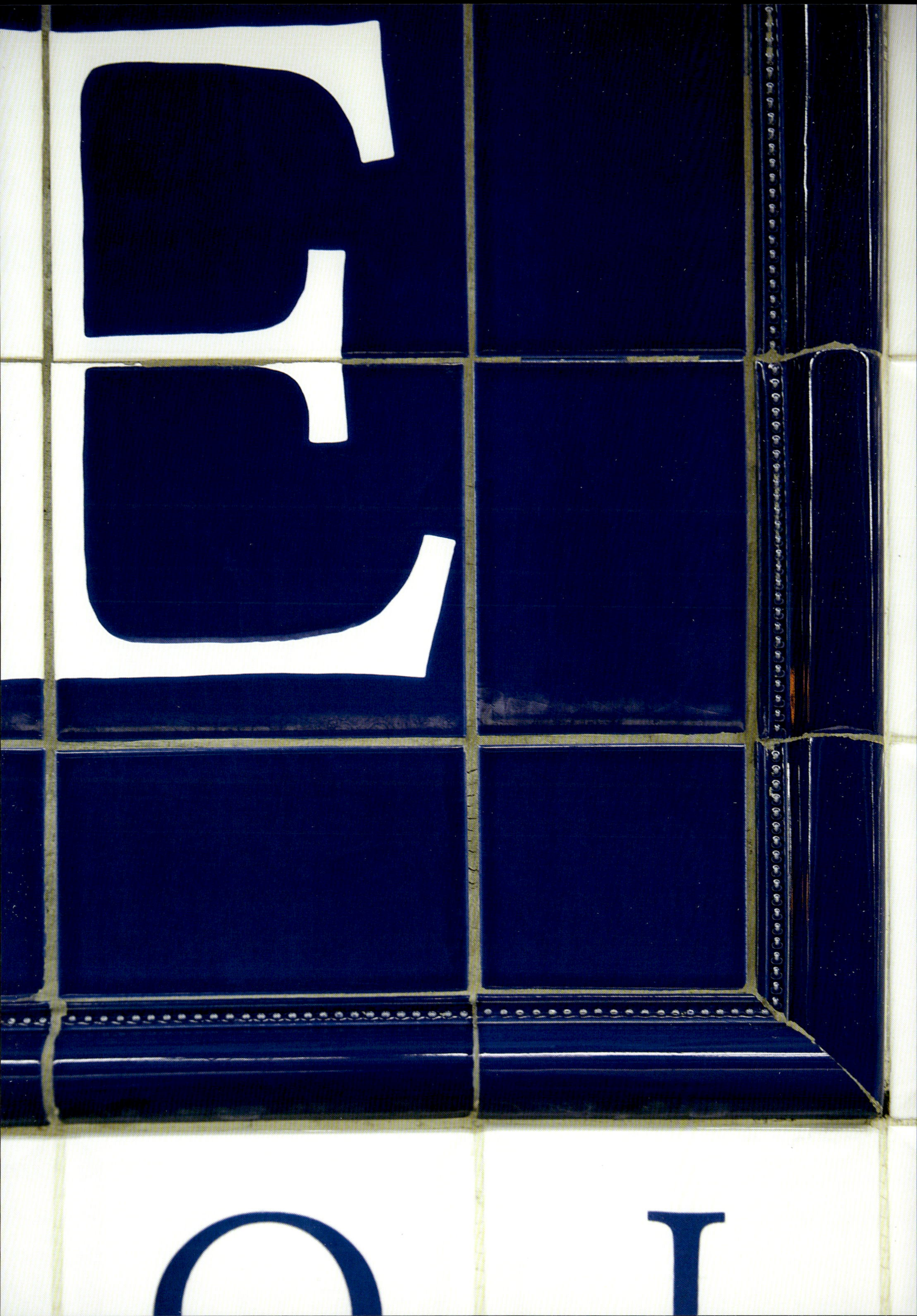

PHILIPPE FAVIER

/ P.I.L.I.

FROM THE LINE 14 PLATFORM, THIS WORK LOOKS LIKE A SUBMARINE PORTHOLE. THROUGH A ROUND WINDOW, A SKY CAN BE SEEN. THE SKY IS PARIS, OR RATHER A MAP OF PARIS THE ARTIST PHILIPPE FAVIER USES TO INVITE US ON POETIC JOURNEYS.

A REMARKABLE INVENTION

P.I.L.I. is a strange name for an artwork but it refers to an object that was familiar to metro users trying to find their way through the urban jungle—it is an abbreviation of *plan indicateur lumineux d'itinéraires*. The earliest such objects date from 1937. There have been several generations of framed metro maps with stainless-steel buttons at the bottom for the different stations. You pressed them, then your itinerary lit up. Today, we might think of them as the distant cousins of the jukebox and the ancestors of online mapping apps. For the young Philippe Favier, who would get off the train from Saint-Étienne at Gare de Lyon, they were reassuring presences: "Just a kid, I wanted to go to the Centre Pompidou and the galleries. The very thought of Paris was complicated, and the P.I.L.I. was a playful object that helped me come to terms with the big city."

CELEBRATING THE MILLENNIUM

Philippe Favier's *P.I.L.I.* dates from the passage to the year 2000, which coincided with the centennial of the Paris metro. "Several artists were invited to compete," he recalls, "including Pierre Buraglio, Sylvie Blocher, and Jean-Michel Othoniel." Then a jury made its choice and Favier designed "a poetic—and useless—object to be placed on the platforms of the very recent line 14 to give the automated surroundings a bit of soul." His *P.I.L.I.* is a journey planner with a twist: "If people use it to get around, they might end up in somewhat exotic locations." Favier invited the Oulipo (acronym for *Ouvroir de littérature potentielle*, literally "Workshop of Potential Literature") poet Jacques Roubaud to design seventy-four routes that lit up on a map when a button was pushed. The names of stations form poetic texts with themes such as music

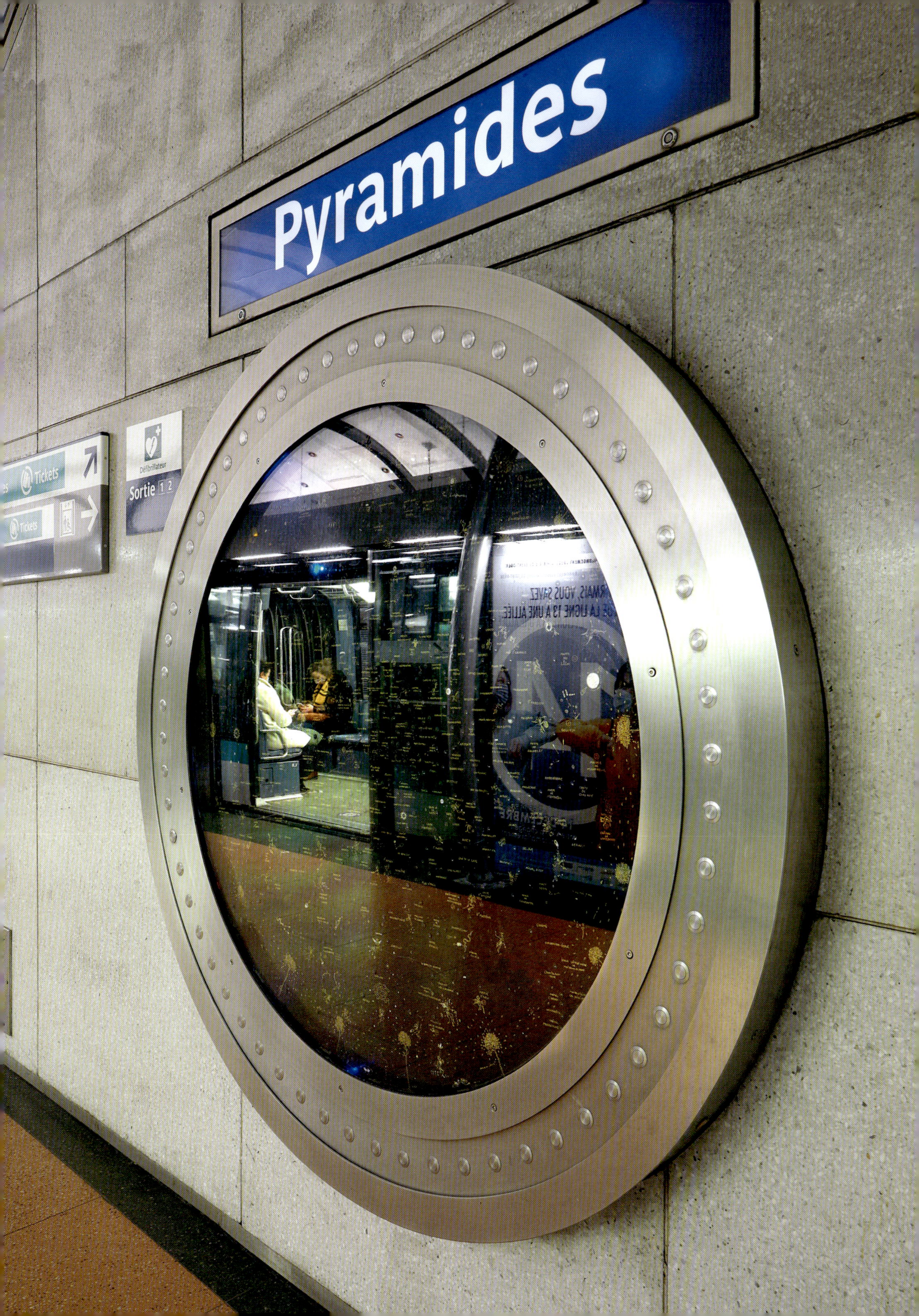
Pyramides
Tickets
Tickets
Défibrillateur
Sortie 1 2

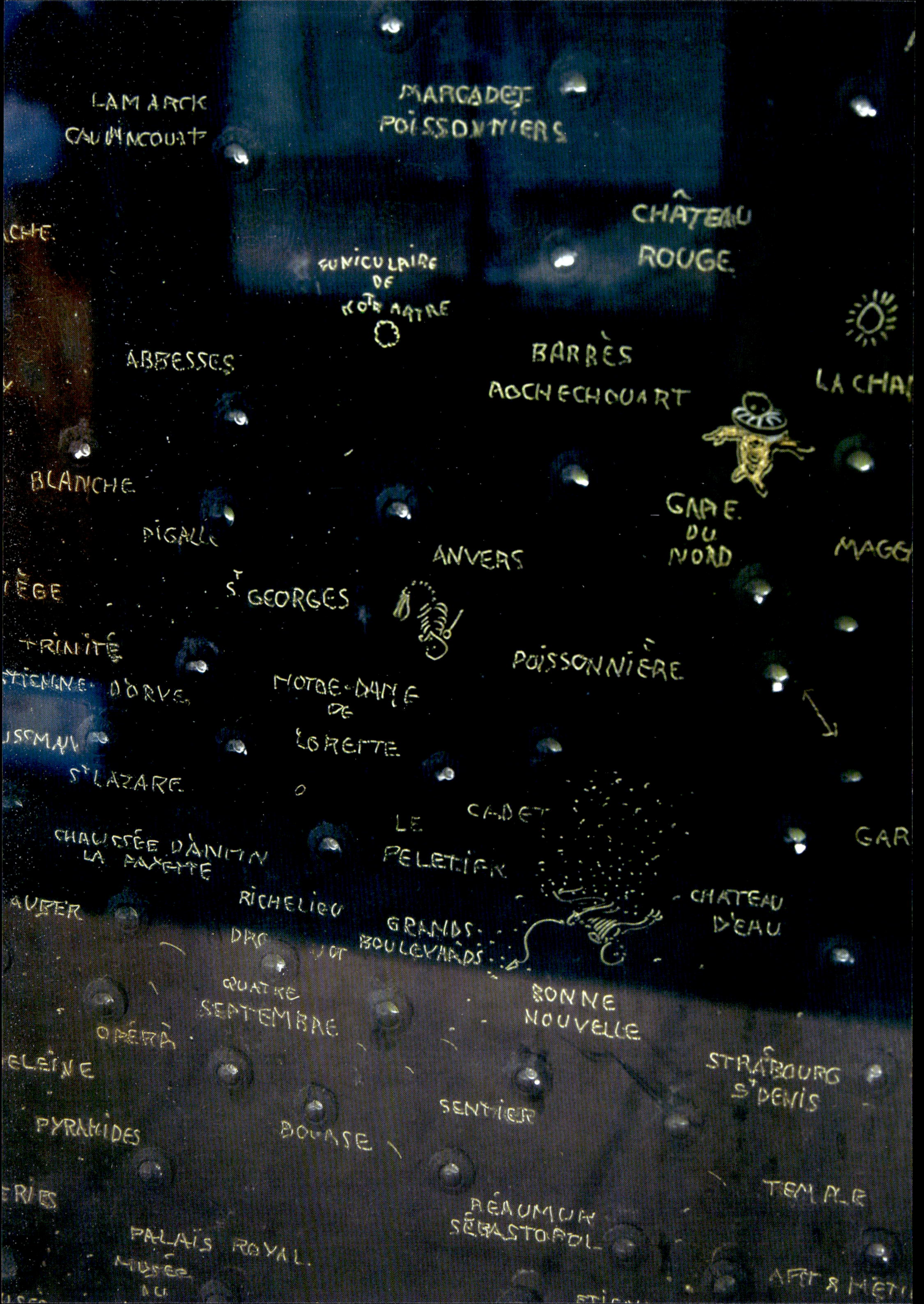
LAMARCK
CAULAINCOURT
MARCADET
POISSONNIERS
CHÂTEAU
ROUGE
FUNICULAIRE
DE
MONTMARTRE
ABBESSES
BARRÈS
ROCHECHOUART
BLANCHE
PIGALLE
ANVERS
GARE
DU
NORD
S^T GEORGES
TRINITÉ
POISSONNIÈRE
NOTRE-DAME
DE
LORETTE
S^T LAZARE
CADET
LE
PELETIER
CHAUSSÉE D'ANTIN
LA FAYETTE
RICHELIEU
GRANDS
BOULEVARDS
CHATEAU
D'EAU
QUATRE
SEPTEMBRE
BONNE
NOUVELLE
OPÉRA
STRASBOURG
S^T DENIS
SENTIER
PYRAMIDES
BOURSE
TEMPLE
RÉAUMUR
SÉBASTOPOL
PALAIS ROYAL

and optimism: Bel-Air, Belleville, Place des Fêtes, and so on. There are also itineraries guided by Oulipian "constraints": for example, a selection of stations whose names begin and end with the same letter. Like the buttons of an accordion, the push buttons surrounding the work are unlabeled. Even though its electronic operation has its ups and down, Favier has a soft spot for this work: "It really is my world."

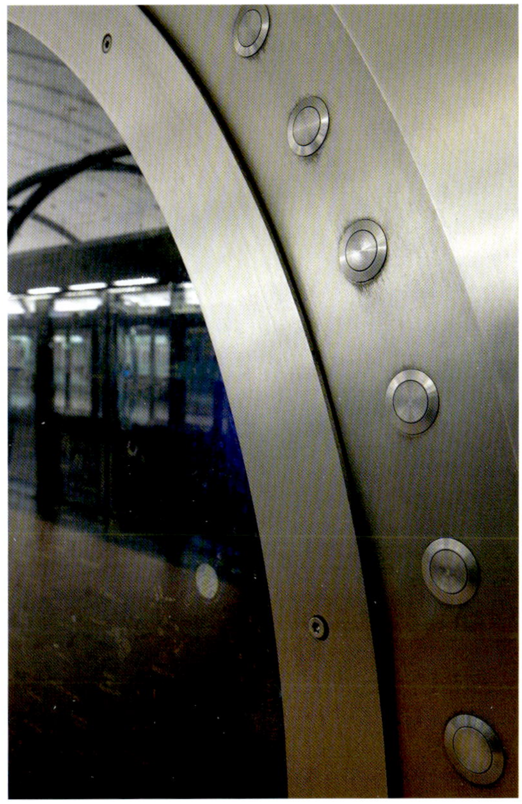

The names of the stations were engraved on a round panel of Plexiglas using a burr. "The technique is fun," says Favier, "with a floppy, gooey feel—a bit like being supervised by a giant earthworm. I poured gold paint into the grooves, then covered the rest in black, which gave a certain preciousness to the whole." The work looks like a constellation or zodiac. Favier often uses the circular form in his work, a reference to *woolloomooloo*, thought to be a transcription of the word for gathering place in an Australian Aboriginal language. In its own way, the Paris metro is also such a place.
Twenty years later, Favier still remembers the commitment and passion of the RATP team that oversaw the production of the work and regularly came to see him at his studio in Saint-Étienne, also visiting the metalworker and electronics engineer involved "with complete confidence and just the right amount of curiosity about the imaginary journeys."

***P.I.L.I.*, 2000**
Metal and Plexiglas
1.9 m × 60 cm × 1.7 m

FRANÇOIS SCHUITEN / *Nautilus*

ENTERING ARTS ET MÉTIERS METRO STATION IS LIKE ENTERING A STRANGE SUBMARINE OR A PROTECTIVE COCOON IN WARM COLORS. WHAT EXACTLY IS THIS CURIOUS NAUTILUS?

THE STORY BEHIND THE WORK

"There was a real alignment of the planets: the moment I entered the station, I had a brain wave. It was obvious," says François Schuiten. Yet, the project saw many twists and turns in its early days. Initially, he and Benoît Peeters had drawn up plans to redesign the Musée du Conservatoire National des Arts et Métiers, a museum for which they both had a passion. Somebody else won that competition, but a member of the museum team had the bright idea of inviting the duo to work on the metro station below, which was also going to be renovated. What were their plans? "To make it look as if the finest machines had pierced the ceiling and seeped into the station, which had become an emanation of the museum." That's why all the walls were covered with copper and brass plates, and large cogwheels were hung from the vault. Then portholes appeared on the platforms, creating effects of scale. Through them, we can contemplate models of emblematic exhibits from the museum: bridges, machines, and figures. "They are machines / sculptures whose aesthetics and materials are extraordinary." Curiously, the reference to the *Nautilus*, the submarine in Jules Verne's *Twenty Thousand Leagues Under the Sea*, did not make an immediate appearance despite the fact that it figures in Schuiten's personal pantheon. With the help of Benoit Peeters,

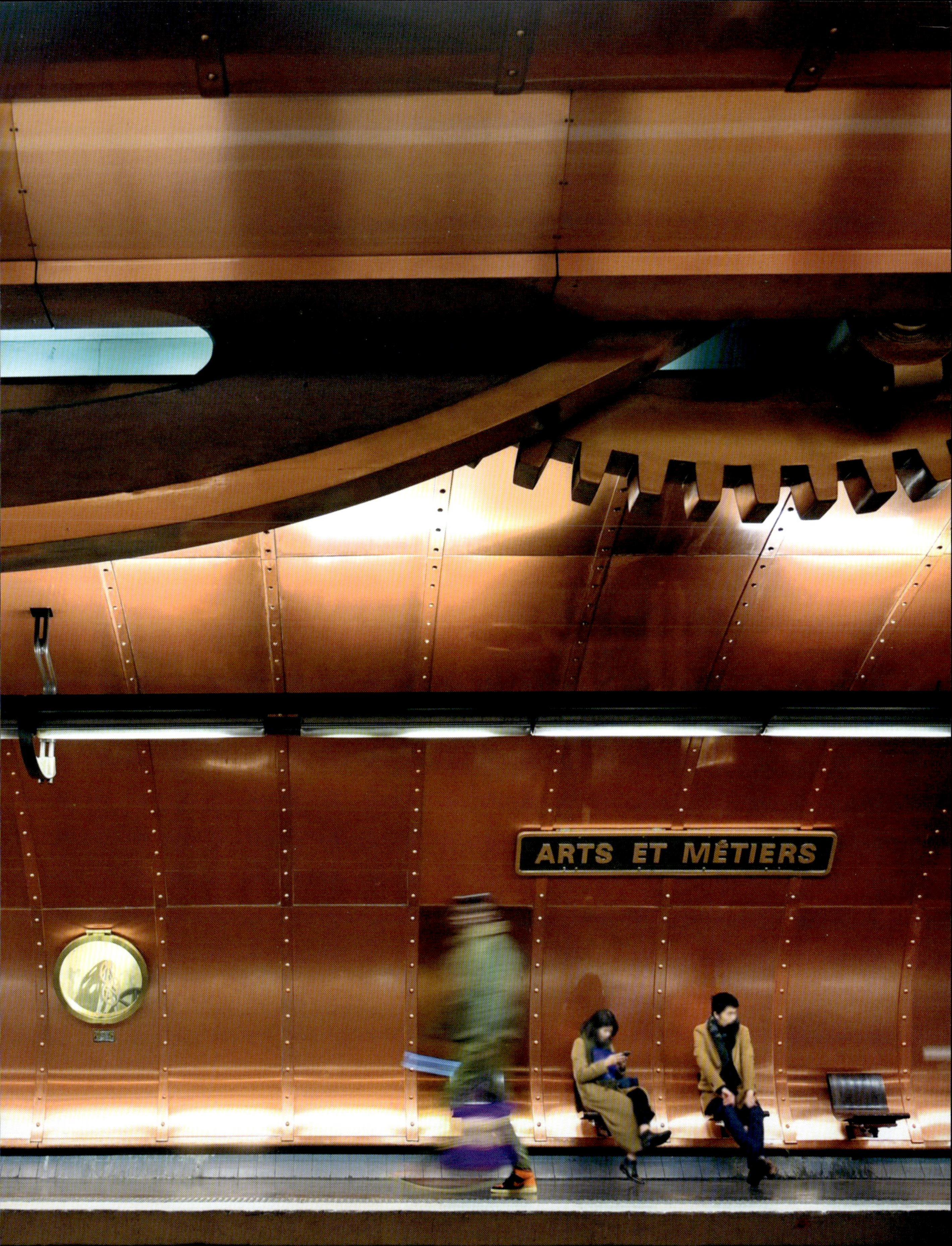
ARTS ET MÉTIERS

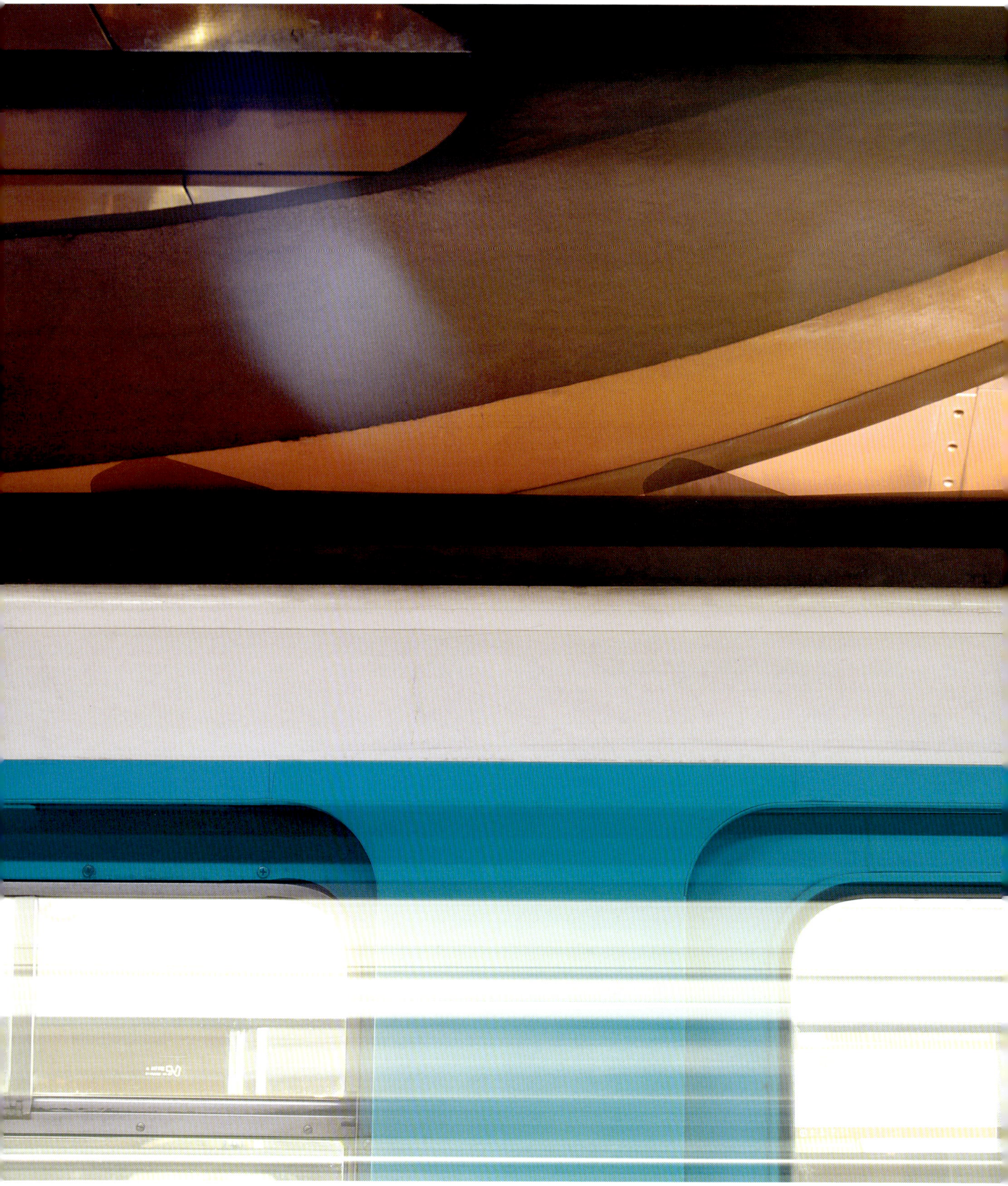

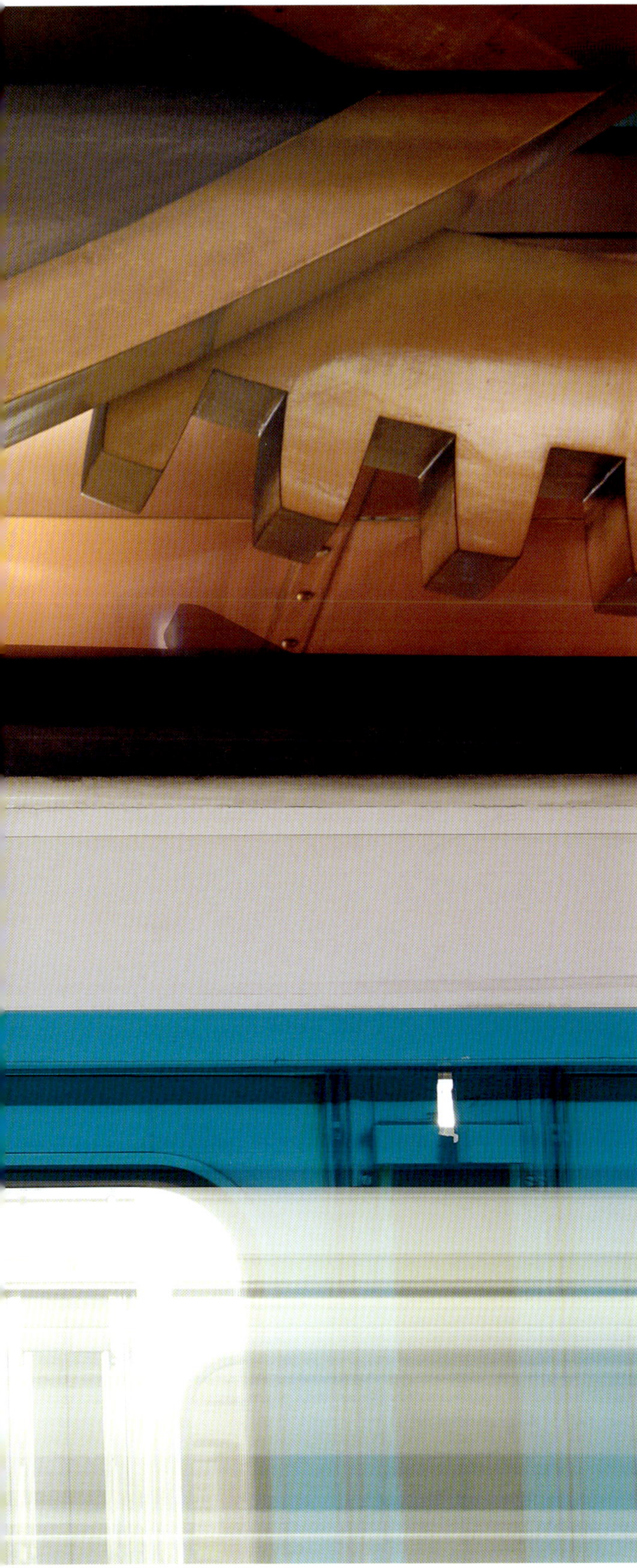

Schuiten—a jack-of-all-trades—has worked in a variety of fields: graphic novels with *Les Cités obscures (Cities of the Fantastic)*; opera set design; urban planning (he was working on Porte de Hal/Hallepoort metro station in Brussels at the same time as this project). First and foremost, however, he is a storyteller. "The metro is a place where you wait, where dreams can get in. In fact, what I love is bringing dreams to places that are not readily porous. With Arts et Métiers station, I wanted to inspire passengers to go up to the museum, not by lecturing but by sparking their curiosity and encouraging them to let their imaginations run wild."

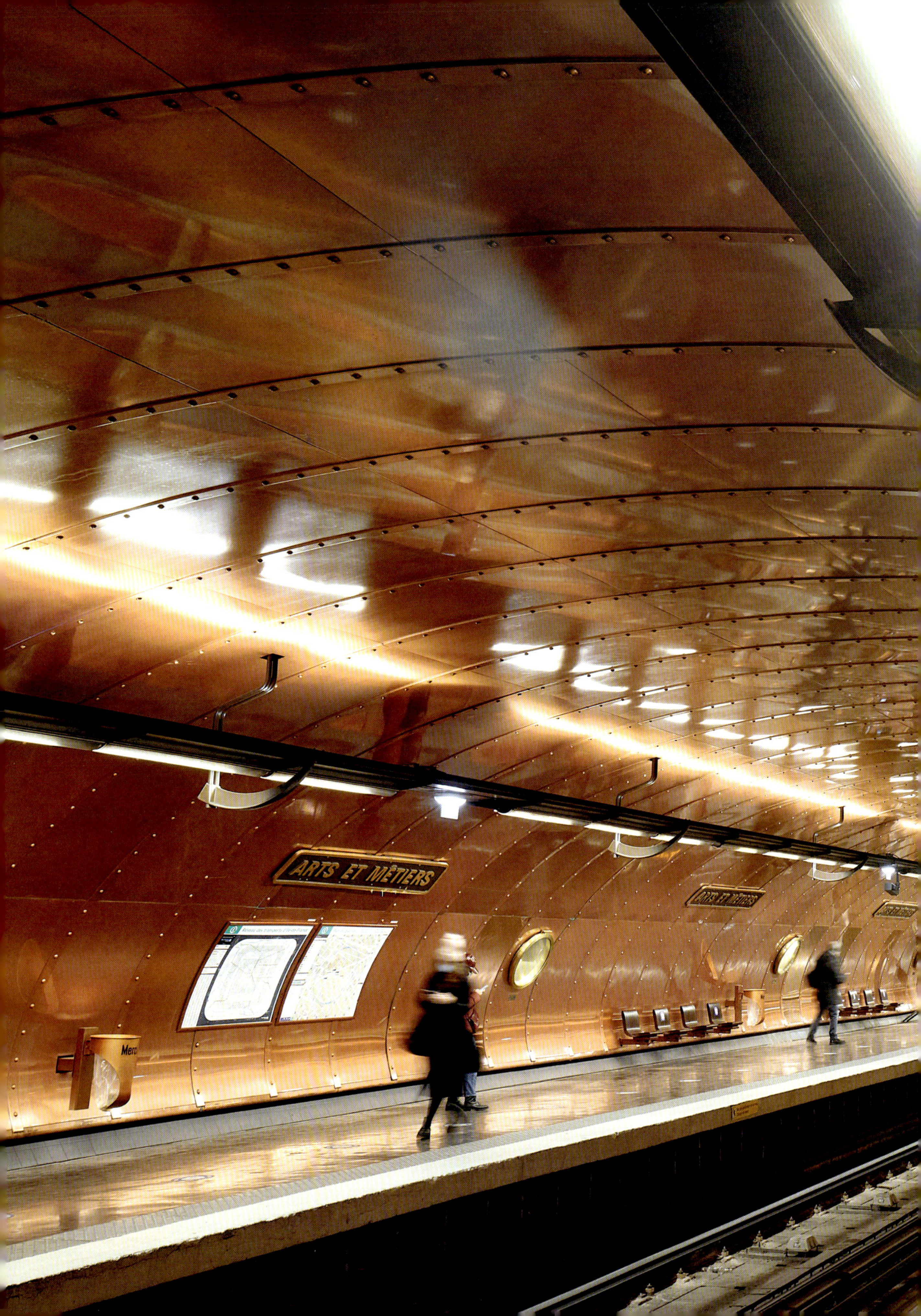
ARTS ET MÉTIERS

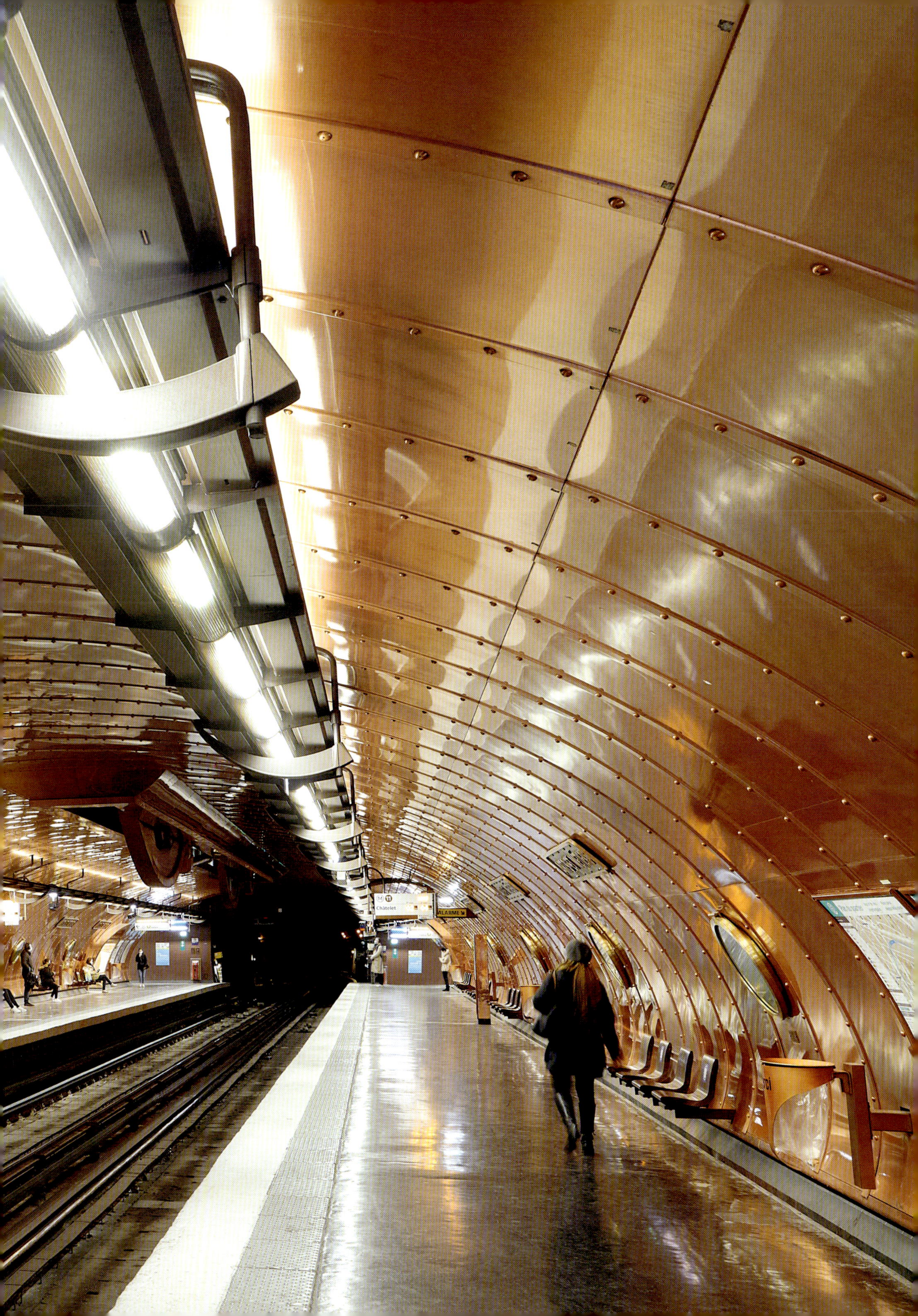
M 11
Châtelet
ALARME

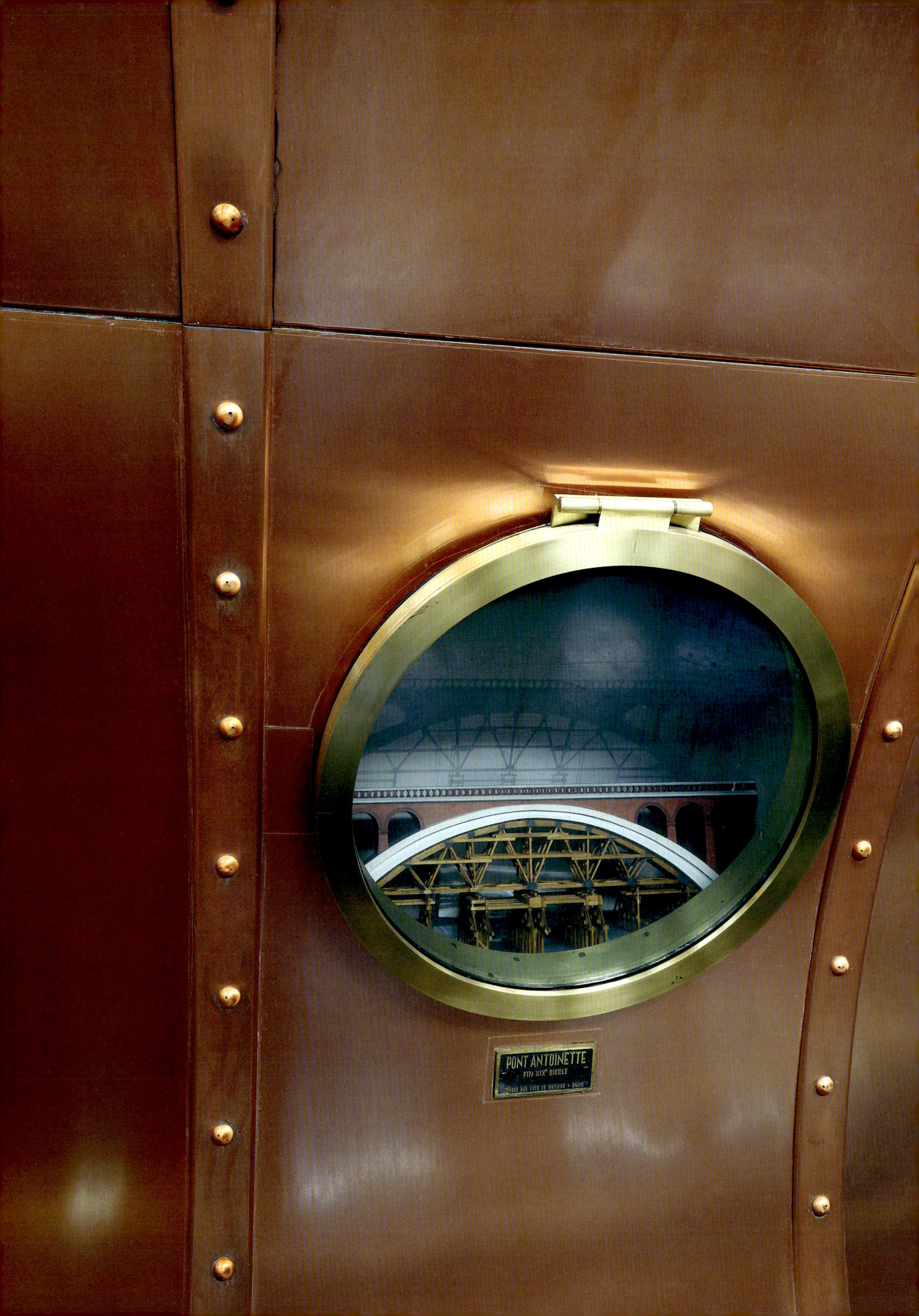
PONT ANTOINETTE
FIN XIXe SIÈCLE
MUSÉE DES ARTS ET MÉTIERS • CNAM

THE REALIZATION OF A VISION

After the initial vision, the preparation was long and fastidious. To convince the RATP to go through with this monumental work, François Schuiten showed them extremely precise drawings, which he had produced alone in the secrecy of his studio. Then he created a 3D image, which was rare at the time, and a full-scale mock-up on a section of wall. He chose the color of the trash cans on the platforms and negotiated so that wenge, a particularly warm wood, would be used for the benches and there that would be no advertising, which is unusual in metro stations. "There were traffic and maintenance constraints, and that was exciting. With the RATP, we found a way. Each project is a blank canvas that gives me the opportunity to relearn my job and work with specific teams. And as the station had to remain open during the works, we hid the finished sections as we went along. So the first time we saw the whole thing was on the morning of the inauguration. The satiny aspect of the copper made it appear womblike—to the wonderment of all." Since then, the station has often been photographed and filmed: it features, for example, in the Wachowskis' TV series. Schuiten whispers that Arts et Métiers is one of the most popular metro stations in Paris.

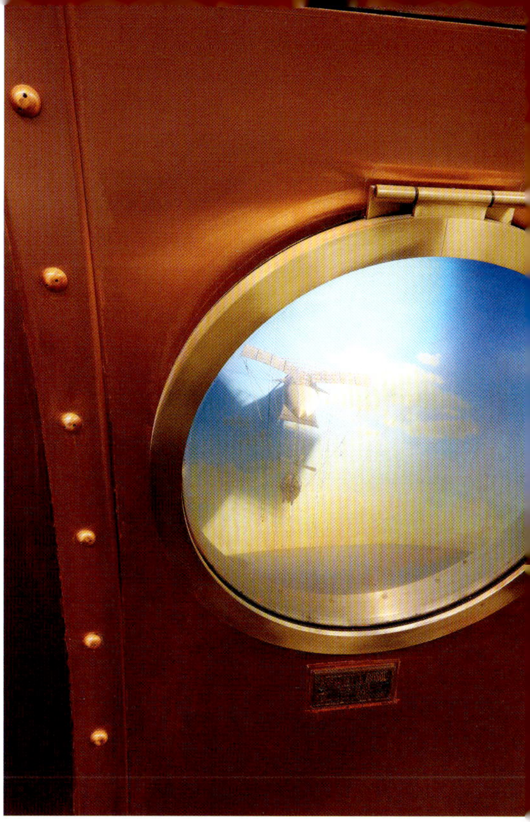

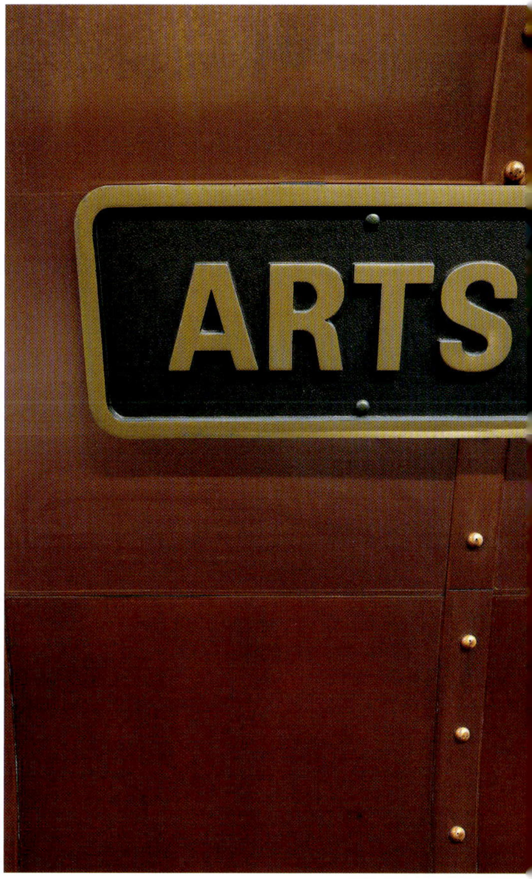

***Nautilus*, 1994**
Copper, brass, wenge, and various materials
75 m long

CARLO SARRABEZOLLES

/ *Monument à la mémoire des agents du Métropolitain morts pour la France*

LOCATED BETWEEN TWO ACCESS CORRIDORS LEADING TO LINE 9, THE MONUMENT TO THE DEAD BY THE SCULPTOR CARLO SARRABEZOLLES IS IMPOSSIBLE TO MISS. INSCRIBED WITH 849 NAMES, IT IS ONE OF THE MOST SOLEMN AND MOVING WORKS ON THE NETWORK.

A TRIBUTE TO FALLEN EMPLOYEES

The *Monument à la mémoire des agents du Métropolitain morts pour la France* in Richelieu-Drouot station is one of the oldest works of art in the metro. With its strong and simple modernist lines—very 1930s—the monumental stela in black granite is an image from another time that has lost none of its emotional impact. Commissioned immediately after World War I, the work was inaugurated by the Compagnie du Chemin de Fer Métropolitain, the forerunner of the RATP, in 1931. It is a tribute to the memory of the 849 employees who died for France during the conflict. An arch flanked by two torchères rises the full height of the corridor.

The imposing caryatid occupying the central section holds up a laurel wreath: one could imagine that it supports the celestial vault on which 849 names are written in gold letters. At the bottom of the work are engraved the names of the main battlefields of World War I: "Marne, Champagne, Artois, Aisne." The word "Libération" was added to the end of this line after 1945 in homage to employees involved in Resistance networks during World War II.

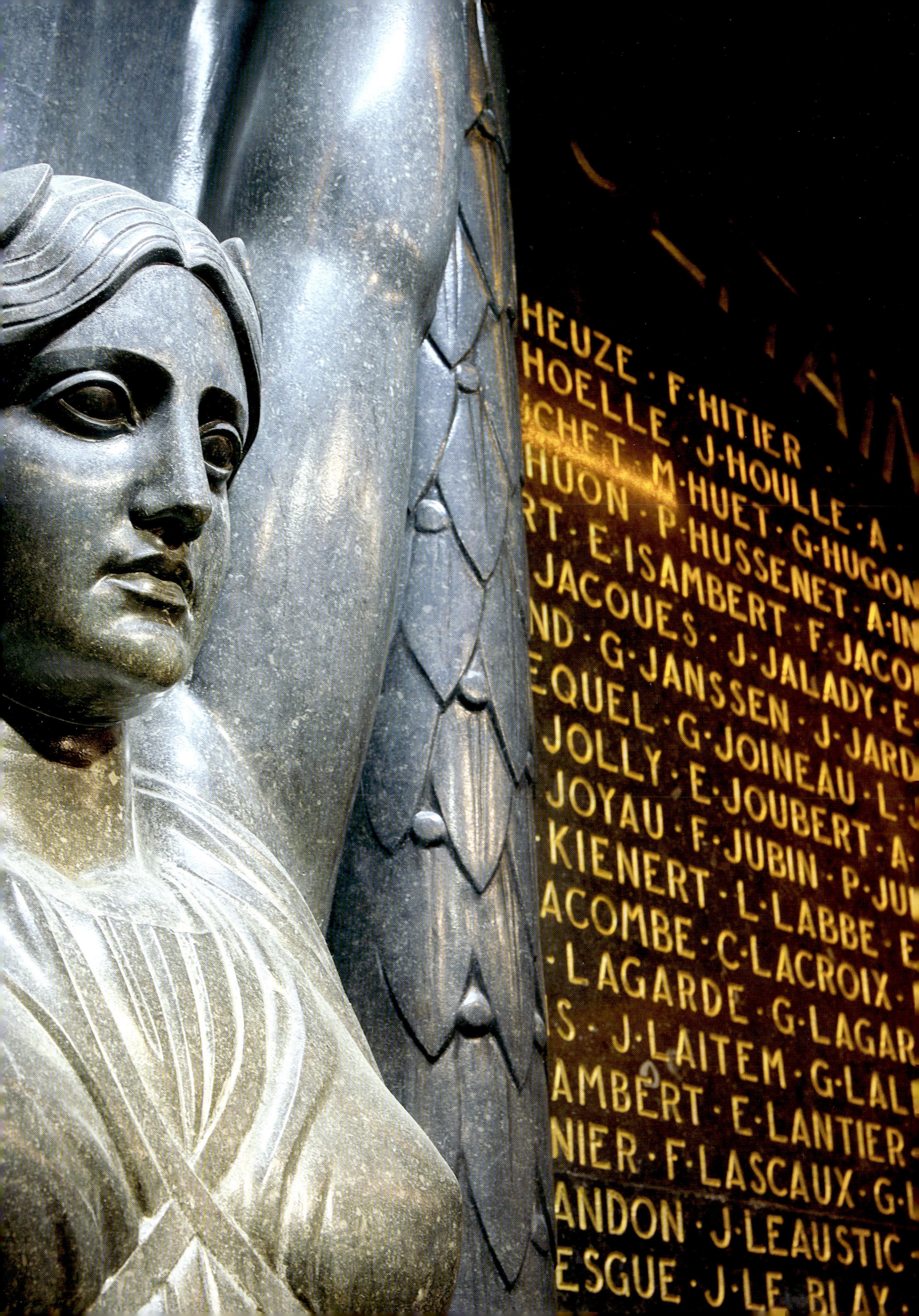
HEUZE · F · HITIER
HOELLE · J · HOULLE · A
HUON · P · HUSSENET · G · HUGON
JACQUES · J · JALADY · E
G · JANSSEN · J · JARD
JOLLY · E · JOUBERT · A
JOYAU · F · JUBIN · P
KIENERT · L · LABBE
ACOMBE · C · LACROIX
LAGARDE · G · LAGAR
J · LAITEM · G · LAL
AMBERT · E · LANTIER
NIER · F · LASCAUX · G
ANDON · J · LEAUSTIC
ESGUE · J · LE BLAY

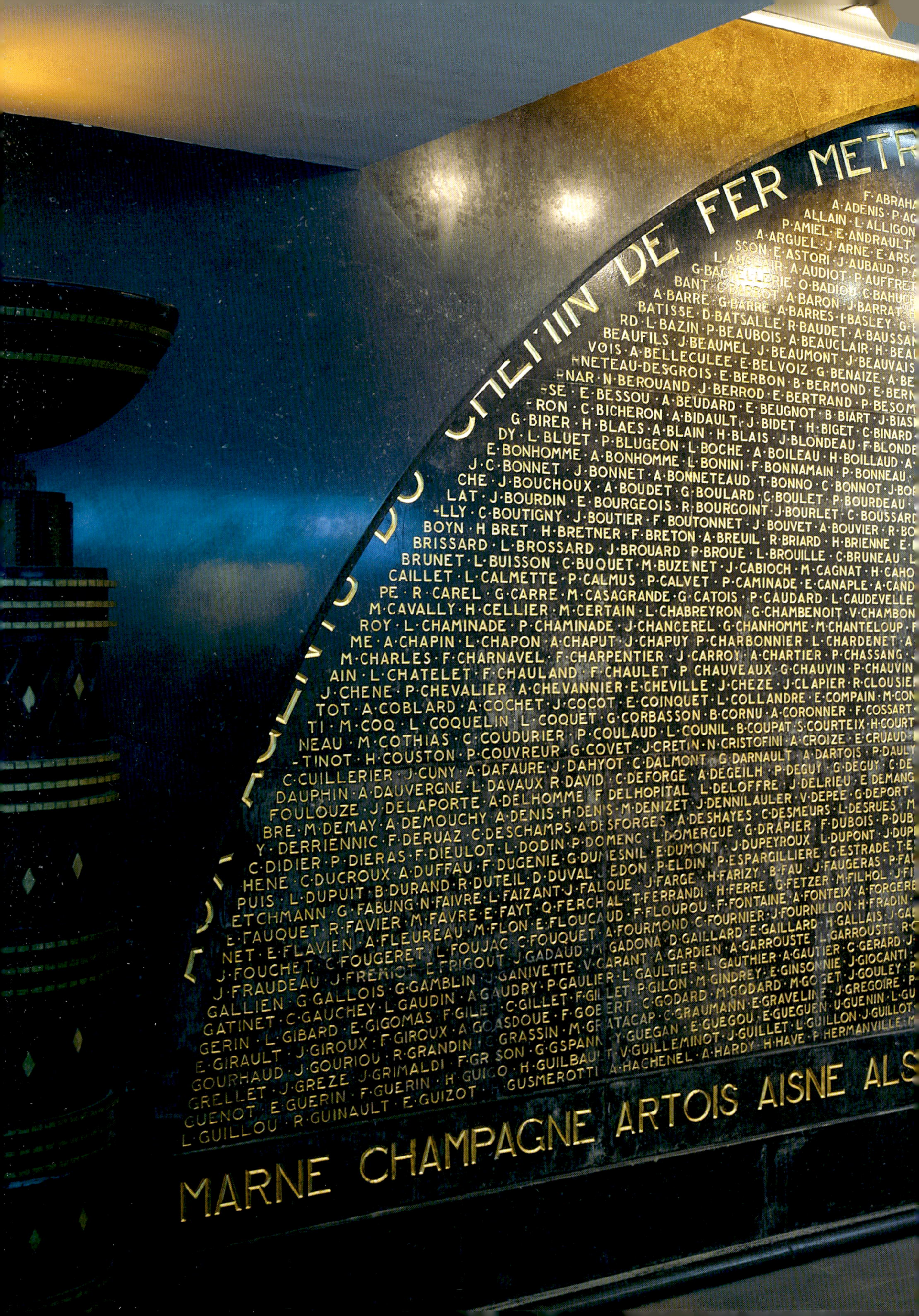
DE FER
MARNE CHAMPAGNE ARTOIS AISNE

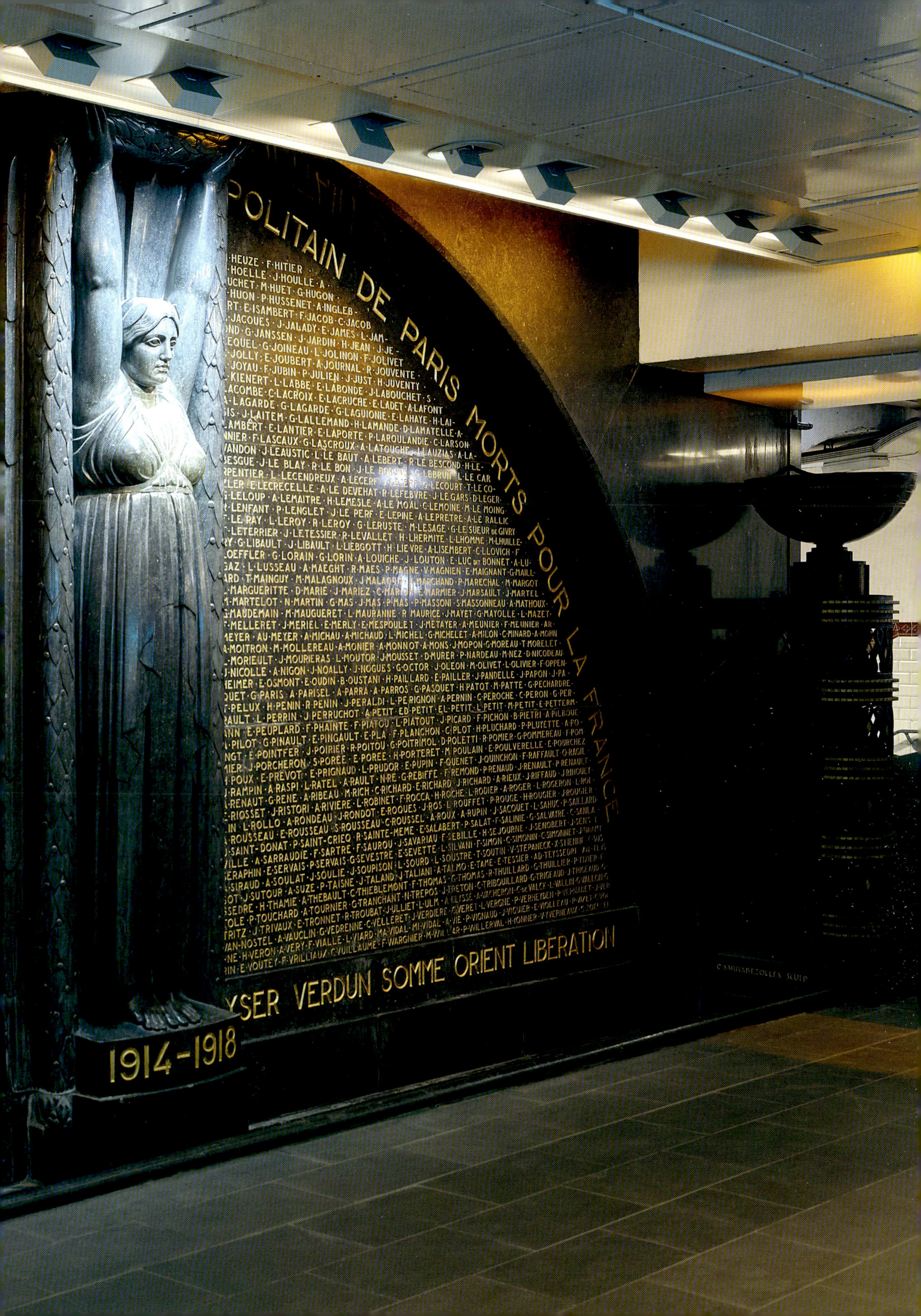
POLITAIN DE PARIS MORTS POUR LA FRANCE
YSER VERDUN SOMME ORIENT LIBERATION
1914-1918

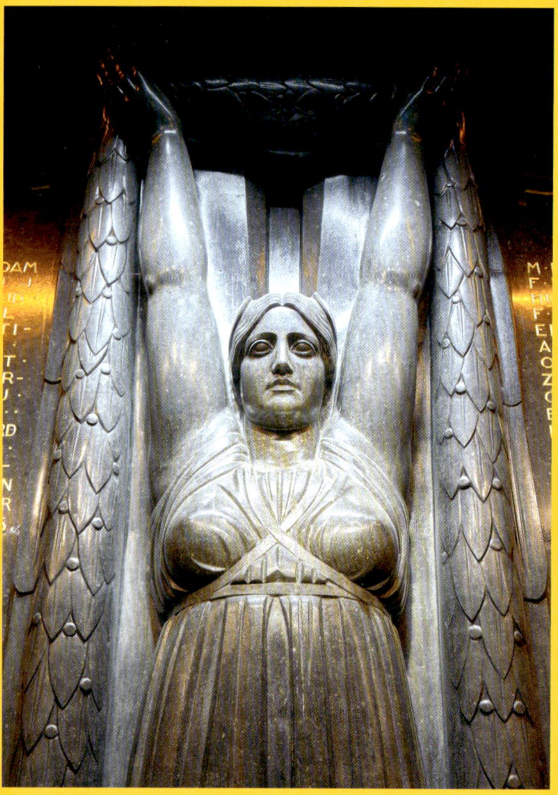

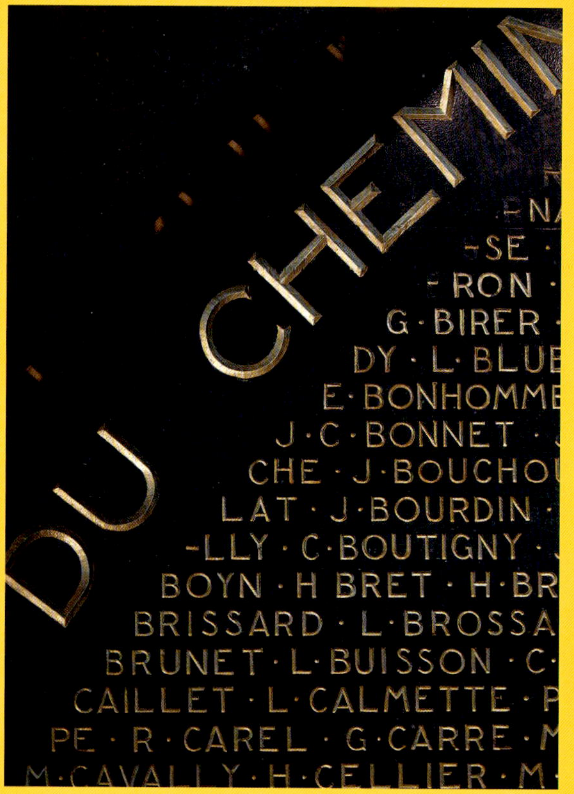
DU CHEMI
SE
RON
G·BIRER
DY · L·BLUE
E·BONHOMME
J·C·BONNET
CHE · J·BOUCHOU
LAT · J·BOURDIN
LLY · C·BOUTIGNY
BOYN · H BRET · H·BR
BRISSARD · L·BROSSA
BRUNET · L·BUISSON · C
CAILLET · L·CALMETTE
PE · R·CAREL · G·CARRE
M·CAVALLY·H·CELLIER·M

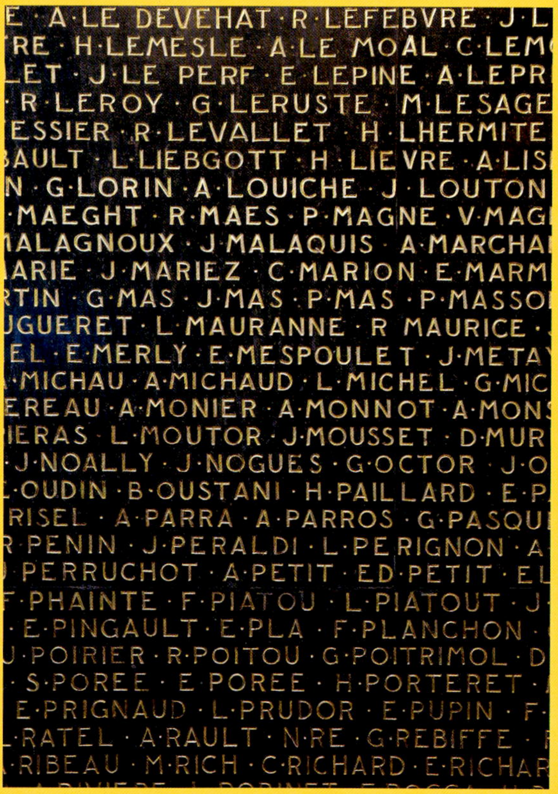
A·LE DEVEHAT · R·LEFEBVRE · J·L
TRE · H·LEMESLE · A·LE MOAL · C·LEM
LET · J·LE PERF · E·LEPINE · A·LEPR
R·LEROY · G·LERUSTE · M·LESAGE
ESSIER · R·LEVALLET · H·LHERMITE
AULT · L·LIEBGOTT · H·LIEVRE · A·LIS
N · G·LORIN · A·LOUICHE · J·LOUTON
MAEGHT · R·MAES · P·MAGNE · V·MAG
ALAGNOUX · J·MALAQUIS · A·MARCHA
ARIE · J·MARIEZ · C·MARION · E·MARM
RTIN · G·MAS · J·MAS · P·MAS · P·MASSO
UGUERET · L·MAURANNE · R·MAURICE
EL · E·MERLY · E·MESPOULET · J·META
MICHAU · A·MICHAUD · L·MICHEL · G·MIC
EREAU · A·MONIER · A·MONNOT · A·MONS
IERAS · L·MOUTOR · J·MOUSSET · D·MUR
J·NOALLY · J·NOGUES · G·OCTOR · J·O
OUDIN · B·OUSTANI · H·PAILLARD · E·P
RISEL · A·PARRA · A·PARROS · G·PASQU
R·PENIN · J·PERALDI · L·PERIGNON · A
PERRUCHOT · A·PETIT · ED·PETIT · EL
F·PHAINTE · F·PIATOU · L·PIATOUT · J
E·PINGAULT · E·PLA · F·PLANCHON
POIRIER · R·POITOU · G·POITRIMOL · D
S·POREE · E·POREE · H·PORTERET
E·PRIGNAUD · L·PRUDOR · E·PUPIN · F
RATEL · A·RAULT · N·RE · G·REBIFFE
RIBEAU · M·RICH · C·RICHARD · E·RICHAR

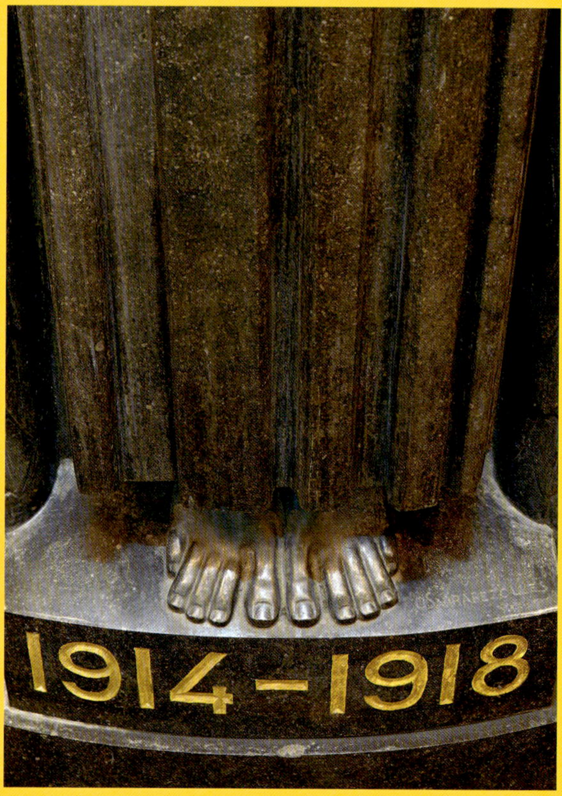
1914-1918

A PUBLIC SCULPTOR

Today, few remember Carlo Sarrabezolles, but he was very successful during his lifetime. Evidence of this is found in the list of his public and private commissions around the world. In Paris, for example, his works include statues for the church of the Saint-Esprit on Avenue Daumesnil in the twelfth arrondissement; *La Danse triomphale de Pallas Athéné* (The Triumphal Dance of Pallas Athena), an example of which can be seen in the Jardins du Trocadéro; interior and exterior medallions for the Institut George-Eastman in the thirteenth arrondissement, and funerary monuments in the cemeteries of Montmartre and Montparnasse. His works also embellish several other cities in France and abroad: a monument to the dead in Sidi Bel Abbès, Algeria; statuary for the grounds of the Du Pont de Nemours residence in Wilmington, Delaware; and *La Douleur* (Grief) for a tomb in Lima, Peru.

A VIRTUOSO

Carlo Sarrabezolles was born in Toulouse in 1888, but it was in Paris that he spent most of his life, after training at the École des Beaux-Arts and trips to Italy and London. In the 1920s and 1930s, he participated in the major international exhibitions that brought many technical innovations in the decorative arts, architecture, and sculpture to light. In 1926 his own great discovery was that of the direct carving of concrete that had not yet set, a process that demanded great technical virtuosity. He occupied the same studio from 1923 until his death in 1971, a pretty brick house at 16 rue des Volontaires in the fifteenth arrondissement. Not far from there, in the square that now bears his name, is *L'Espérance* (Hope), his statue of a woman with raised arms. It is reminiscent of the statue at the center of his Richelieu–Drouot metro station monument to the dead.

***Monument à la mémoire des agents du Métropolitain morts pour la France*, 1931**
Black granite
4 × 8 m

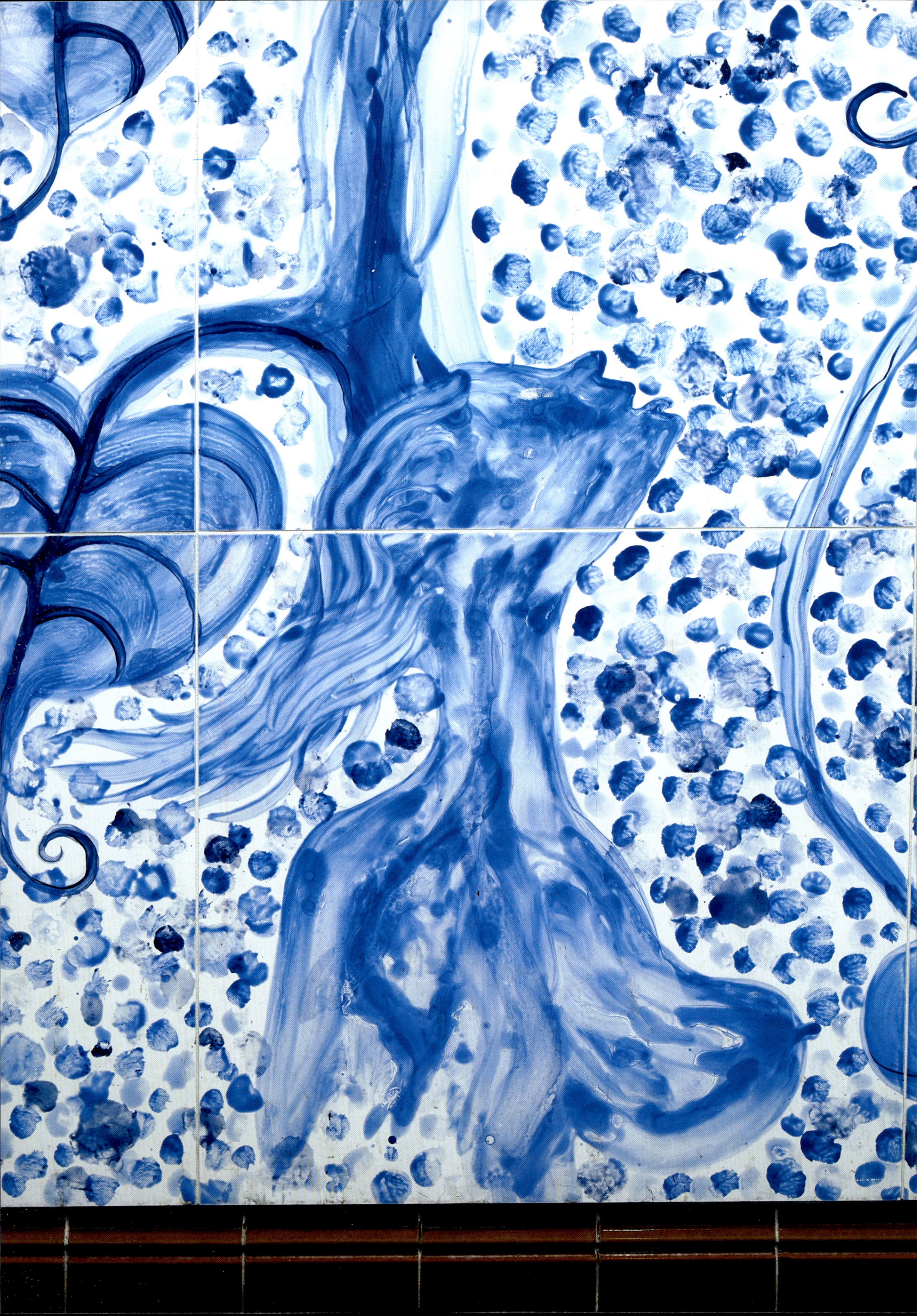

BARTHÉLÉMY TOGUO

/ Célébrations

FOLIAGE IN A BEAUTIFUL SHADE OF BLUE FORMS THE BACKDROP TO THE TO-ING AND FRO-ING OF PASSENGERS IN FRONT OF THE TICKET OFFICE. THE TREES ARE BARTHÉLÉMY TOGUO'S AND THE LARGE FRESCO, WHICH EMANATES HUMANITY, HIS FIRST ARTWORK IN FRENCH PUBLIC SPACE.

A TRIBUTE TO THE NEIGHBORHOOD

Célébrations is a tribute to the Château Rouge neighborhood of cosmopolitan streets where the Marché Dejean attracts customers from all over Paris with its stalls selling cassava, mangoes, and tilapia. Barthélémy Toguo knows the neighborhood well because he lived there from 1998 to 2002. His large ceramic fresco features tall trees springing out of archetypal heads. "I wanted to celebrate life," he says. "Vegetation is the celebration of a new world. The figures rub shoulders, a reflection of what happens at Château Rouge metro station where people of many nationalities mix."

Featuring motifs in which the human and the botanical merge, the work is also "a reflection on the problems of access to water and the depletion of natural resources." It also echoes an ongoing project in Cameroon: since 2008, Toguo has been managing a residence for artists called Bandjoun Station (named after the town where it is located), where he conducts experiments in art and organic farming.
Born in 1967, the Franco-Cameroonian moved to Paris after studying art in Grenoble and Düsseldorf. A major figure on the international art scene, Toguo travels around the planet to set up his exhibitions. At a time when museums and galleries are becoming increasingly interested in the creative endeavors of the African continent, one of his main preoccupations is the labeling of his work.

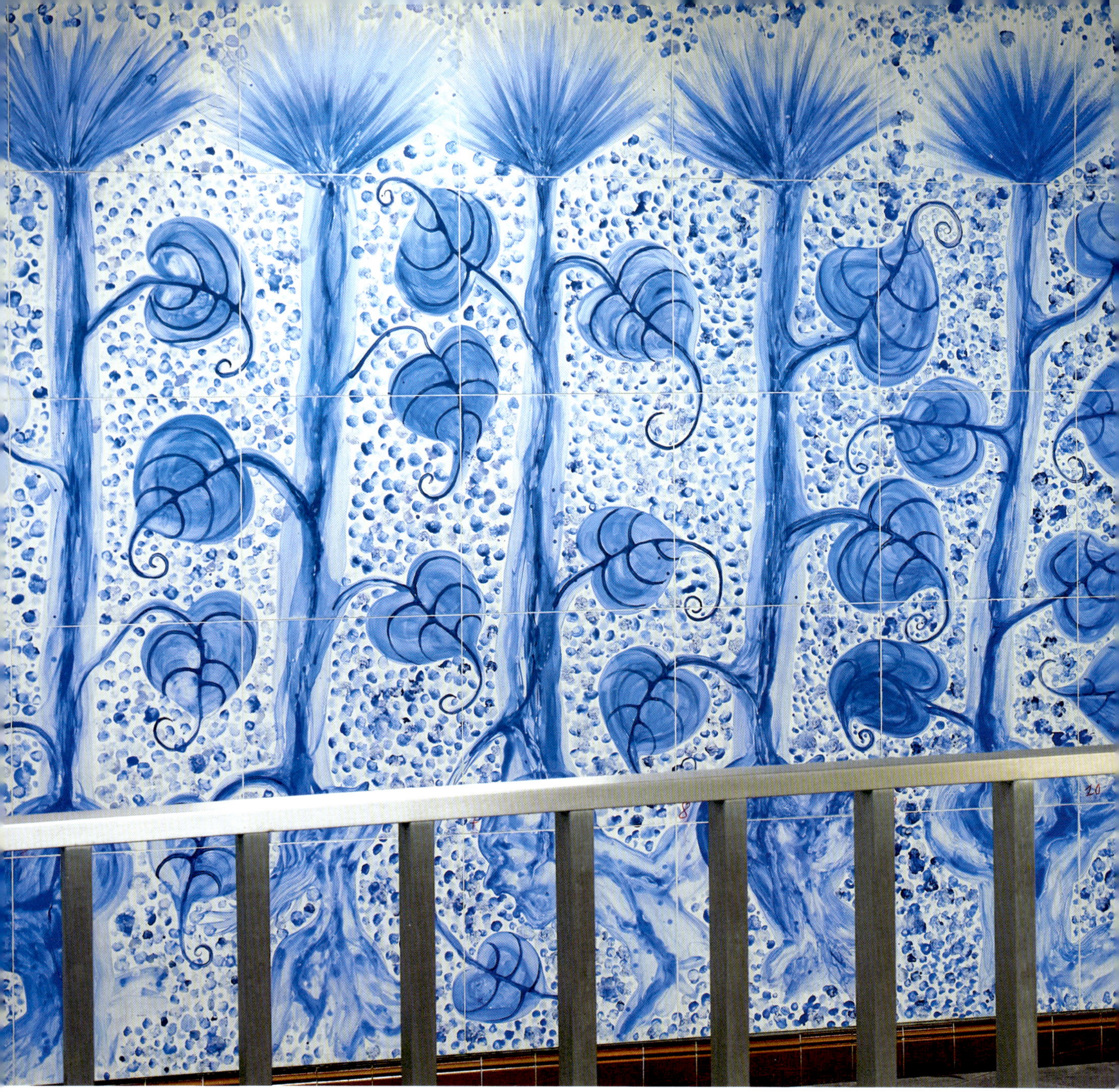

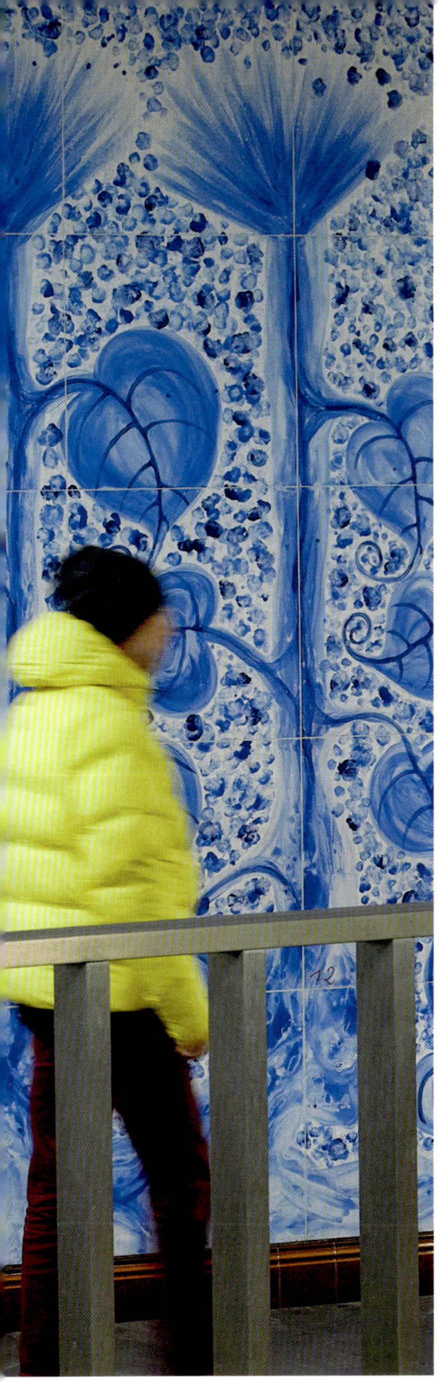

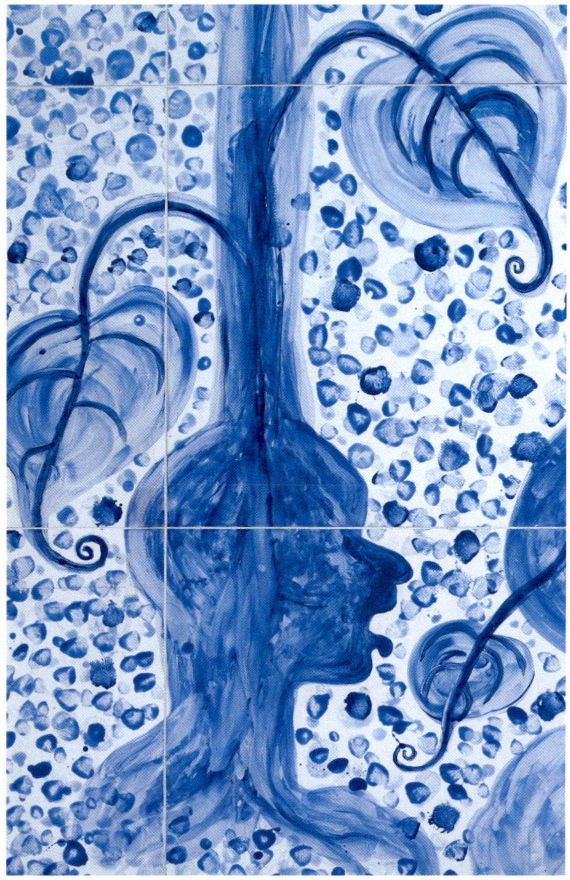

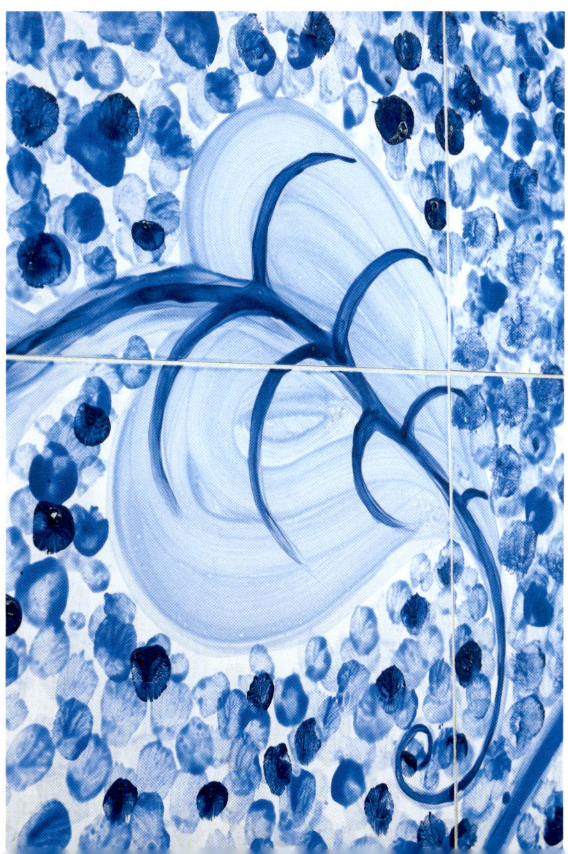

A MAJOR COMMISSION

Barthélémy Toguo was chosen for this project from a group of five internationally renowned artists. The RATP commissioned the work to accompany a renovation of the entire station, including the construction of a new entrance on Rue Custine and a new ticket office. A vibrant, durable material was required. Ceramic tiles resonated with the heritage of the Paris metro. And the idea of a collaboration with the Manufacture de Sèvres came up. Toguo worked with craftspeople associated with the manufactory, an institution whose savoir-faire has been handed down from generation to generation since the eighteenth century. First, he drew sketches, thought about using red, and finally decided on a blue that was developed specially for him and now bears his name: "Toguo blue." The soothing shade is both warm and delicate. After several tests, the 110 ceramic tiles were made in the manufactory's high-fire kilns. Toguo blue is fired at temperatures over 1,000°C and contains no lead or other toxic materials. Your thoughts may turn to International Klein Blue (IKB), patented by Yves Klein in 1960, but Toguo has taken a diametrically opposite approach: "My blue is open to others," he laughs.

The inauguration of the work was quite an event, a real celebration. It took place on October 17, 2017, in the presence of the artist and the mayor of the eighteenth arrondissement. *Célébrations* was immediately embraced by passengers and station employees alike. Apparently, when the work was being installed, some employees asked for a fragment of tile to take home as a souvenir. Barthélémy Toguo pursues this generous approach in all his work. The idea is to generate individual and collective emotions—and propose and share new ways of looking. "The artist should show, should challenge preconceptions, but should never lecture. I've always known that my art should have a strong social dimension. My art is people-oriented."

Célébrations, 2017
Ceramic tiles
3 × 10 m

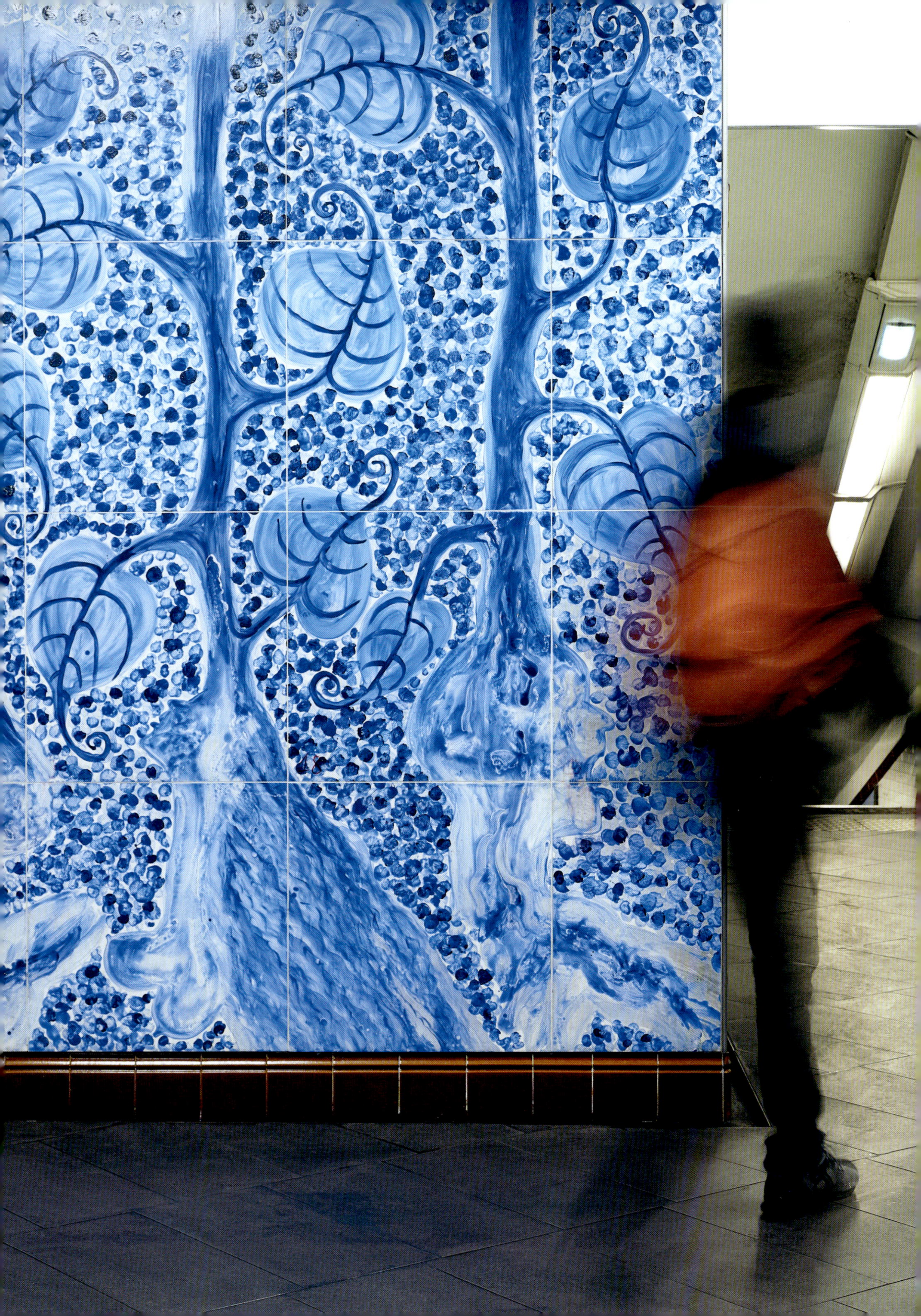

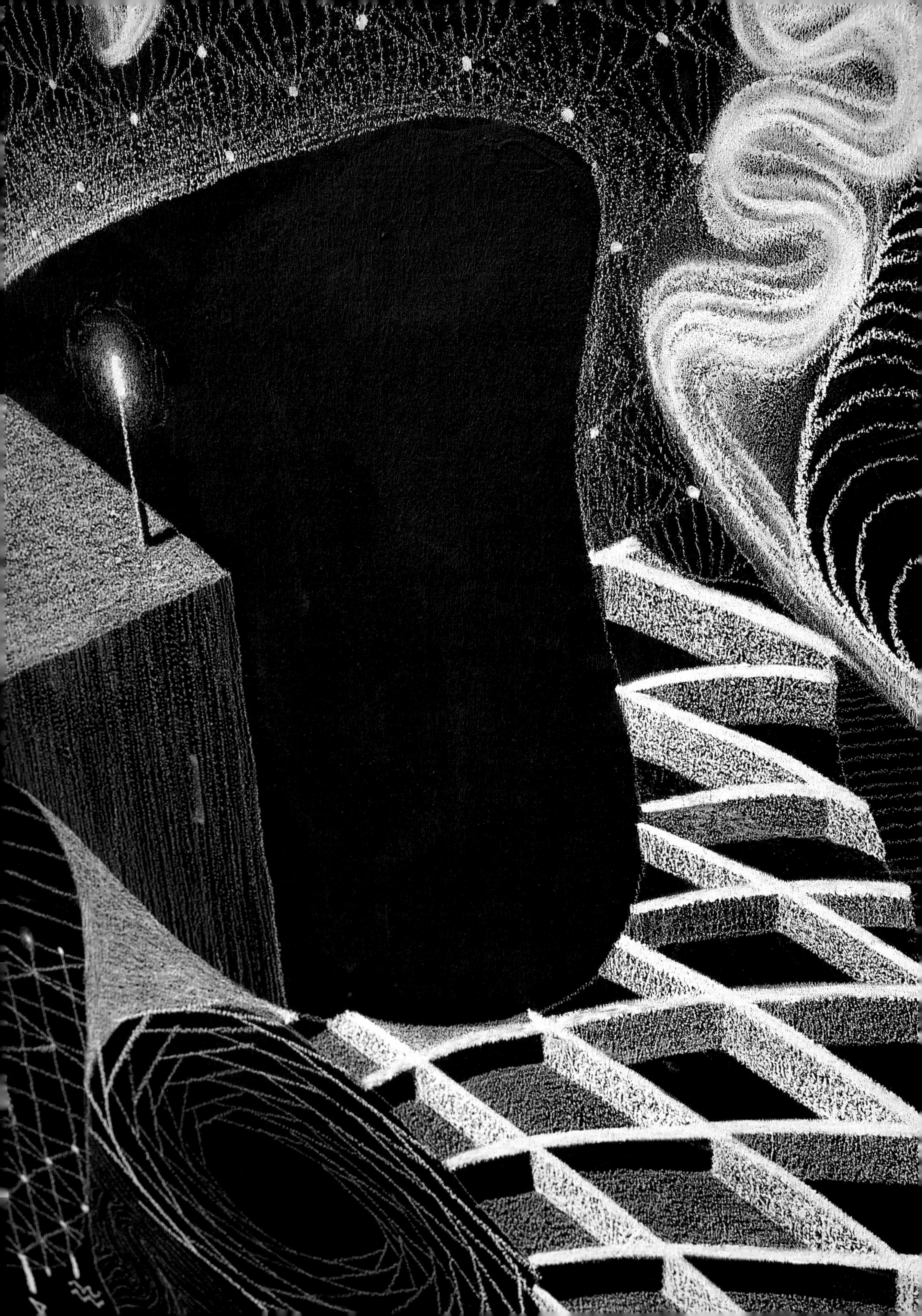

INNER JOURNEYS

IN THE CONCOURSE OF CHÂTELET–LES HALLES RER STATION, NEAR THE PORTE LESCOT EXIT, A FEW FLASHES OF GOLD CATCH THE ATTENTION OF HURRIED PASSENGERS. IT IS A BAS-RELIEF IN PATINATED AND POLISHED BRONZE WHOSE TITLE CONVEYS THE ATMOSPHERE OF THE PLACE: *ÉNERGIES.*

PIERRE-YVES TRÉMOIS

/ *Énergies*

THE QUEST FOR SIMPLICITY

A singular figure in French art, independent and unclassifiable, Pierre-Yves Trémois—who passed away, aged ninety-nine, in August 2020—always seemed to embody the role of the gifted young man. In 1938 he enrolled in the École Nationale Supérieure des Beaux-Arts de Paris in the studio of one of Gustave Moreau's former pupils; in 1942 he competed for the Prix de Rome—and was not chosen, rumor has it, because of his overly erotic interpretation of the subject. He competed again the following year, successfully that time, but left the Villa Médicis and Rome after just one year, instead of three. He also cut short his sojourn at the Casa de Velázquez in Madrid. That was when he decided to devote himself entirely to engraving, an art form that occupied him for the rest of his life. He liked the hieratic style of Egyptian art and Japanese prints, as well as the Italian primitives Andrea Mantegna and Piero Della Francesca. "The burin taught me simplicity, and simplicity is overwhelming," he wrote. In the aftermath of World War II, he produced a series of illustrated books in collaboration with authors, a great many of whom later became his friends, including Henry de Montherlant, Paul Claudel, and Jean Giono, as well as the biologist Jean Rostand and the filmmaker Federico Fellini. He also designed monumental sculptures, engraved gold jewelry, and ceramics, notably during a sojourn in Vallauris, the village of potters where Marc Chagall, Pablo Picasso, and Henri Matisse also worked.

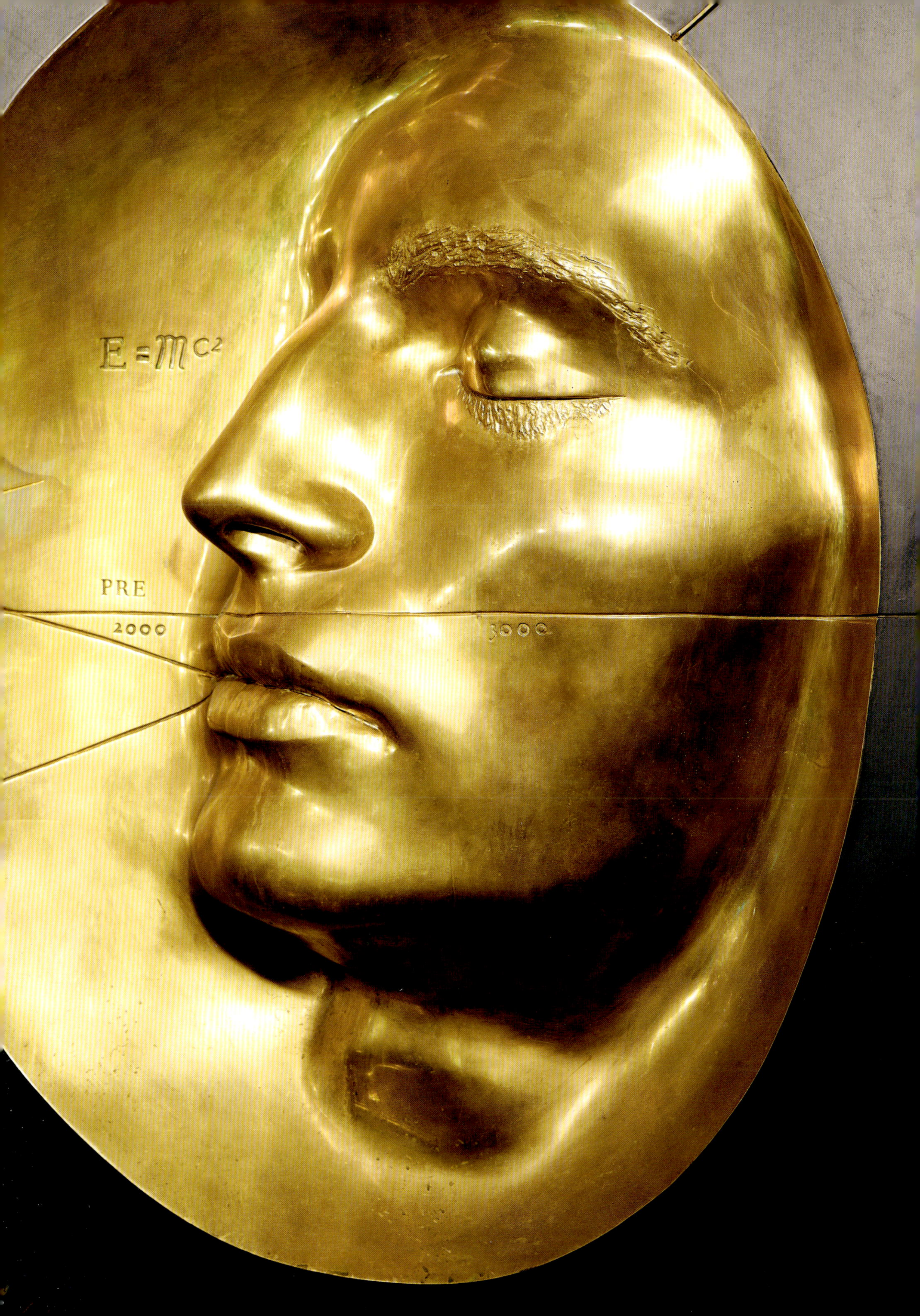
E = mc2
PRE
2000
3000

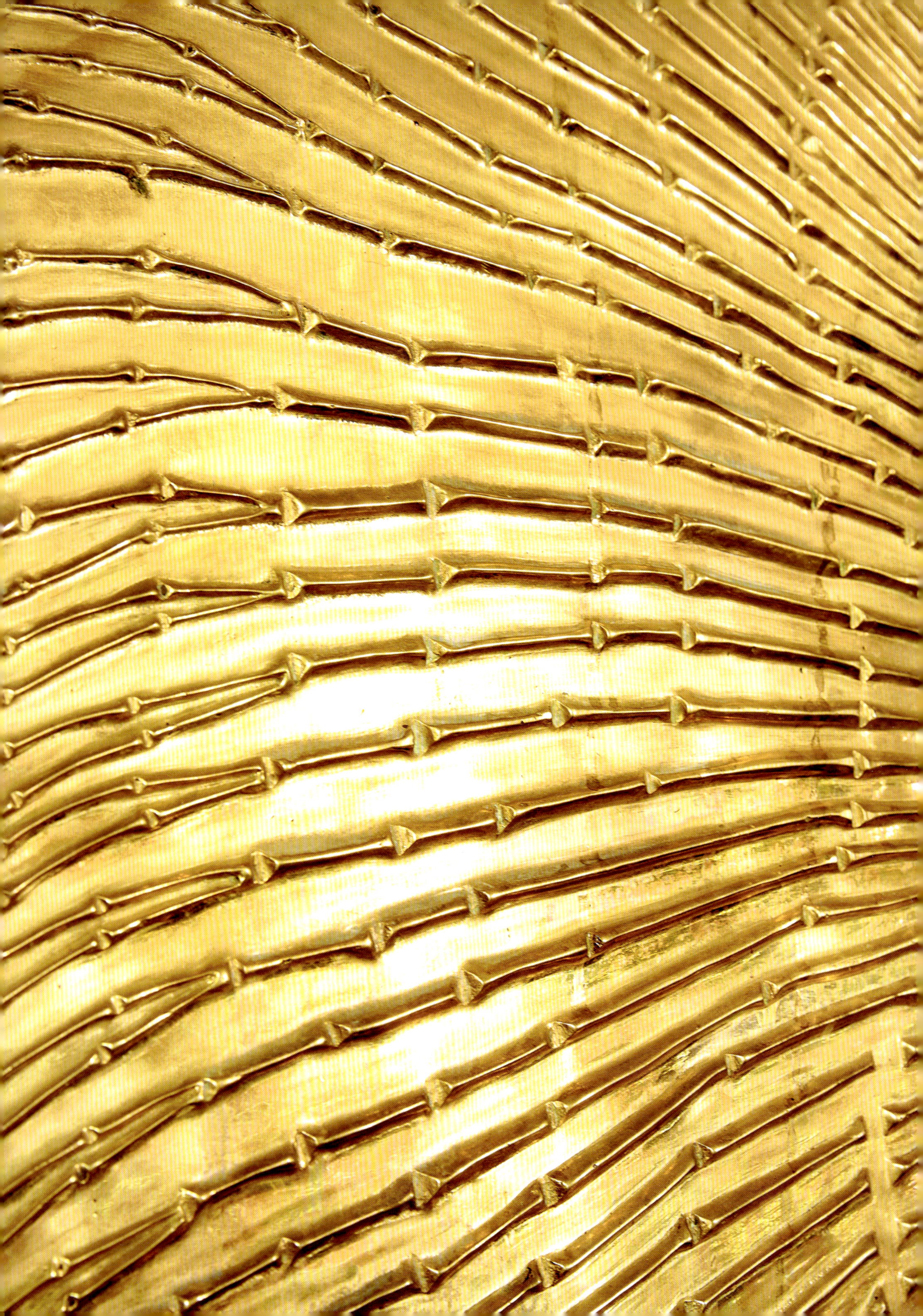

RADIANT ENERGY

It was in 1977 that the RATP commissioned a spectacular work for Châtelet–Les Halles RER station. The station, which connects RER lines A, B, and D, is the hub of the Paris public transportation system. The monumental concourse is the largest in Europe. The light-spangled work is titled *Énergies*, a patinated and polished bronze bas-relief measuring 8 meters wide and 3 meters high. It was made at the Susse foundry in Malakoff, just outside Paris; founded in 1758, it is the oldest French foundry still in operation. Many of the official sculptures of the Third Republic were cast there, as were works by Auguste Rodin, Antoine Bourdelle, Salvador Dalí, and César; several contemporary sculptors still work there, including Ousmane Sow and Wang Keping.

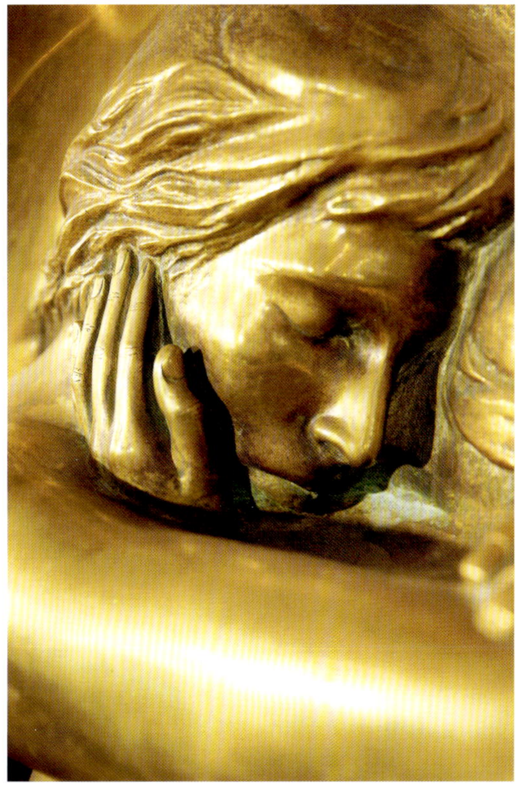

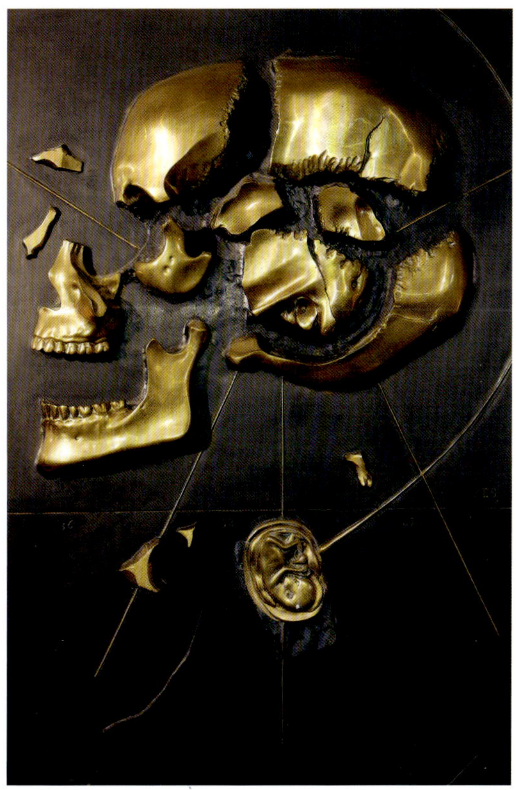

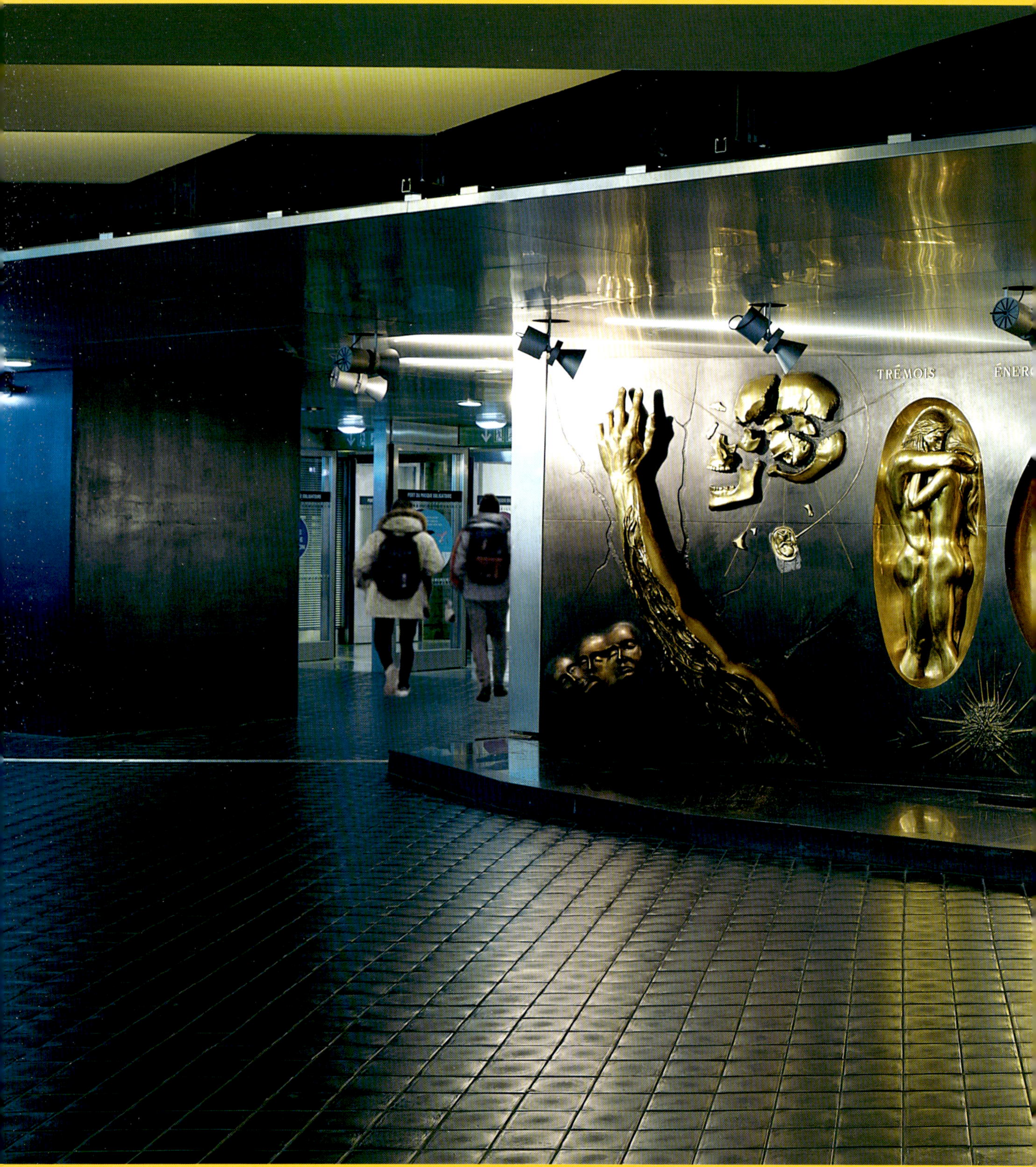
TRÉMOIS

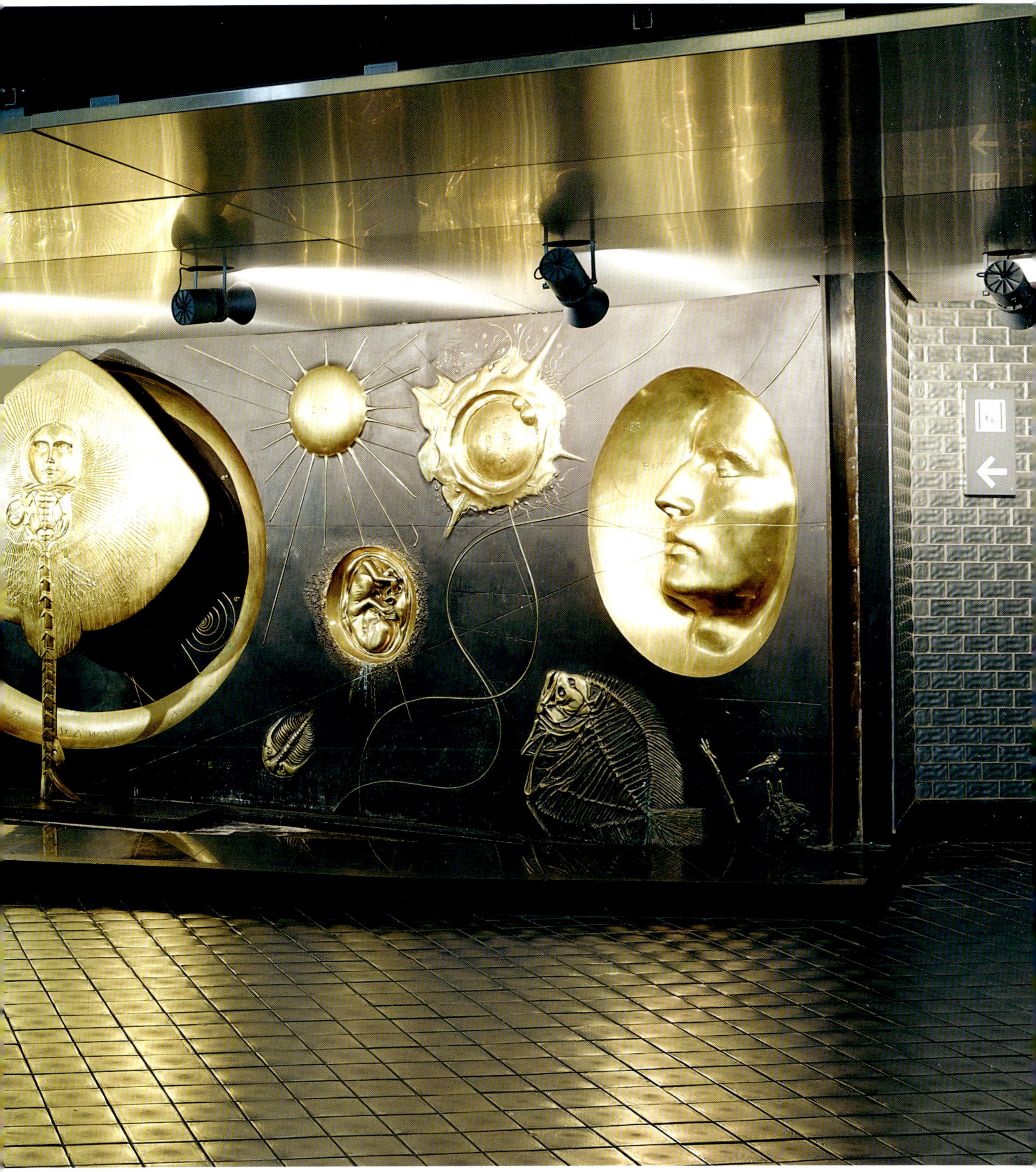

PIERRE-YVES TRÉMOIS, *ÉNERGIES*

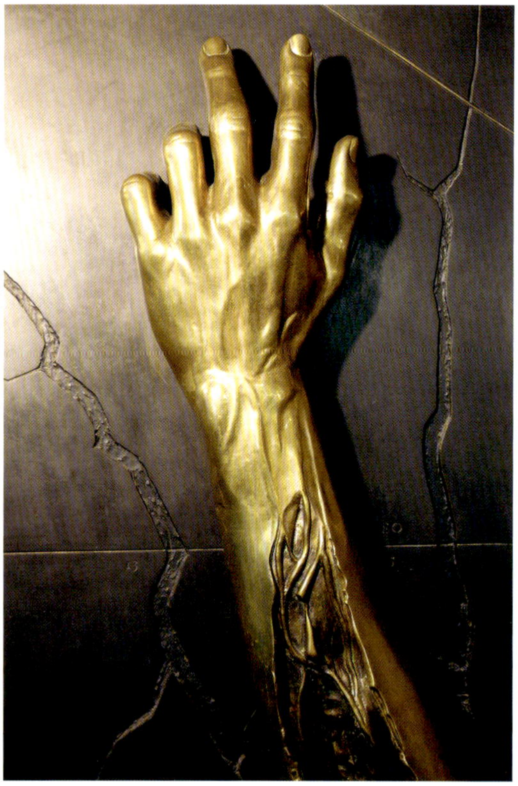

Gold spangles reflected on the ground, a ray of light, a flayed arm raised to the sky, a fetus, a skull, a star, a man and a woman embracing, faces, and fish: *Énergies* is full of erudite symbols. In the center, on the back of the large golden skate, are the inscriptions "I am radiant energy" and "I make myself shadow and light." The lead type came from the Imprimerie Nationale. The Schrödinger equation and two of Heisenberg's inequalities also appear, demonstrating Pierre-Yves Trémois' curiosity for science and interest in philosophical questions pertaining to the animal world and the origins of man. That same year, he executed *Bestiaire fabuleux* (Fantastic Bestiary), eighteen bronze sculptures of animals that were exhibited at Thoiry zoo in 1980. He also designed three stamps at the request of the French post office. In 1978 he was elected to chair II of the Engraving section of the Académie des Beaux-Arts. He had the following inscription engraved on his academician's sword: "The line is my lot."

Énergies, 1977

Patinated and polished bronze
8 × 3 m

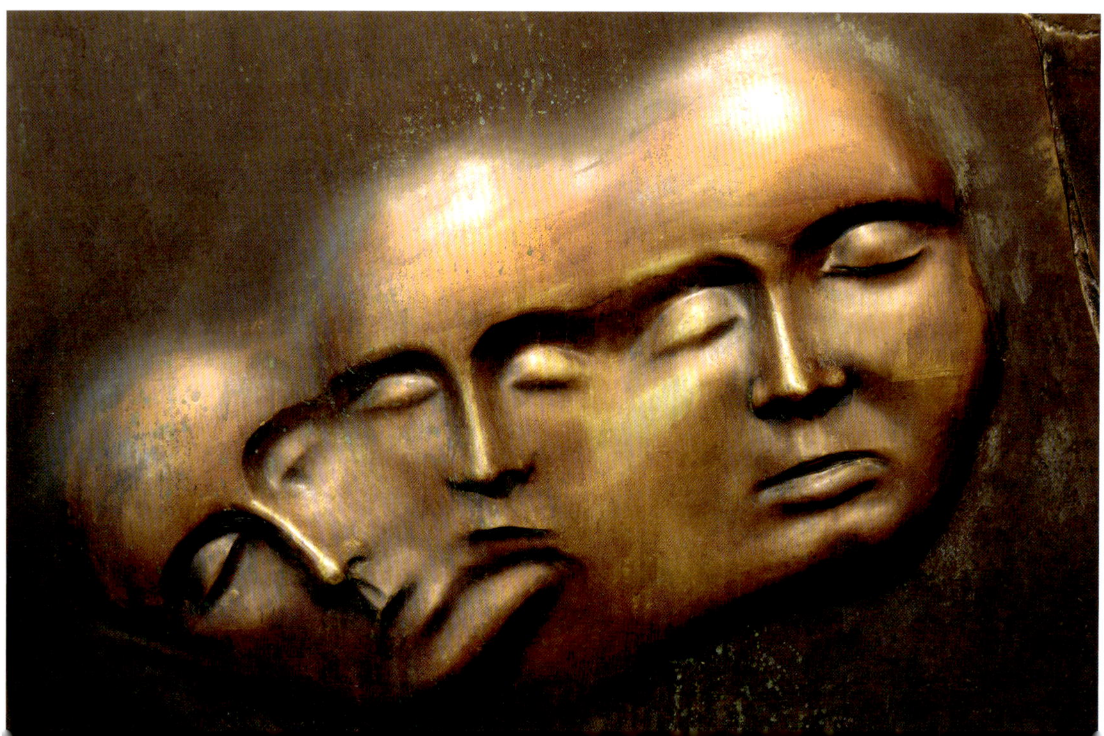

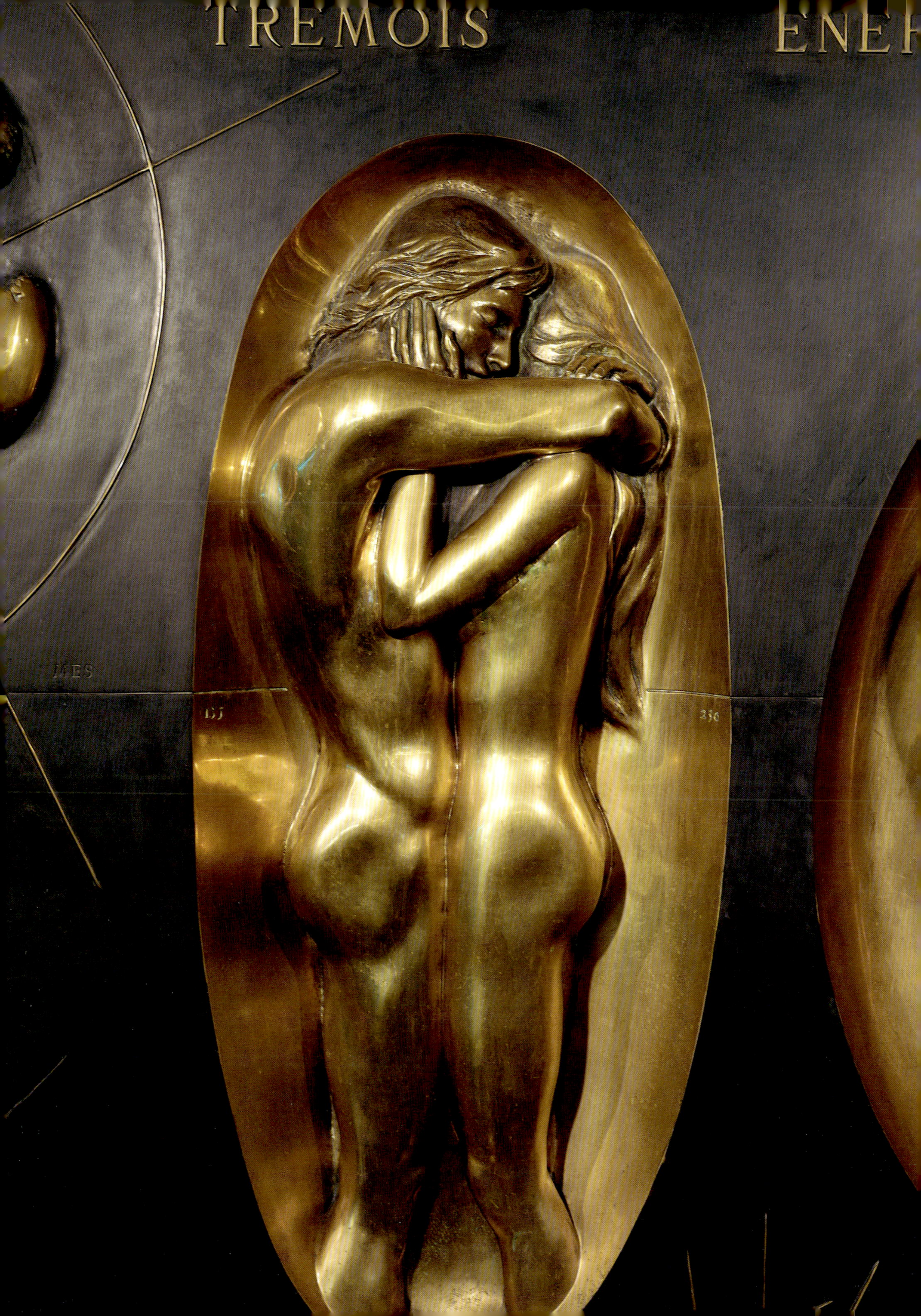
TREMOIS
ENER
MES
DJ
236

WHEN YOU WALK ALONG THE CORRIDOR LINKING THE CHAMPS-ÉLYSÉES TO CHARLES DE GAULLE–ÉTOILE STATION, COLORFUL DOTS CATCH YOUR EYE. THEY FORM A STAR, PERHAPS A LUCKY ONE.

NEIL WOOD

/ *Et toi là, attrape ton étoile*

A STAR IS BORN

The corridor has been given a new lease on life. In 2015 the RATP communications department called in Neil Wood to come up with ideas for an artwork for the 50-meter-long space, which connects the most famous avenue in the world to the metro. "I replied in a few weeks," he says, "and went into overdrive to produce the designs. In the corridor, untouched since the 1960s, there was an impressive to-ing and fro-ing of passengers. I wanted to accompany them in both directions, with a work that interacts with visitors and makes their journeys more agreeable. When we travel, our minds are more open, our thoughts freer, so when we create works for the metro, we should free ourselves of any tendency to lecture, and invite visitors to let themselves be carried away."

Thus, the idea of a star that can be read in both directions was born. The artwork comprises a series of disks, 20 centimeters in diameter, in the colors of the network lines, including RER red and RATP green, against a dark backdrop. Its invites passengers to place themselves under a lucky star and is inspired by the sometimes-enchanting nighttime atmosphere on the Champs-Élysées created by the lights of the cars and the illuminated trees. Wood's artwork also gives the place a touch of tranquility. "It has always been respected," he says, "even during the tense moments we have recently been through." Wood used spray paint for the preliminary drawings, then switched to the computer. Elements of his handmade approach are still evident in the modeling and shading of the colors: "You don't really know how it was done, and I like that," he says.

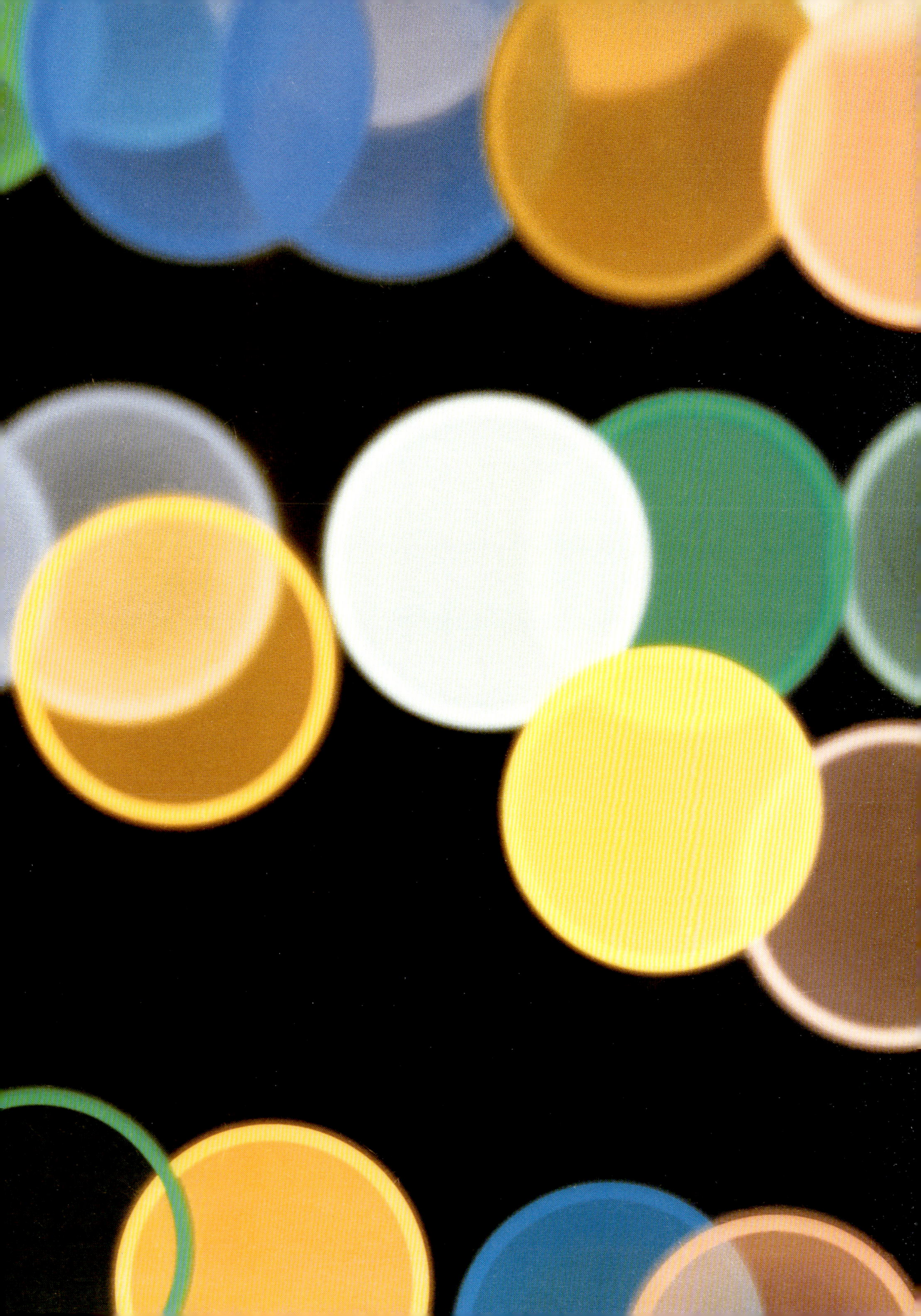

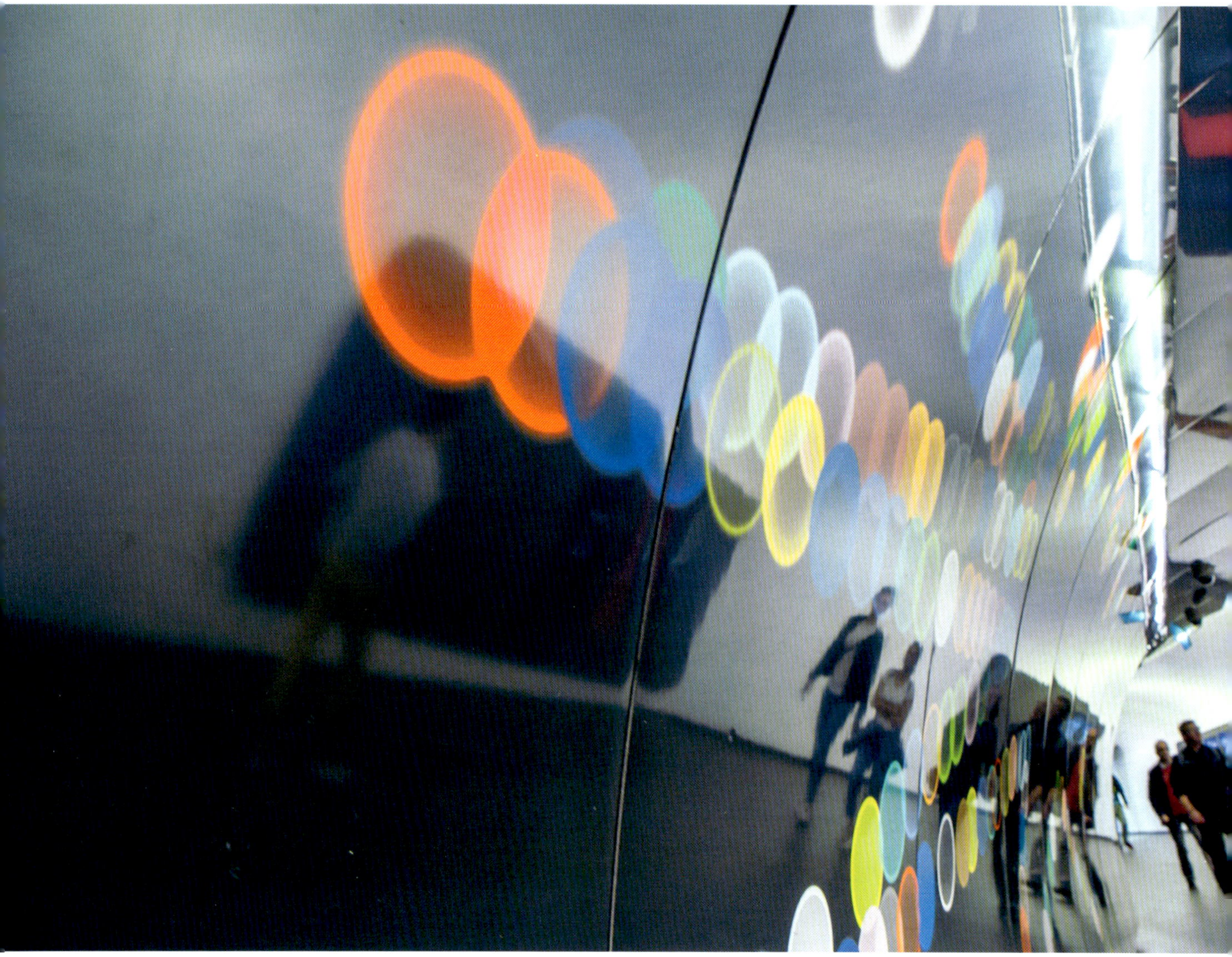

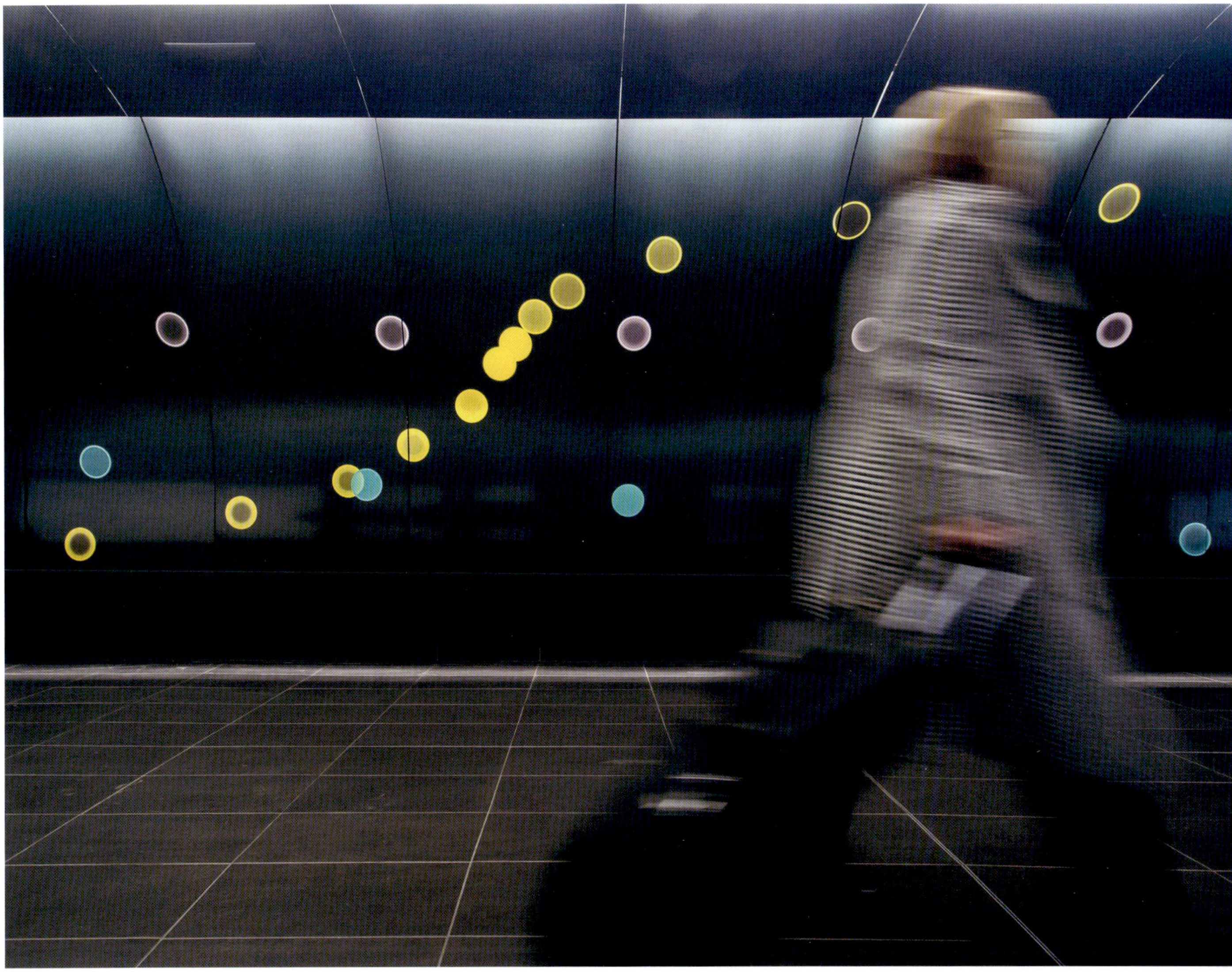

NEIL WOOD, *ET TOI LÀ, ATTRAPE TON ÉTOILE*

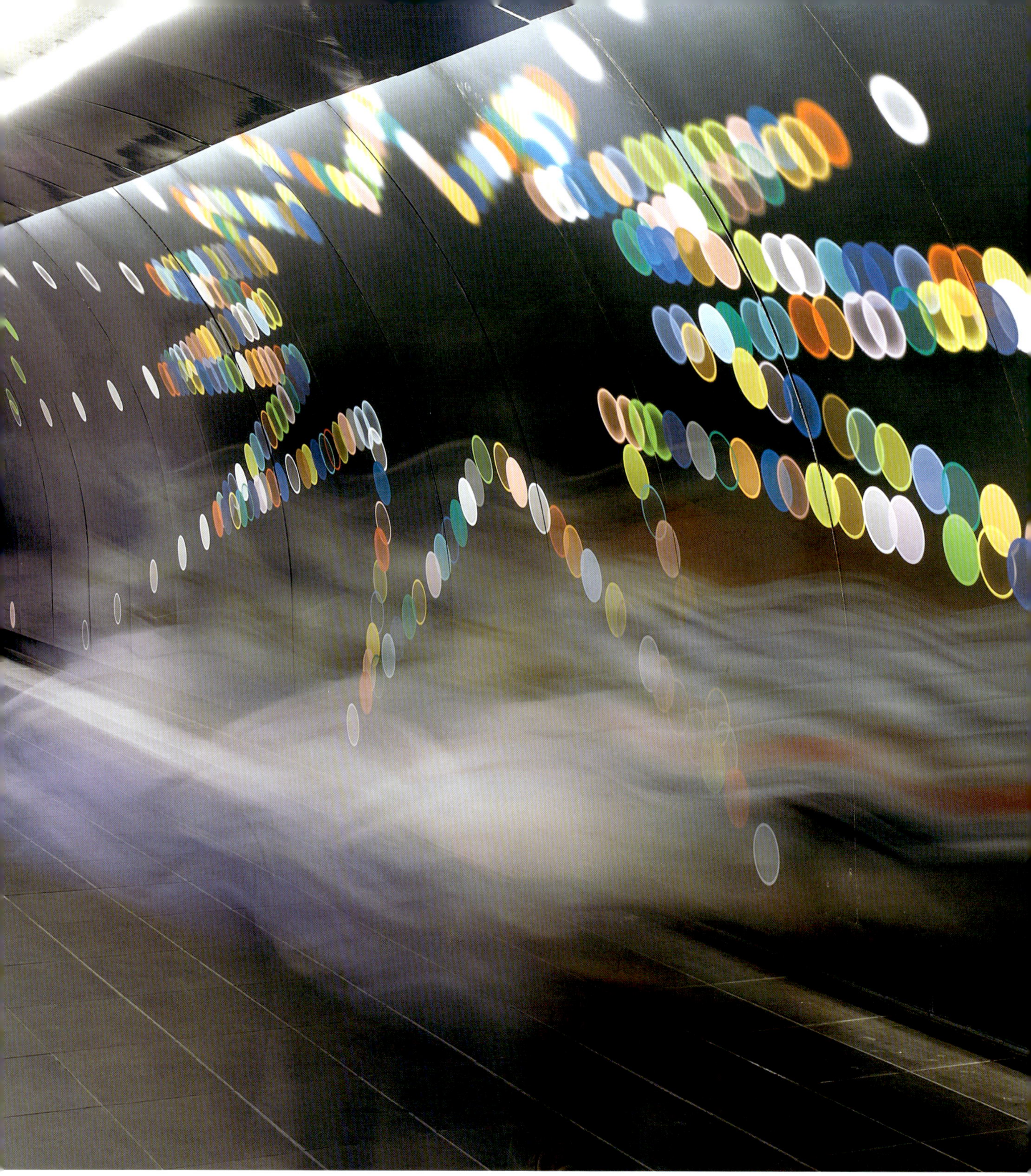

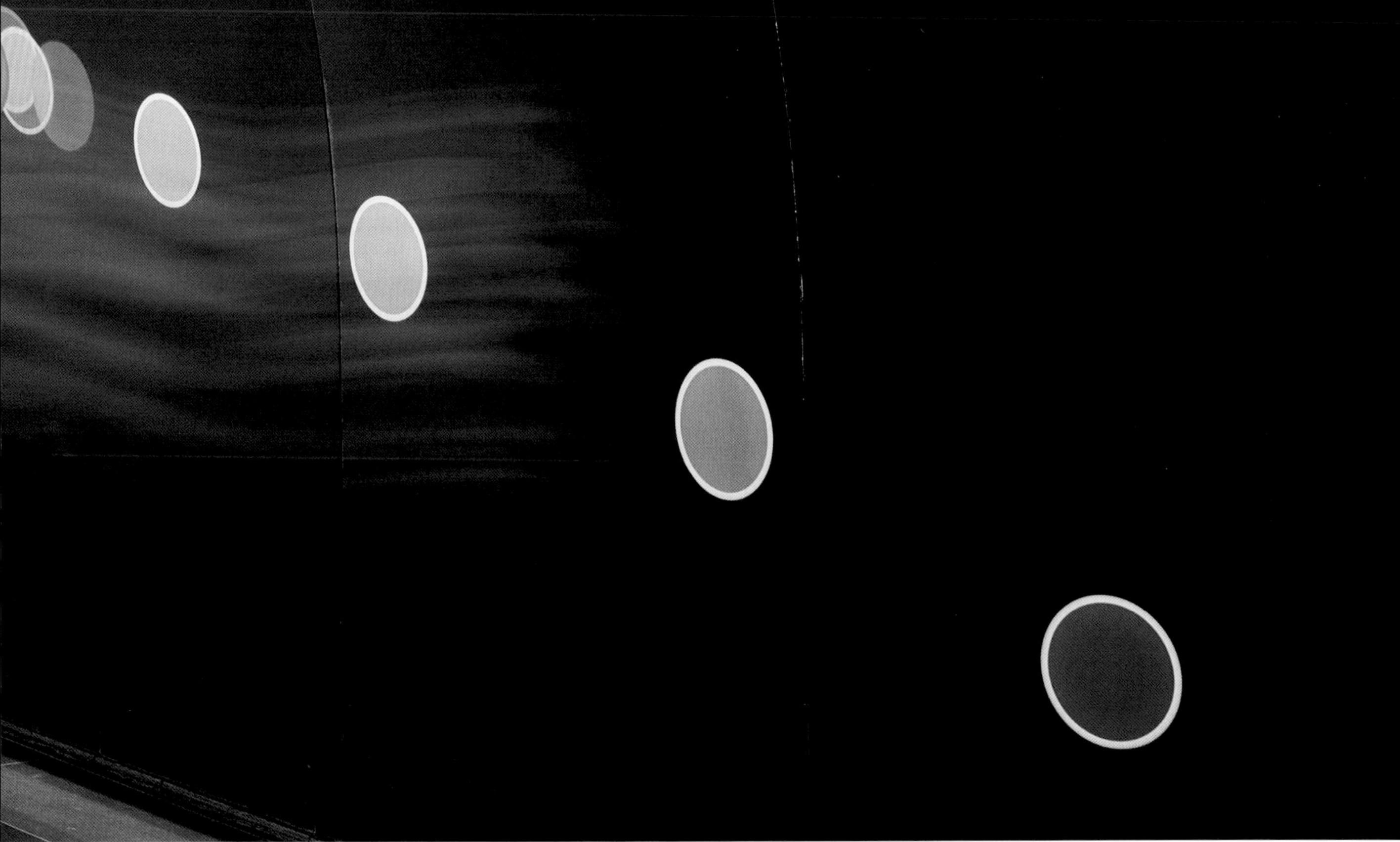

NEIL WOOD, *ET TOI LÀ, ATTRAPE TON ÉTOILE*

A POETIC PRACTICE

It took nearly two years of preparation to bring this monumental cosmic vision to life. The enameled steel panels, 1.1 meters wide and 3 meters high—bearing in mind the unevenness of the corridor—were manufactured in the Belgian workshops of PolyVision. On site, Neil Wood realized that he had to revise his palette as certain colors could not be used for environmental reasons—cadmium red, for example. Then the installers and lighting engineers came in. While the artist was working, a team of architects were busy with the huge task of redeveloping the station.

When the RATP approached Wood in 2015 the company already had a long-standing relationship with him: on several occasion, he had competed to take part in the network's temporary or permanent graphic design and artistic projects. In 2008 he designed a mural installation for Assemblée Nationale station, *50 ans de vie politique* (50 Year of Political Life), and contributed to *J'avance, donc je pense* (I Move, Therefore I Think) at Montparnasse–Bienvenüe: the long corridor at that station greatly inspired his work for Charles de Gaulle–Étoile.

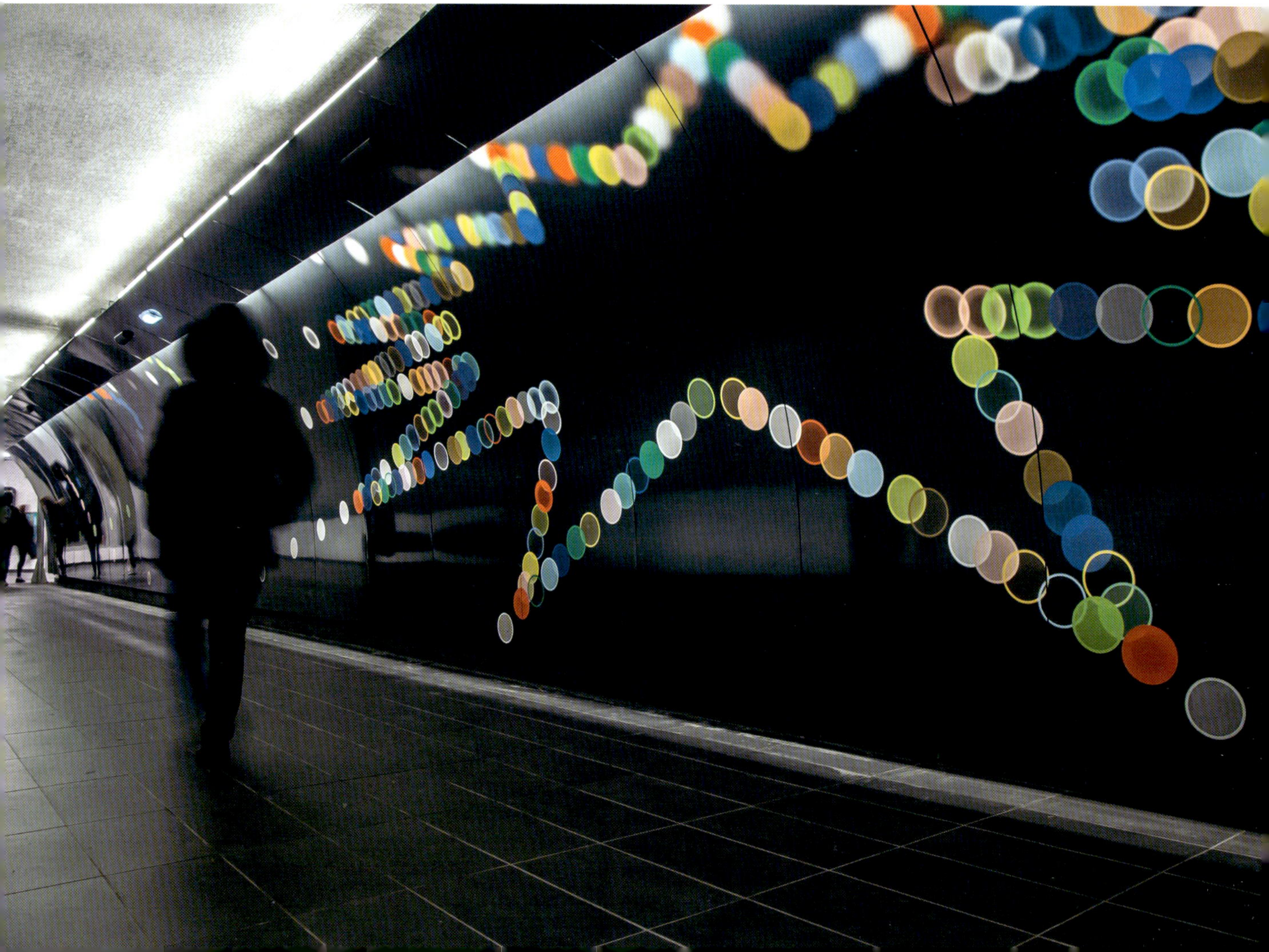

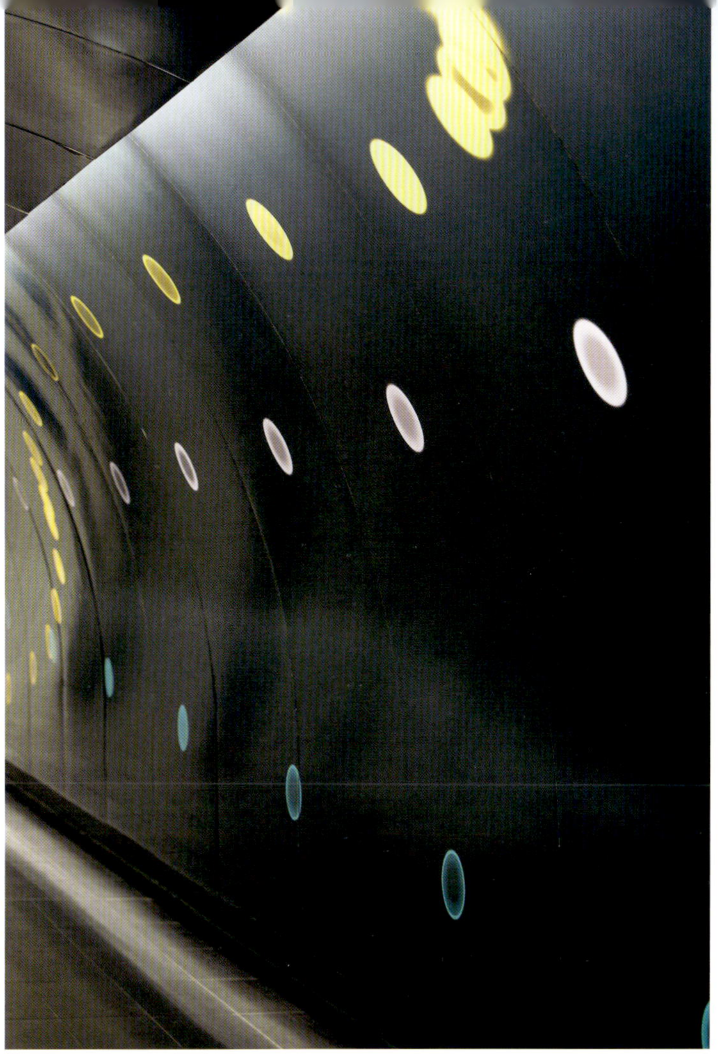

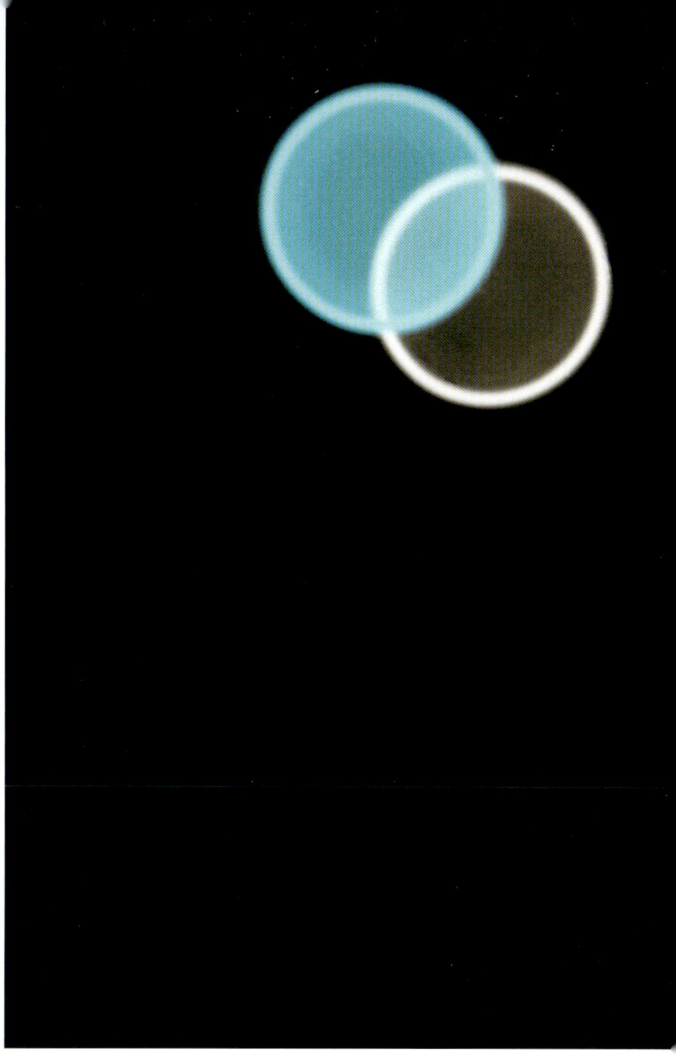

Wood was born in Britain in 1963. He started out in design and fashion, then founded his own studio in 1991 and moved into typography, silk-screen printing, printmaking, and photography. He now incorporates poetic, almost haiku-like, language into his practice: the title of this artwork is *Et toi là, attrape ton étoile* (Hey You, Catch Your Star).

Et toi là, attrape ton étoile, 2017

Digital print on enameled steel panel
3 × 50 m

HUGUES REIP / *Périple*

A WHOLE WORLD TO EXPLORE. A FUNNY CATERPILLAR ON A BRANCH LIKE THE ONE IN *ALICE IN WONDERLAND* OBSERVES YOU, AN UNDERWATER LUNAR LANDSCAPE, BOULDERS DIGITALLY PRINTED ON THE ESCALATOR HANDRAILS LEADING TO THE TICKET HALL, TRANSLUCENT AMBER AND QUARTZ WALLS, A FEW IMAGES OF FOSSILS ON THE FLOOR, AND CELESTIAL PROJECTIONS ABOVE THE TRACKS.

A TREASURE HUNT

Hugues Reip has transformed Mairie de Montrouge metro station into a fairyland. The artist, who was born in 1964, collects pebbles and rare stones, and likes discreet gestures and simple shapes. His artistic practice includes video works, photography, installations, and sculpture. For his metro *Périple* (Journey), he decided to create an ensemble of works instead of a single monumental one. We discover them one by one on a treasure hunt of sorts. "I had already worked with landscape architects in peri-urban areas. For Montrouge, the idea was to give the impression that a scree slope was descending from street level to the bowels of the Earth. I wanted to evoke a journey to the center of the planet, a little like in a book by Jules Verne or Jonathan Swift."

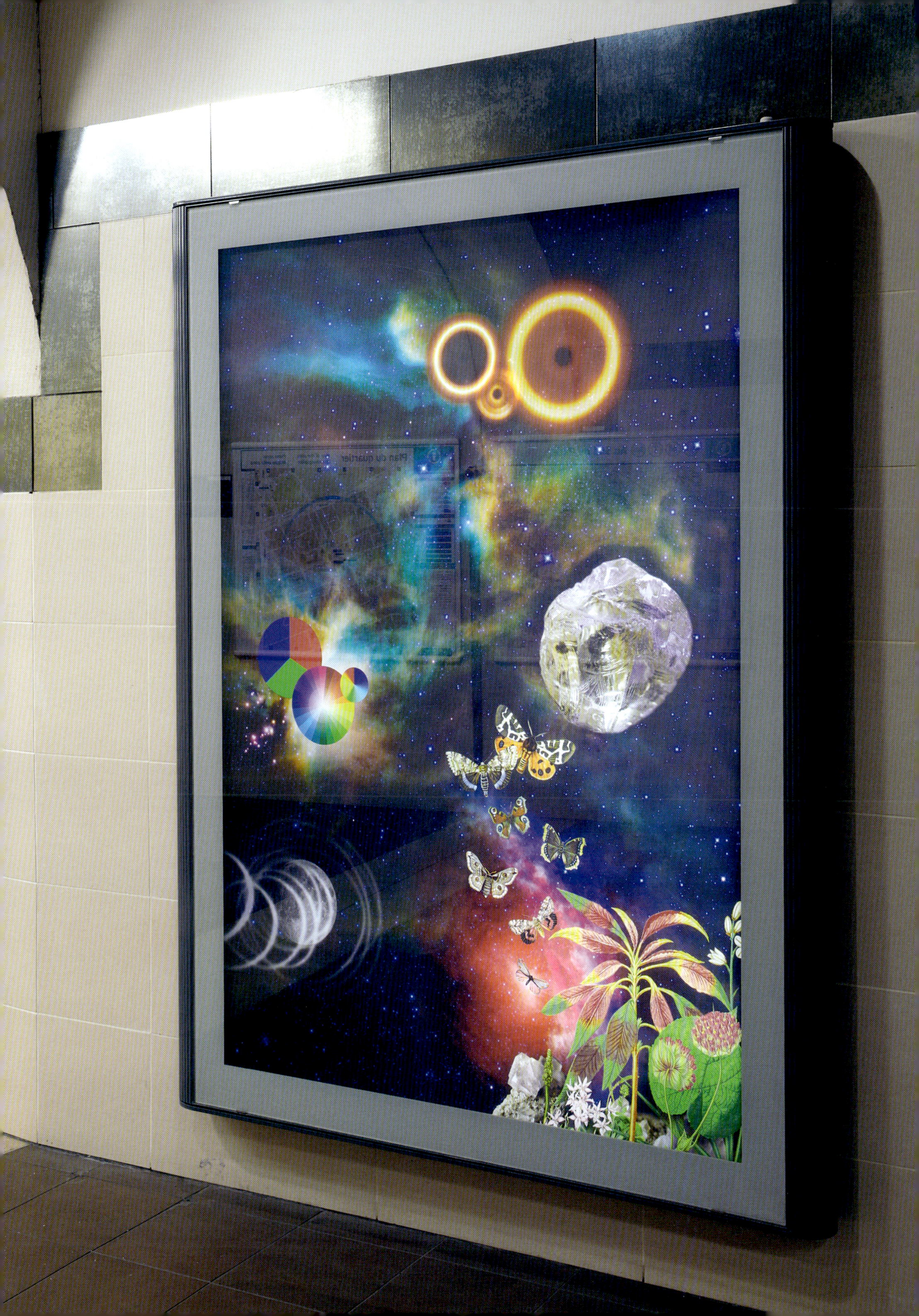

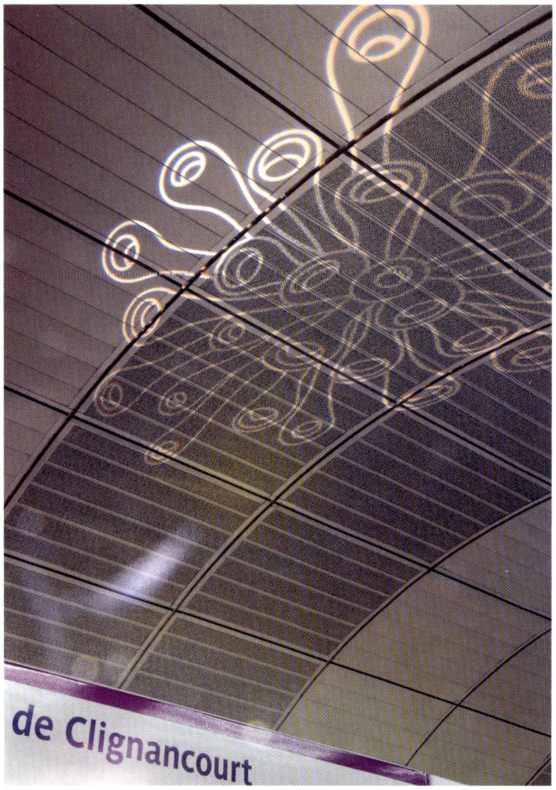
de Clignancourt

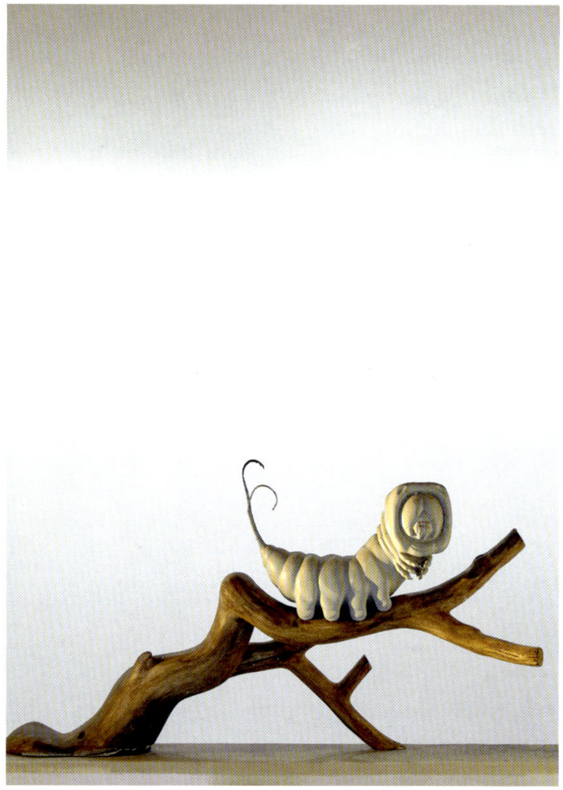

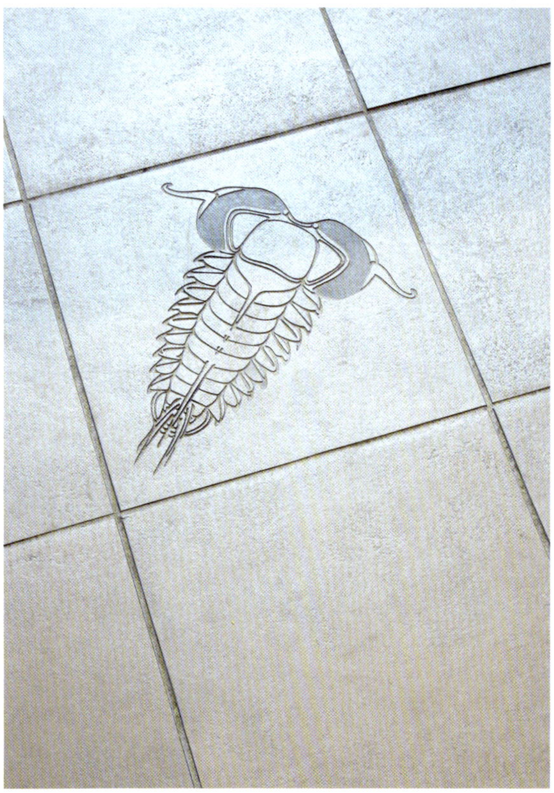

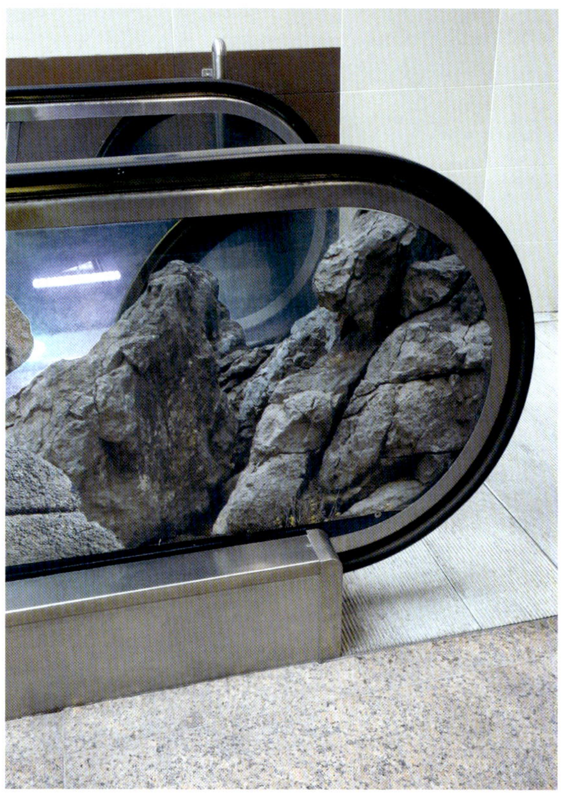

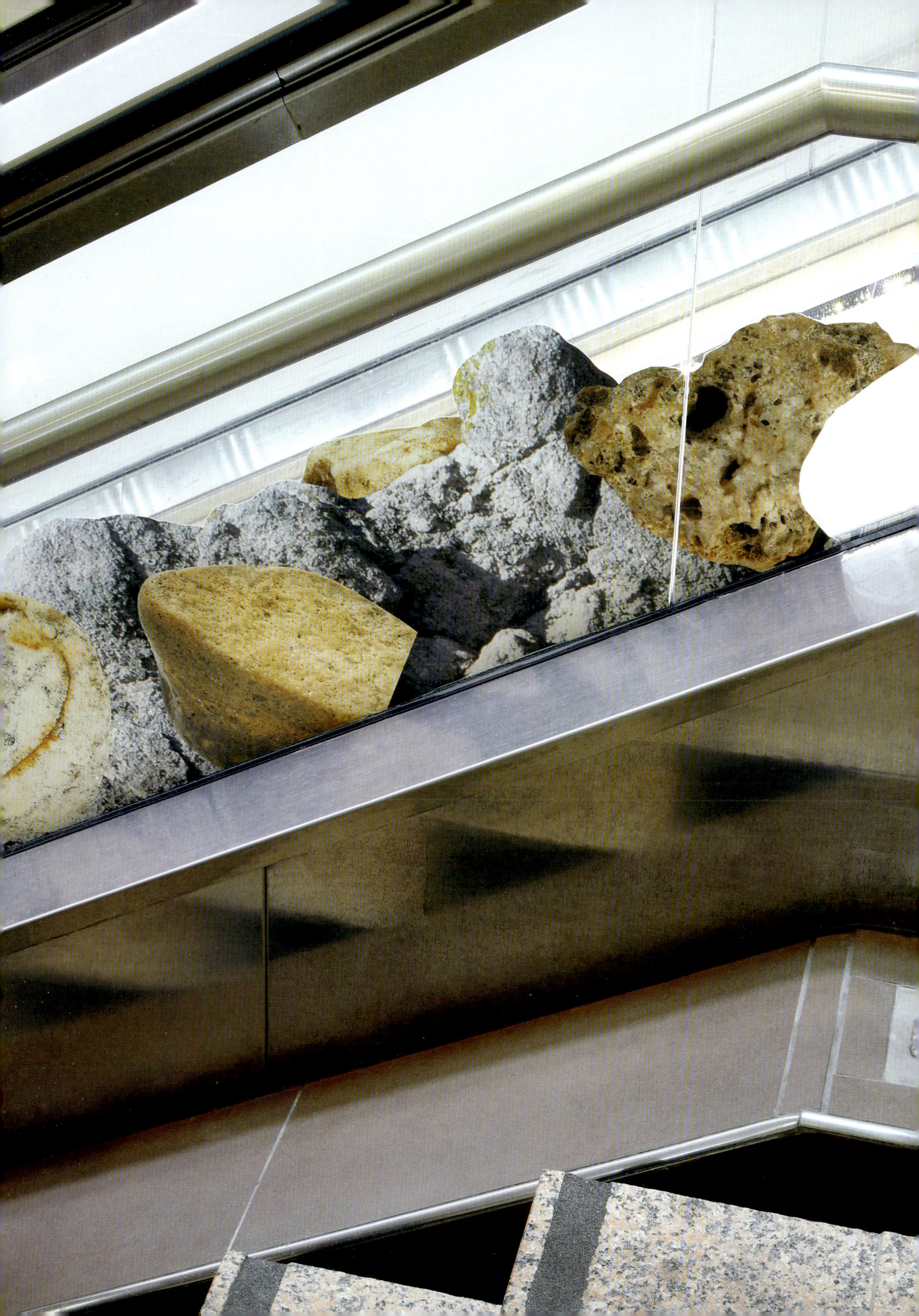

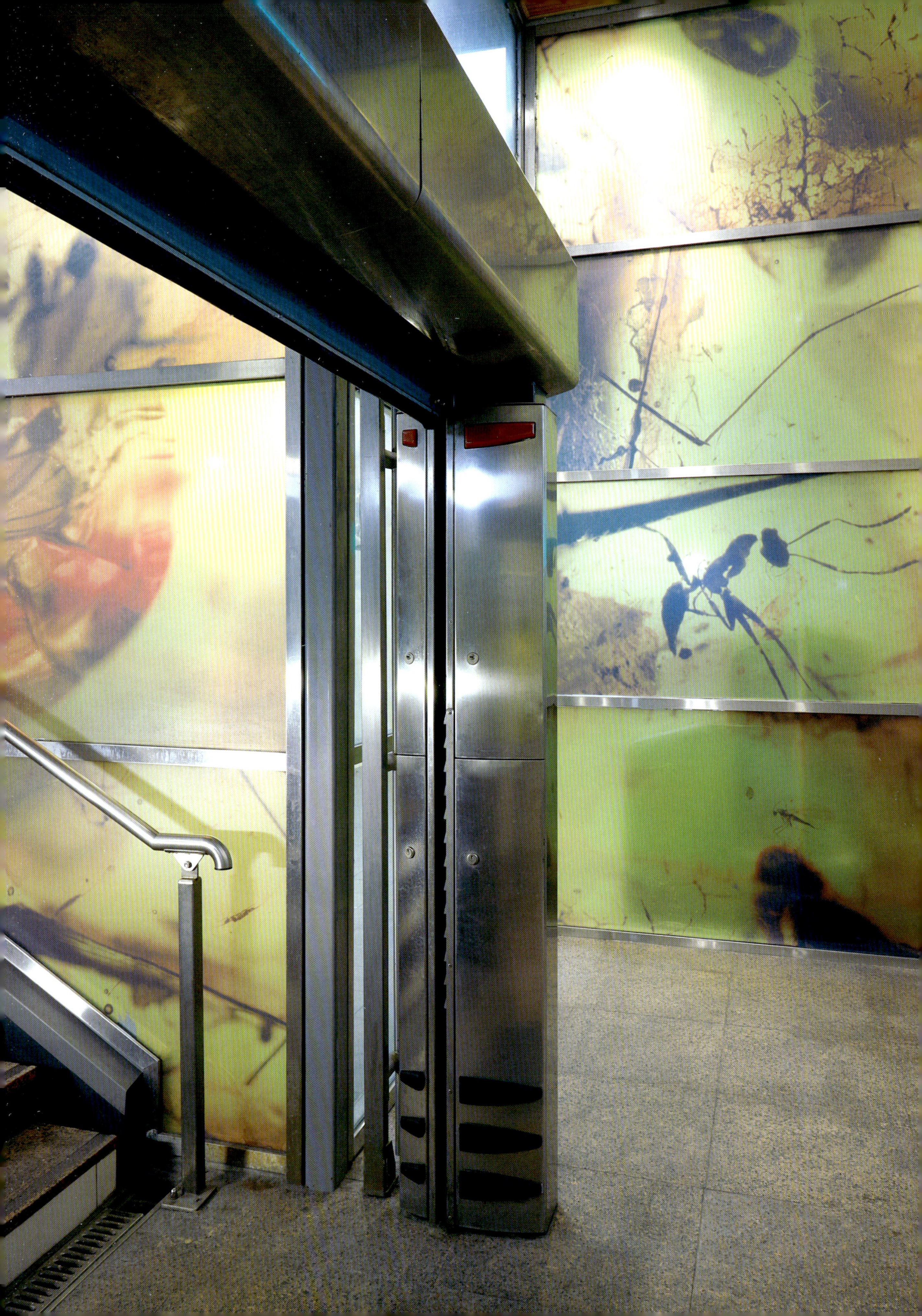

AN IMAGINARY LANDSCAPE

Unlike other works installed in places steeped in history, this artistic commission dated from the same time as the new station. "When I was chosen," he recalls, "the site did not exist yet. I even had the chance to see the drill digging the tunnel." It was a production company, Arter, that suggested he respond to the RATP call for tenders. His project was chosen by a committee made up of RATP teams and the mayor of Montrouge, just outside Paris. "Then there were three phases of construction, which lasted three years. The ticket hall was, for example, delivered before the platforms: that allowed me how to gauge how my works were received. We were also able to test the video projections in the station itself. It was the first time we used etched glass slides." The designs evoke both a celestial vault and somewhat shamanic wall paintings.

Périple, 2013

Les cailloux: Digital prints on translucent polyurethane film, varying dimensions
L'ambre: Digital prints on translucent polyurethane film, varying dimensions
Le quartz: Digital print on translucent polyurethane film, varying dimensions
Suspens II: Polyester resin
Trilobites: Engraved porcelain stoneware tiles
Butterflyer: Digital print, advertising panel
Darkslides: Gobo light projections, varying dimensions

A CHANCE TO PLAY

Hugues Reip's subtle works seem to be inviting passengers to play. An advertising panel displays a travel agency ad for a fantastic journey that will never take place. Another reveals a landscape that comes to life with the coming and going of passengers. Reip says that, one day, he even received a message from a passenger thanking him for making her daily commutes less tedious because she enjoyed looking for tiles engraved with trilobite fossils. "You make my day every morning when I go to work," she wrote.
Reip enjoys playing with scale because of the strangeness created. The variations also offer him a chance to be playful, and all his works are reversible. "There is no bronze statue bolted to the ground, the content of the panel can be replaced, the caterpillar can be taken down, and if the light under the vault is switched off, the projections disappear." His works are like apparitions that appear and disappear, as if by magic.

AN OWL, A WOLF, AND A GORILLA APPEAR ON PILLARS AS YOU MOVE AROUND THEM. PHILIPPE BAUDELOCQUE HAS CREATED A WHOLE BESTIARY IN THE CONCOURSE OF CHÂTELET–LES HALLES RER STATION, ONE OF THE BUSIEST PLACES ON THE NETWORK.

PHILIPPE BAUDELOCQUE

/ *Du corps au fruit, du fruit au corps*

ORIGIN STORY

"When you're an artist, there are works that you are commissioned to do and those that you dream of doing." It was Philippe Baudelocque who initiated his ephemeral intervention at Châtelet–Les Halles station by inviting the RATP teams to come see one of his monumental works. He had just installed *Brève Histoire du cosmos* (Brief History of the Cosmos), a fresco rising the entire height of a staircase serving five levels, at the Palais de Tokyo. "I noticed that several spaces that had just been renovated, and that there were panels painted black on the columns. It was the perfect support for a drawing!"

So he was able to realize his dream of taking over a space that 800,000 people passed through every day—by way of comparison, the Venice Biennale welcomes 200,000 people over a period of a few months. "It's popular place and I like that," he says. "I often pass by there myself. I thought of all the people going to work who passed by it every day and wanted to create something light-hearted and poetic in a place that seemed to be lacking those qualities."

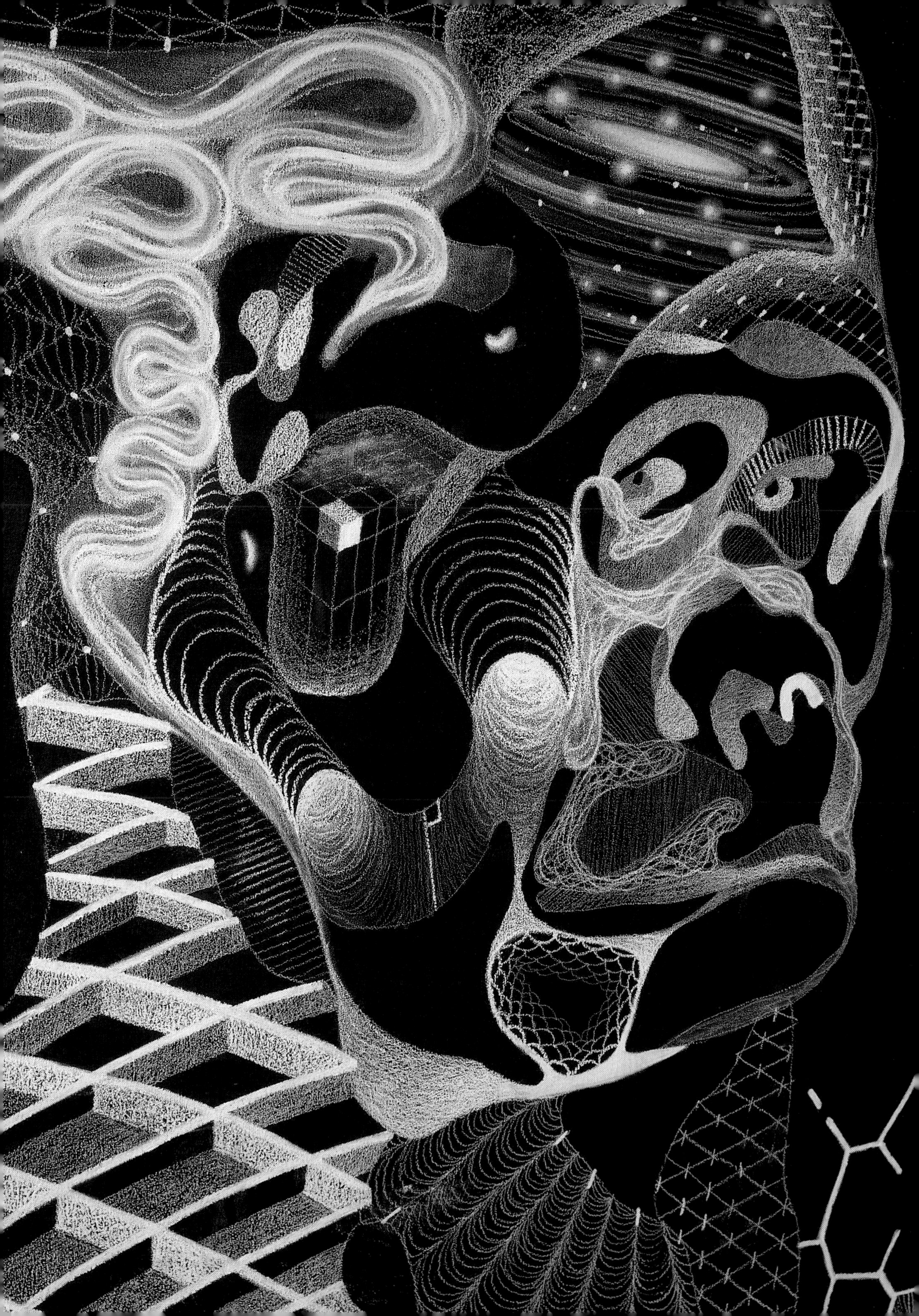

LIVING CREATURES EMERGE

Baudelocque's RER station artworks are apparitions of sorts. They can be read in thousands of ways. "Children immediately see animals and stars, an owl, a wolf, a gorilla," he says. "Their parents often mention the molecular dimension of my drawings, sometimes the relationship between the infinitely large and the infinitely small. What interests me most is the question of energy or electromagnetic networks. With these drawings, I wanted to do things that I had never done before." From a distance, the mural drawings installed between the Porte Lescot and the Porte Rambuteau exits look like they were drawn with chalk, but they were made using oil pastel, which takes three days to dry. "In a mineral context such as the station, simply using sophisticated drawings that can be touched introduces a poetic dimension."

He says that many passersby are worried about their fragility. From the beginning of the project, it was understood that the work would not be permanent and some of the twelve initial panels of the work have now disappeared.

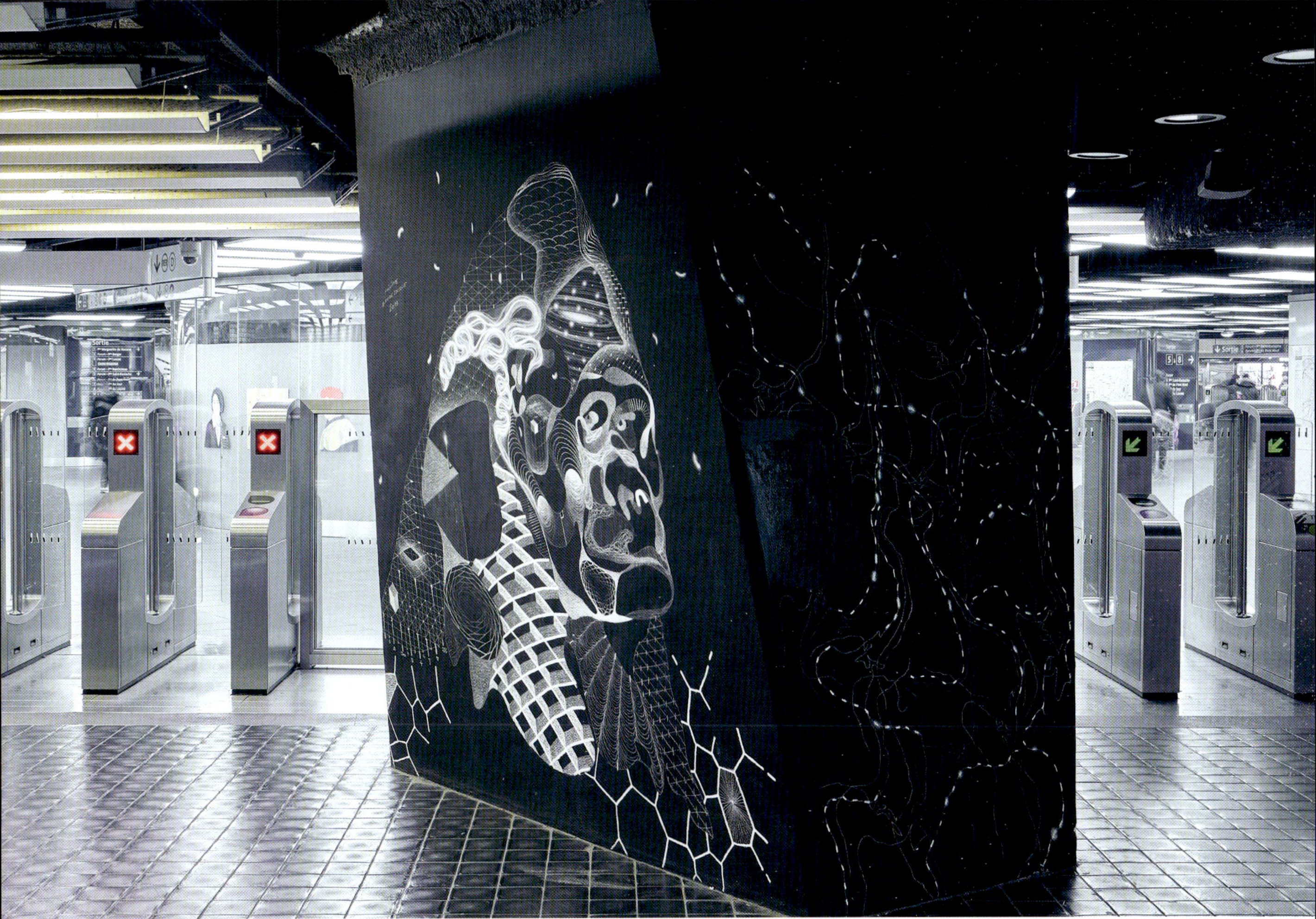

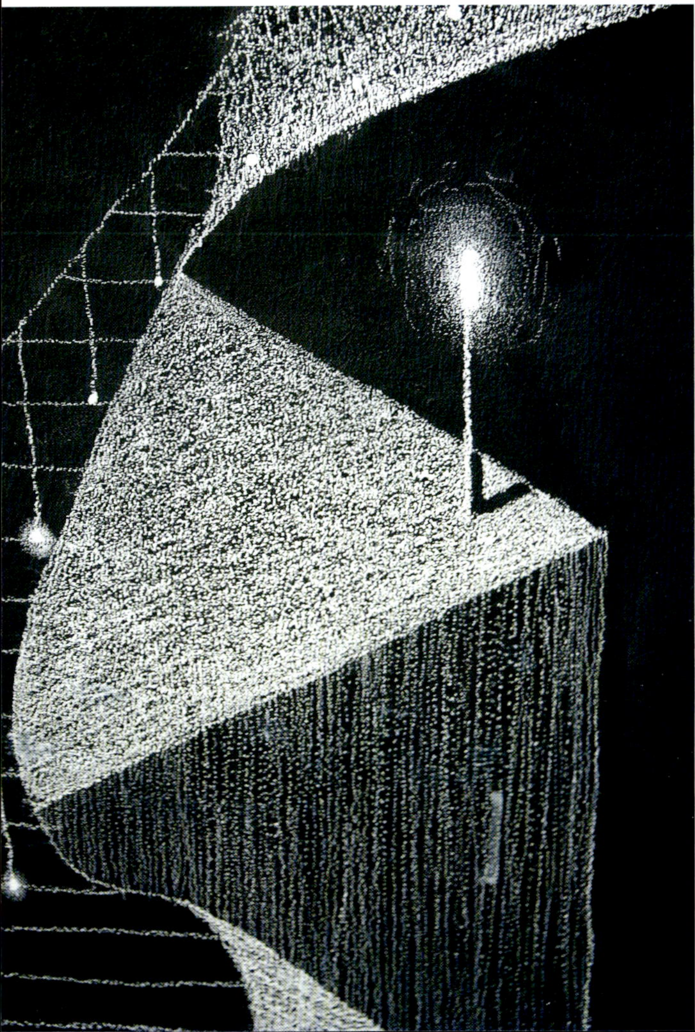

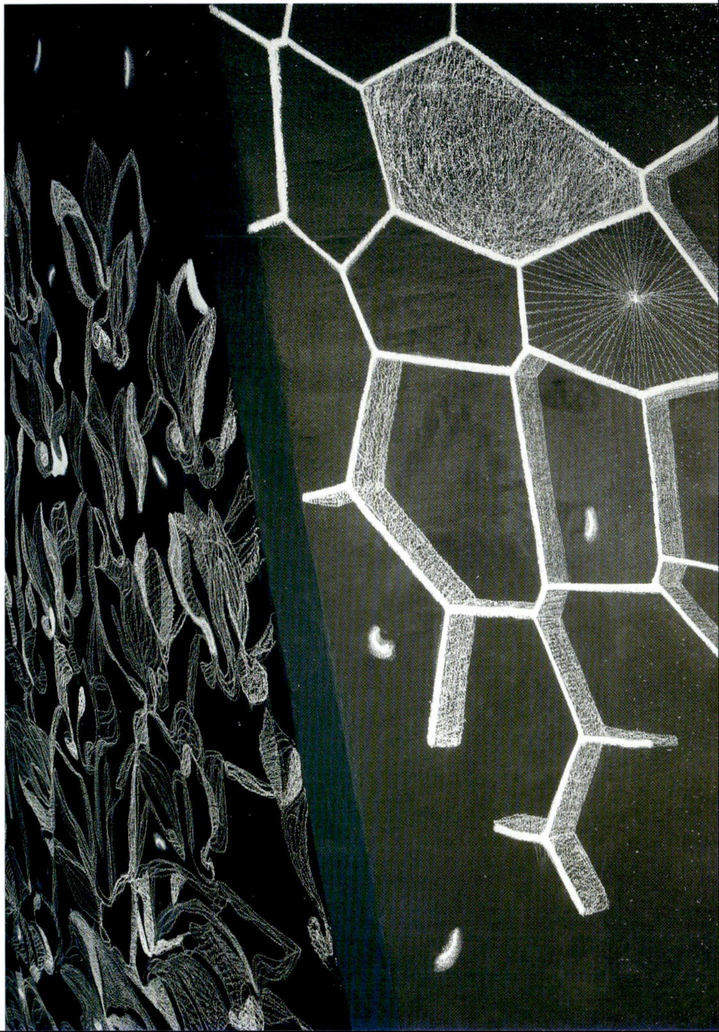

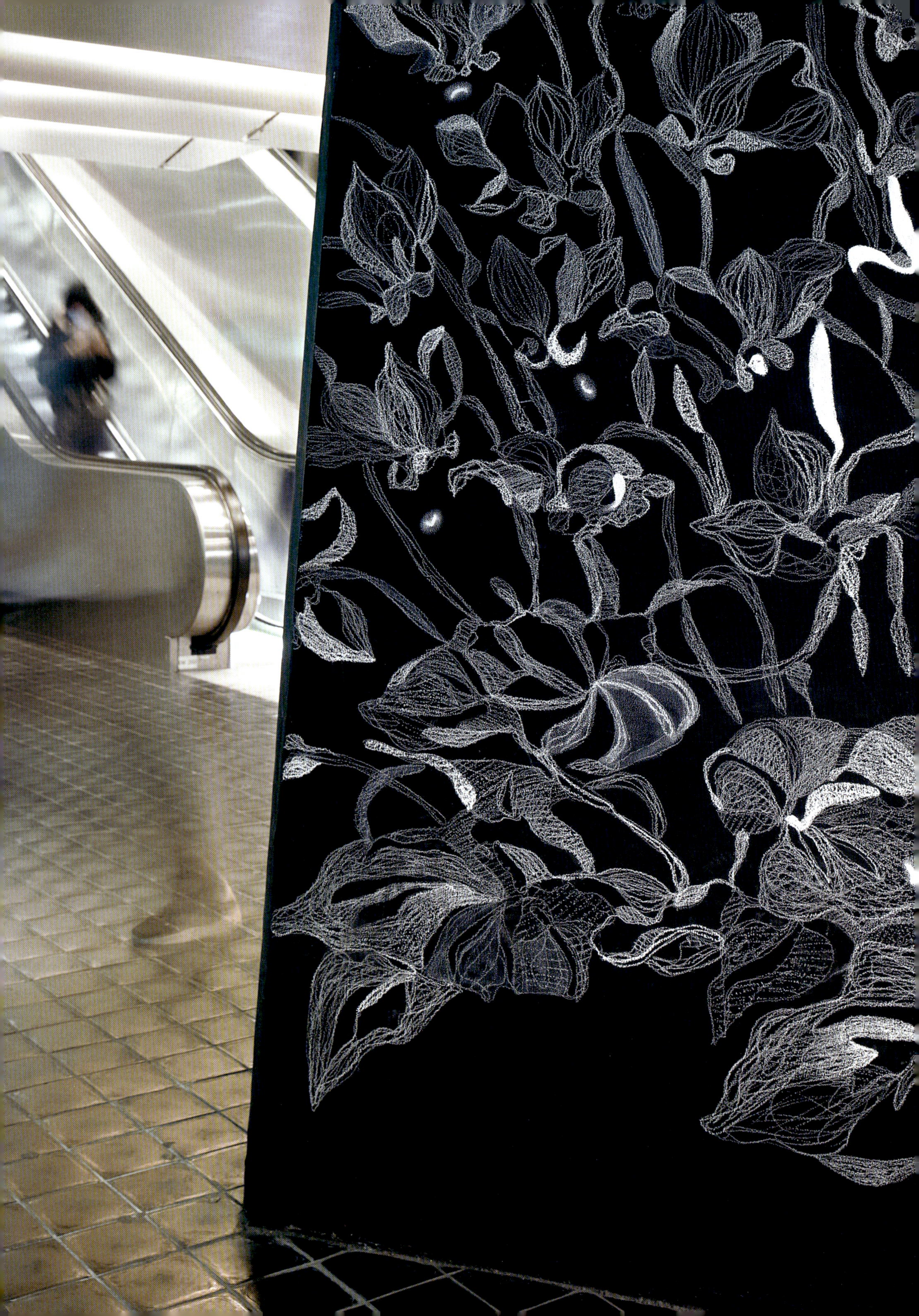

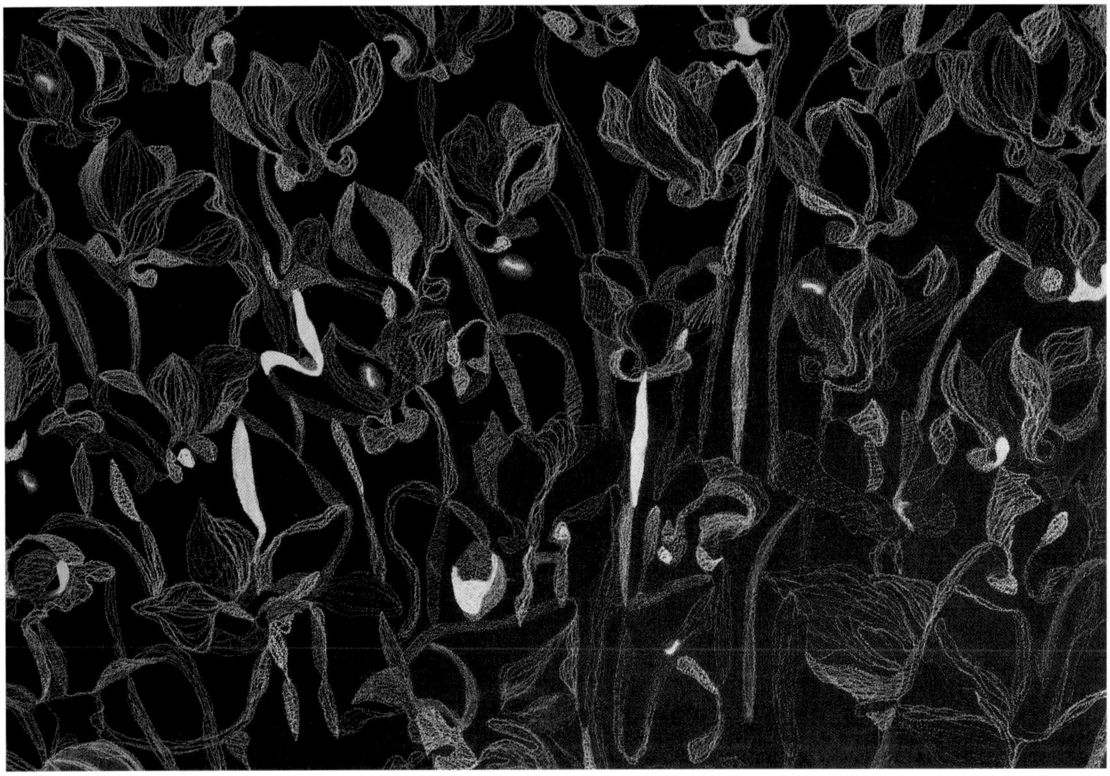

AN ARTIST APART

"When we were kids," says Baudelocque, "my brother and sisters and I were given books instead of games: history; geography, natural sciences. Knowledge was essential." Baudelocque was a graffer when he was a teenager—graffiti gave him a taste for making works in public and for the public space. "What I removed from my drawings was the New York feel, someone in the Bronx with a ghetto blaster. In Paris, it did not ring true. So I introduced my own culture into my work while preserving the energy of my experiments of my tagging days. Today, my drawings can be found on T-shirts, canvases, or panels in the metro—the only thing that changes is the people who see them. My discourse remains the same."

—

Du corps au fruit, du fruit au corps, 2018

Oil pastel on wall painted black

2.7 × 2.4 m and 2.7 × 1.2 m

JACQUES TISSINIER

/ Tissignalisation n° 14

IT IS A SKY ABOVE OUR HEADS, A CONSTELLATION COVERING THE VAULTS OF PYRAMIDES AND MADELEINE STATIONS. THESE LITTLE "SIGNS" INDICATE NOTHING, OR EVERYTHING: THEY ARE AN INVITATION TO DAYDREAM.

MAN OF THE SOUTHWEST

Jacques Tissinier was born in the Aude department of southwestern France in 1936. That's where he grew up and produced his early works. Even after setting up his studio in Bagnolet, outside Paris, where he lived from the1970s to his death in 2018, he kept close ties with the region where he was born. After training at the École des Beaux-Arts de Toulouse, Tissinier set off for Paris and enrolled in the painter Marcel Gromaire's classes at the École Nationale des Arts Décoratifs, where he met Georges Braque and André Malraux. After a stint at the École des Beaux-Arts, he went to the Casa de Velázquez in Madrid.

FROM ART TO GRAPHIC DESIGN

For Jacques Tissinier, painting was not the result of solitary contemplation. He always preferred lively streets to silent museum spaces. He wanted to create a new language that could be used in the domestic space as well as in urban furniture and public spaces. "Where better than the street, a collective, special place, for experimenting with my most profound motivations." In his compositions, he used "signs" to shift his work from painting to signage, signage that is not cold but charged with symbols and poetry.

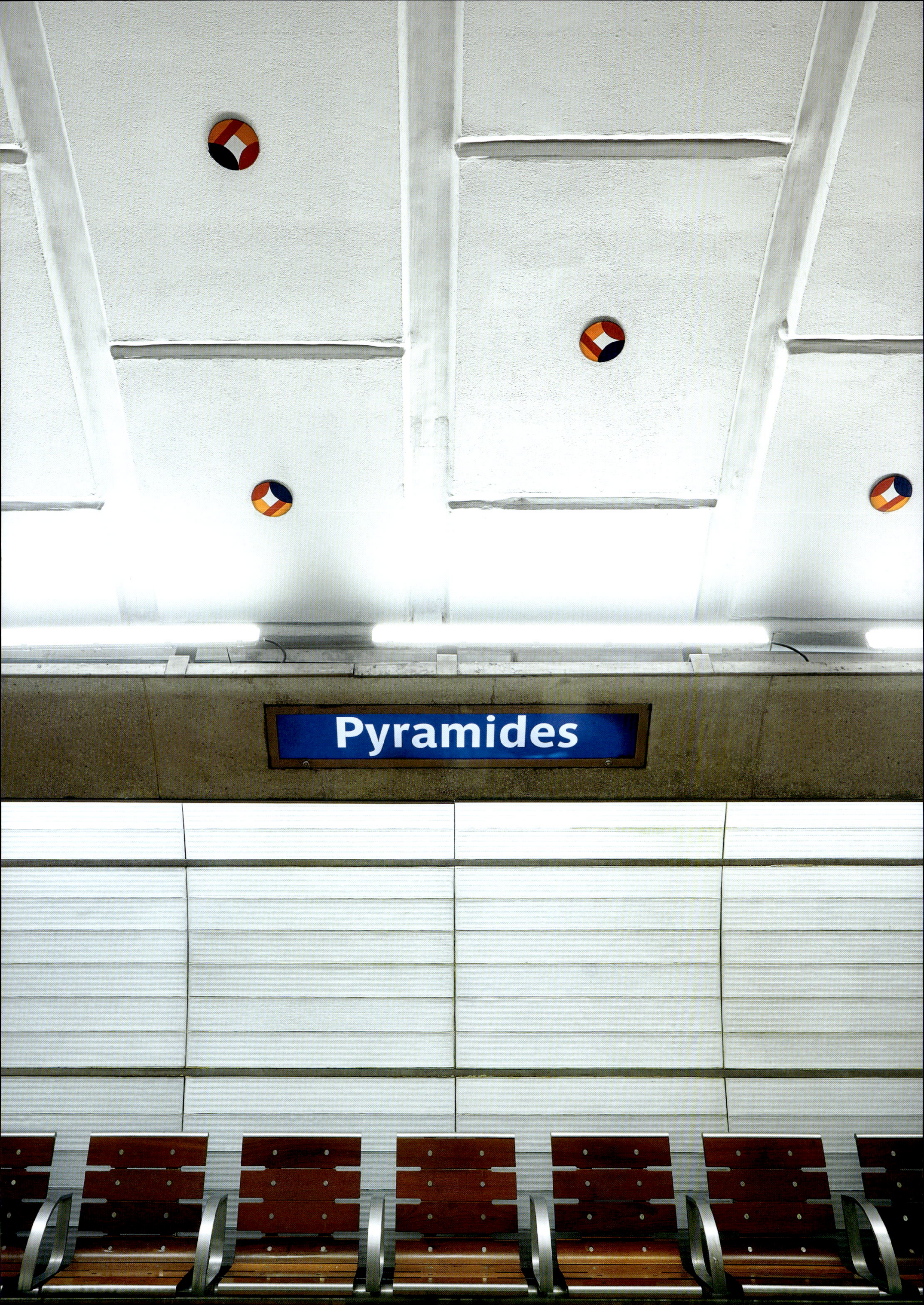
Pyramides

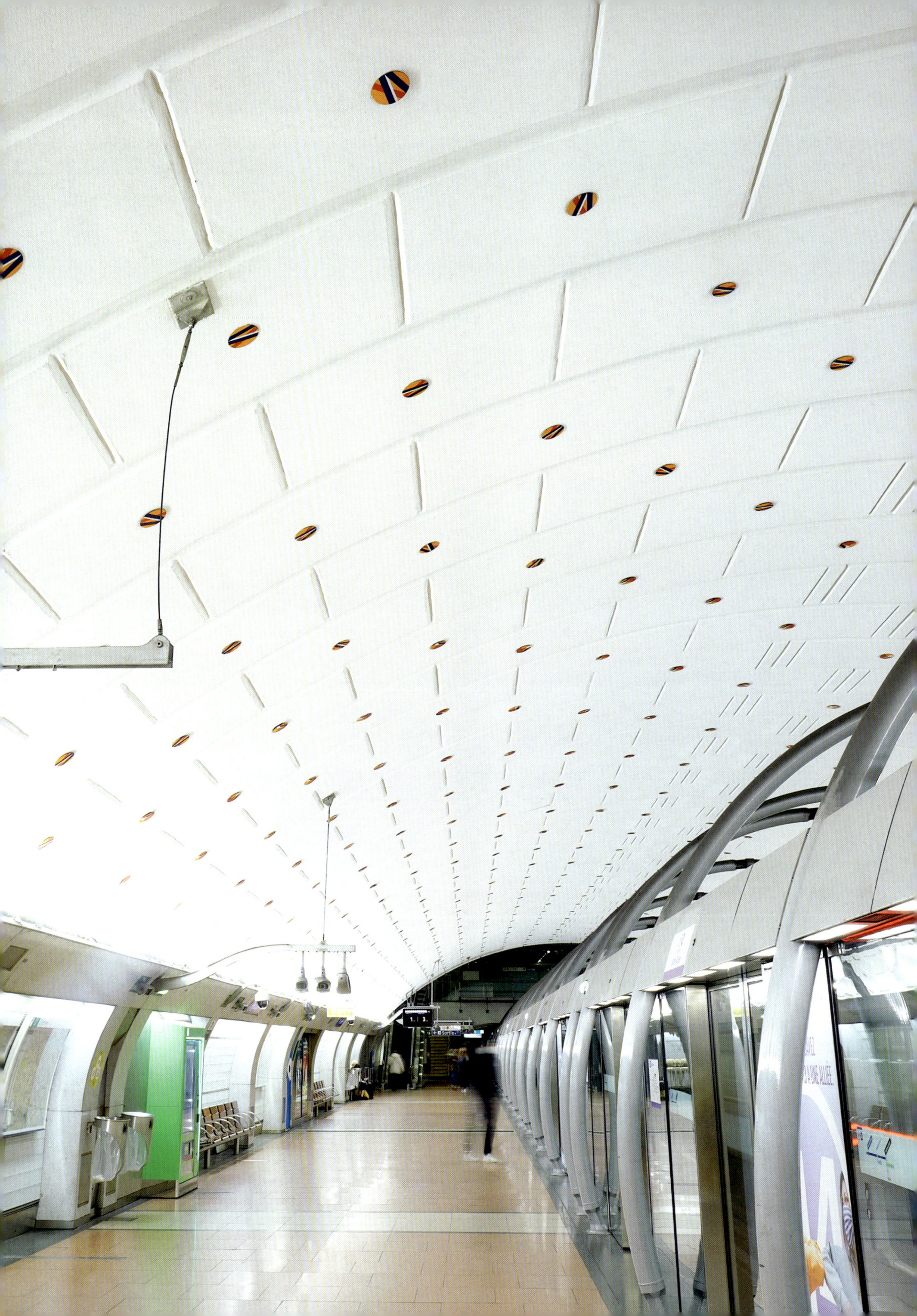

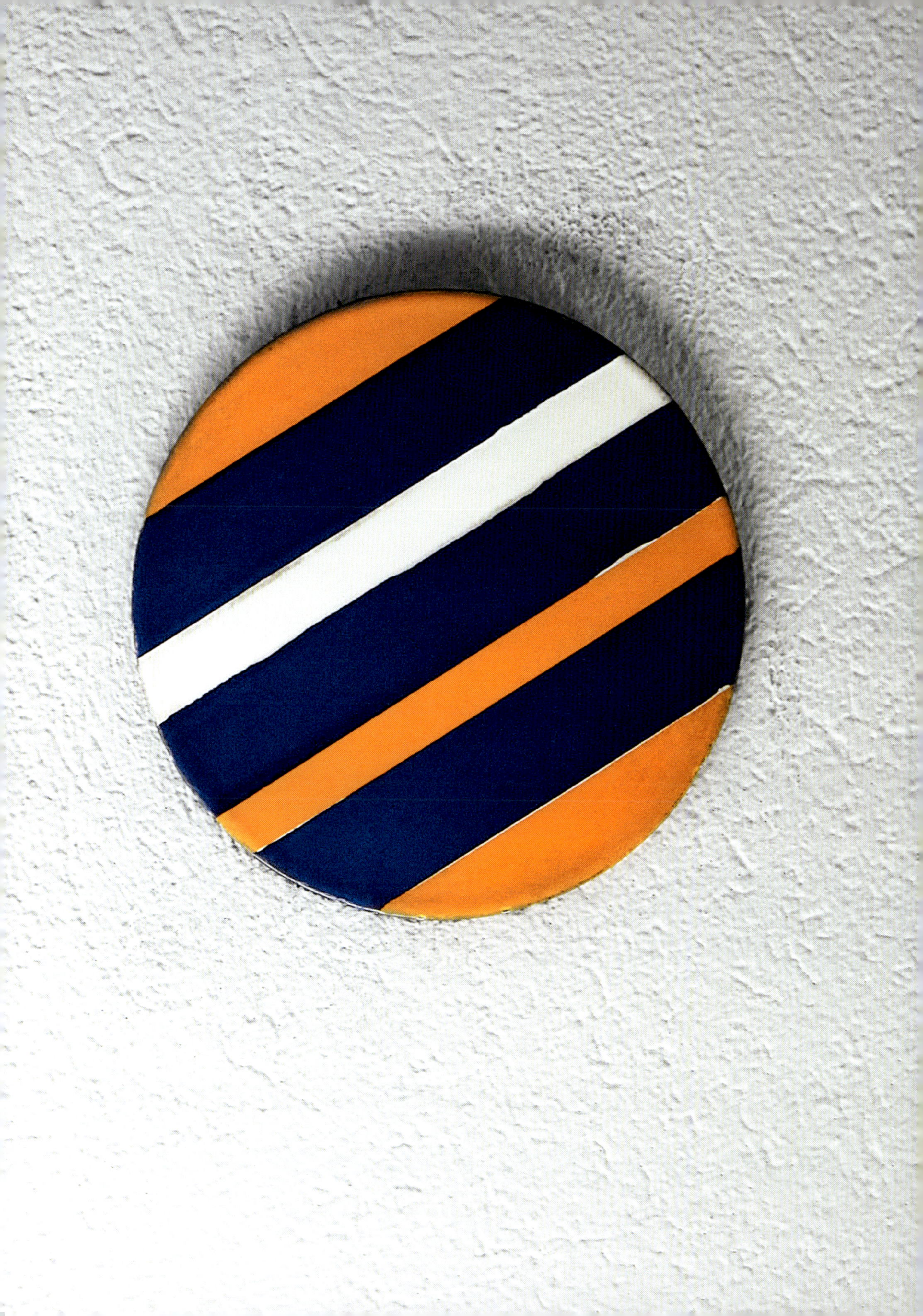

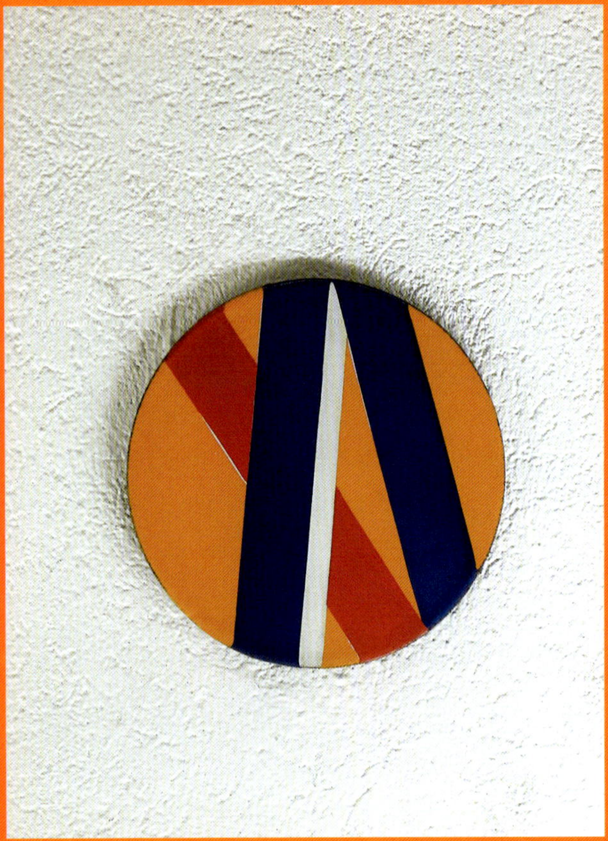

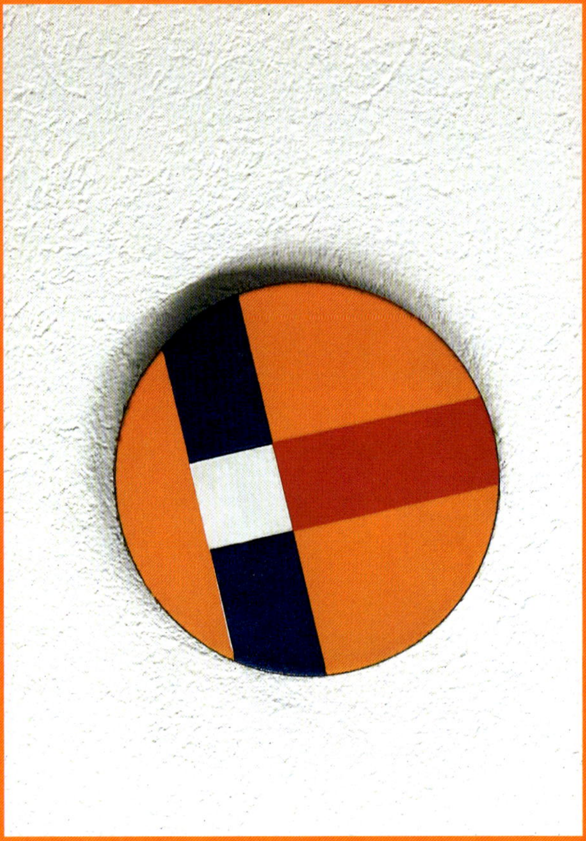

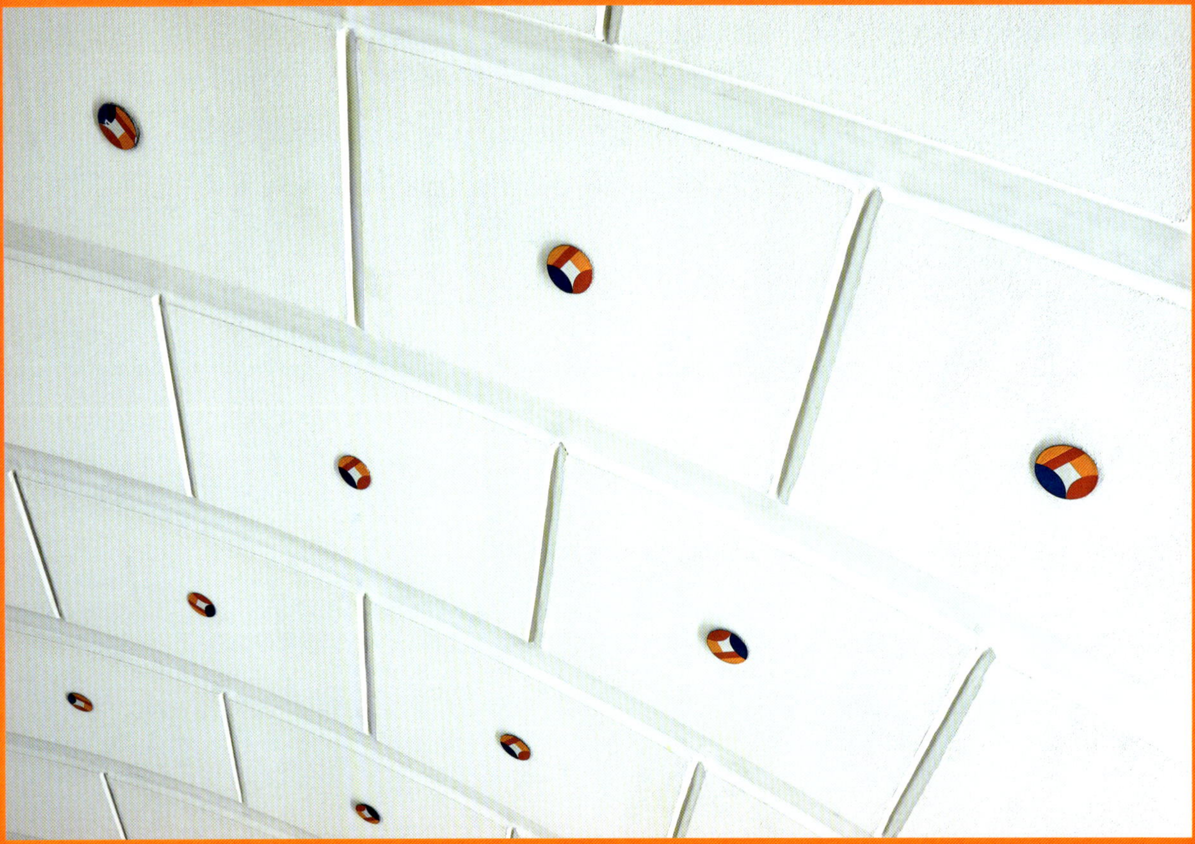

THE MAIN URBAN PROJECTS

One of his first murals, for the Abattoirs de Pamiers in southwestern France in 1968, features automotive paint. At the time, the choice of medium was revolutionary. The following year, the architect charged with redeveloping the seaside resort of Port-Leucate, Georges Candilis, commissioned him to design bus shelters. Tissinier's designs featured solid blocks of black, red, and white. Candilis had this to say about their project: "It was above all, a question of destroying the monologue of a work of architecture or a painting and replacing it with a dialogue, that is to say, mutual understanding and a common language. Legendary French adman Jacques Séguéla pointedly referred to Tissiner as "public artist number one". Pursuing his ideal of art accessible to all, Tissinier made his bus-shelter designs available as stacking tables and stools, which were produced and sold by the inexpensive department store Prisunic in 1973. Later, Tissinier's works could be found in places such as highway A61 near Narbonne—*Chevaliers cathares* (Cathar Knights, 1980)—and in Toulouse and Paris, in front of the Centre Pompidou and in the Parc de la Villette—*Crayons libertaires* (Libertarian Pencils, 1972–89).

TISSIGNALISATION N° 14

The work for line 14 commissioned from him by the RATP in 1997 heralded a new phase. The brand-new metro line was the first whose architecture featured such large volumes. These exceptional volumes were further enhanced by the works commissioned for the line's stations. Tissinier was chosen for Pyramides and Madeleine. The vaults, dotted with a thousand red, white, blue, and orange enameled steel disks, look like starry skies. Each of the disks at Pyramides station features a stylized papyrus leaf that evokes both the natural world and the hieroglyphic writing of ancient Egypt. As was his wont, Tissinier gave signage a twist, making it somewhat superfluous and thus absolutely necessary. His disks invite us to embark on thousands of inner journeys.

***Tissignalisation n° 14*, 1997**
Enameled steel
Diam. 16 cm

JULIAN OPIE

/ *Passage*

The frieze will comprise four 60-meter-long and 3-meter-high frescoes on various supports: printed ceramic tiles adorn the walls and black vinyl film has been applied on the glass surfaces. The work depicts eighty-eight figures in motion and makes passengers a part of an immersive and dynamic installation in which they become the protagonists. Julian Opie talks about his work:

"I want to create a kind of frieze that you can walk along and through, echoing the passageways and temples of the ancient world where rows of warriors or servants would line the walls. The passengers themselves would form part of the flow of bodies and combine with the implied movement of my drawings.
I have drawn the people from the streets so they have a contemporary and public quality, holding phones and bags and reflecting the current styles and fashions of clothes and accessories.

I have made many works using glass as the support structure. Glass is a common but magical material that still conjures a sense of awe and confounds our bodies' understanding of the world. Glass turns the world beyond it into a view, a picture. It flattens the world beyond and abstracts it. By putting all four parts of the work behind glass I invite the passengers to enter into a virtual representation, a shift from the present into an image of the present.

THIS WORK BY THE BRITISH ARTIST WAS DESIGNED TO HIGHLIGHT THE IMPRESSIVE VOLUMES OF THE CONCOURSE AT PORTE DE CLICHY STATION.

The trick with installations is to make a work that seems to dictate the surroundings—as if the building was made to present this particular artwork, as if the artwork could only exist if these circumstances were built to house it. I tried a number of solutions here and found this idea growing out of the particularities of the site.

Much of my work focuses on the balance between the public and the private, the way we navigate the exterior world from our individual interiors. I use the language of modern urban signage, graphics and architecture to depict individuals and personal details. The passing passengers will not have the time or inclination to stop and gaze at an artwork in this environment, instead I invite them to keep going on their journey and to let the artwork become a part of that motion to use our natural instinct to navigate and to look at other people as the dynamic of enjoying and engaging in the artwork."

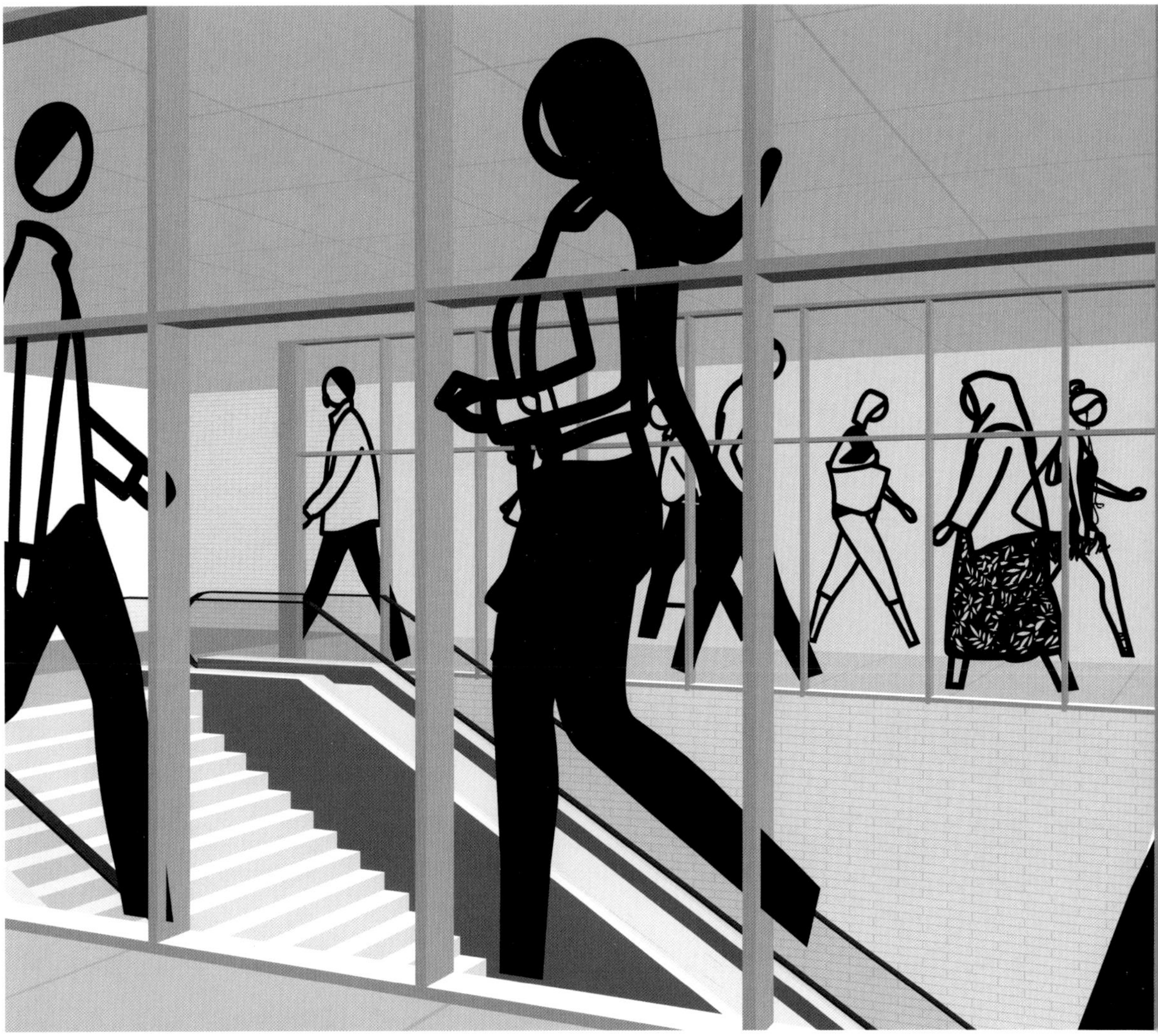

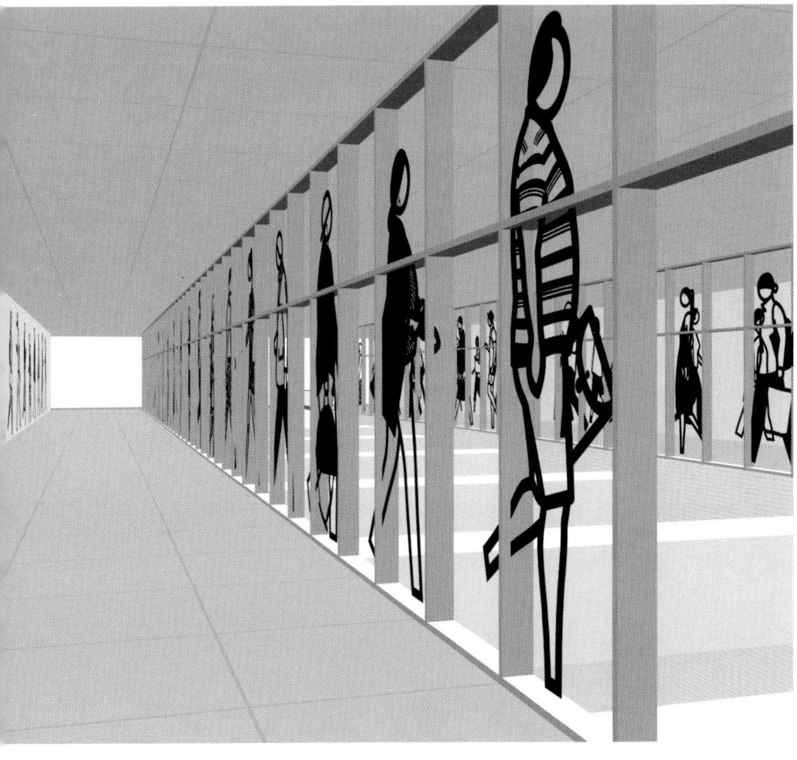

***Passage*, 2022**

Ceramic tiles, glass, black vinyl
60 × 3 m

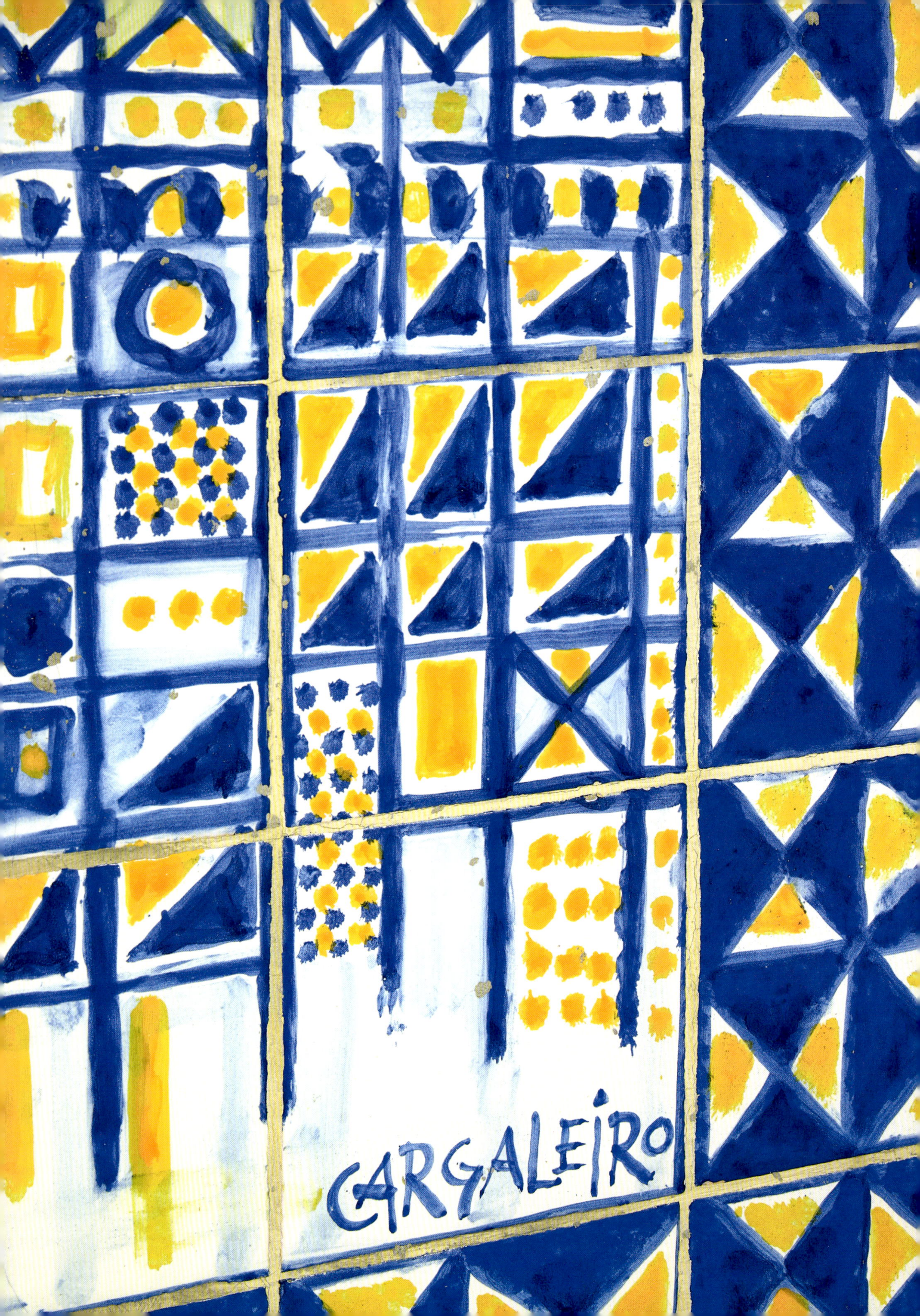
CARGALEIRO

Open to the World

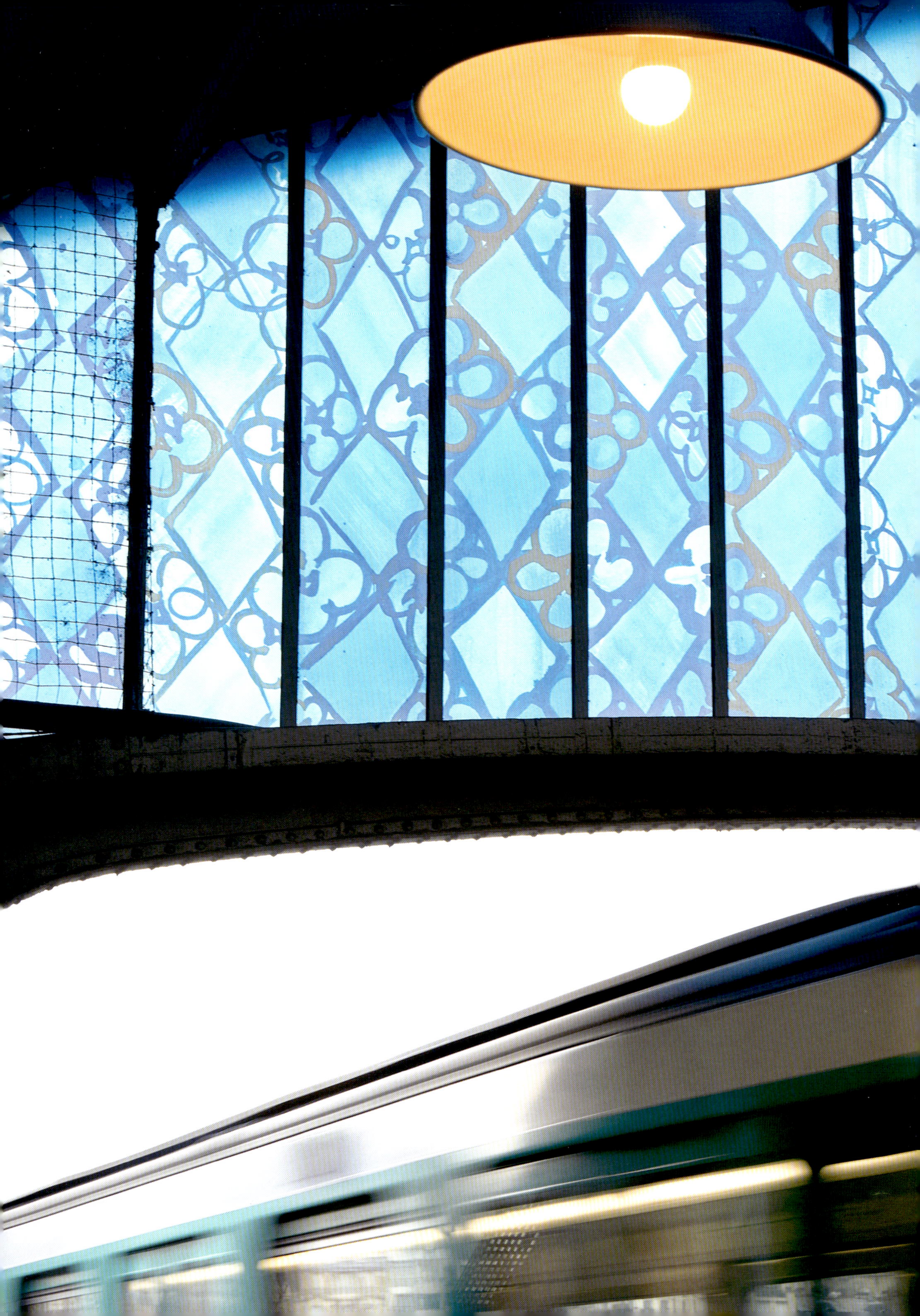

JUDY LEDGERWOOD

/ *Night and Day*

DAY ON ONE SIDE AND NIGHT ON THE OTHER: JUDY LEDGERWOOD'S ARTWORK INVITES PASSENGERS TRAVELING THROUGH BIR-HAKEIM STATION ON AN INNER JOURNEY THAT VARIES WITH THE DAYLIGHT.

STAINED-GLASS LANDSCAPES

From the platforms, you can see the sky. Bir-Hakeim is one of the twenty-six elevated metro stations in the Paris network. You can even see the sky filtered by two canopies, one blue and one yellow, which color the clouds whatever the weather. *Night and Day* is an invitation to imagine landscapes, seas, and mountains. The artist, Judy Ledgerwood, was born in the state of Indiana in the American Midwest in 1959. "The light of day and the artificial light of night interact with the work. Like a stained-glass window, it whispers tales to travelers' pupils that are renewed, time after time." The two large Parisian stained-glass windows constitute her first work for a public space: "I really conceived this piece for the widest possible audience, as a real sensorial experience."

PAINTERLY INSPIRATION

In a real dialogue with the architecture, *Night and Day* is installed in the tympana of Bir-Hakeim station—inaugurated in 1906—in the heart of the iron structure covering its tracks. What is most surprising is the fact that the images, based on very small gouaches, were digitally printed on glass. Judy Ledgerwood has many strings to her bow: she is known for teaching skills as well as her large pink, red, blue, yellow, and green canvases. Her inspirations include Mark Rothko's colorful abstract painting and those of the Light and Space movement led by a handful of Californian artists in 1970s.

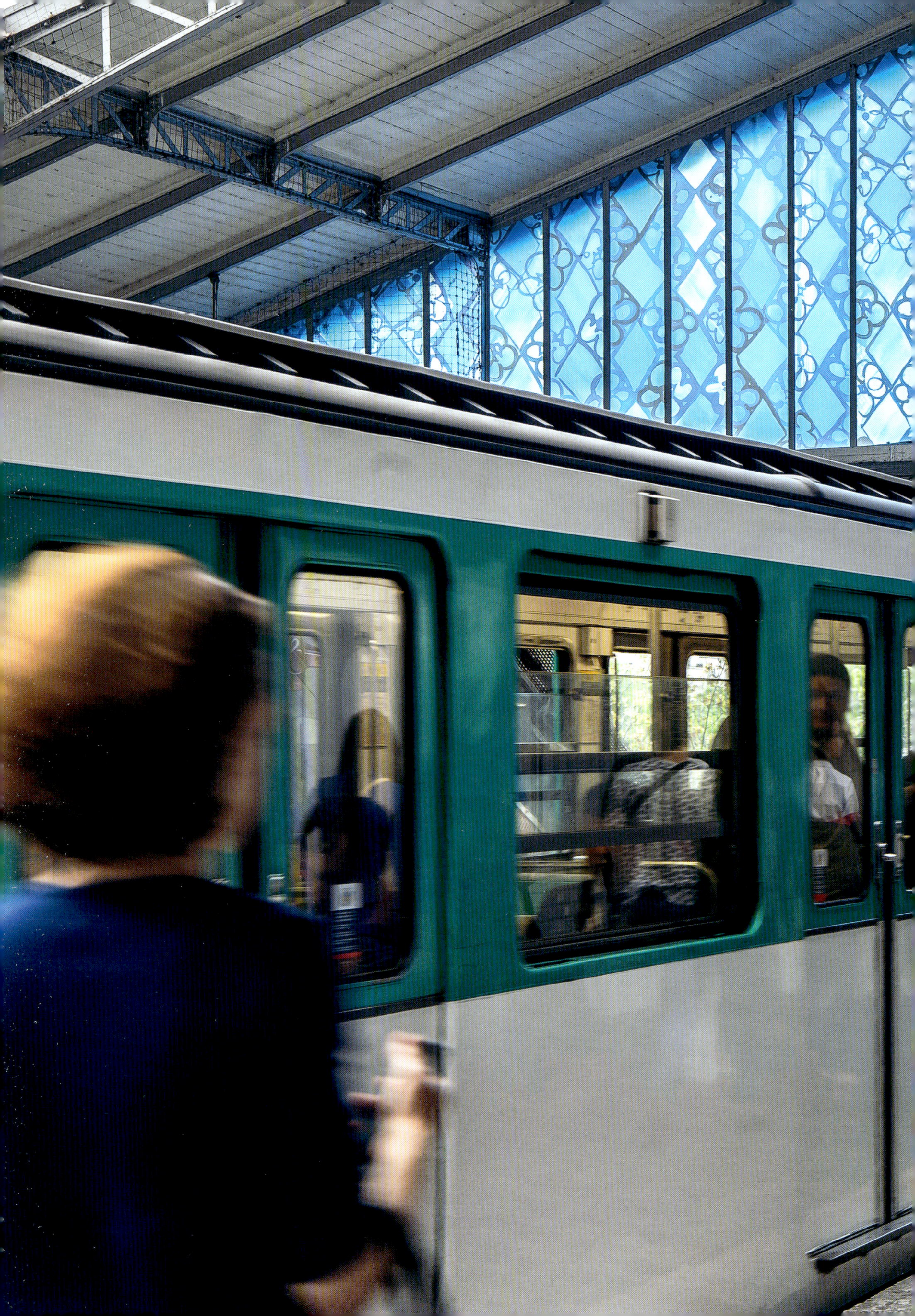

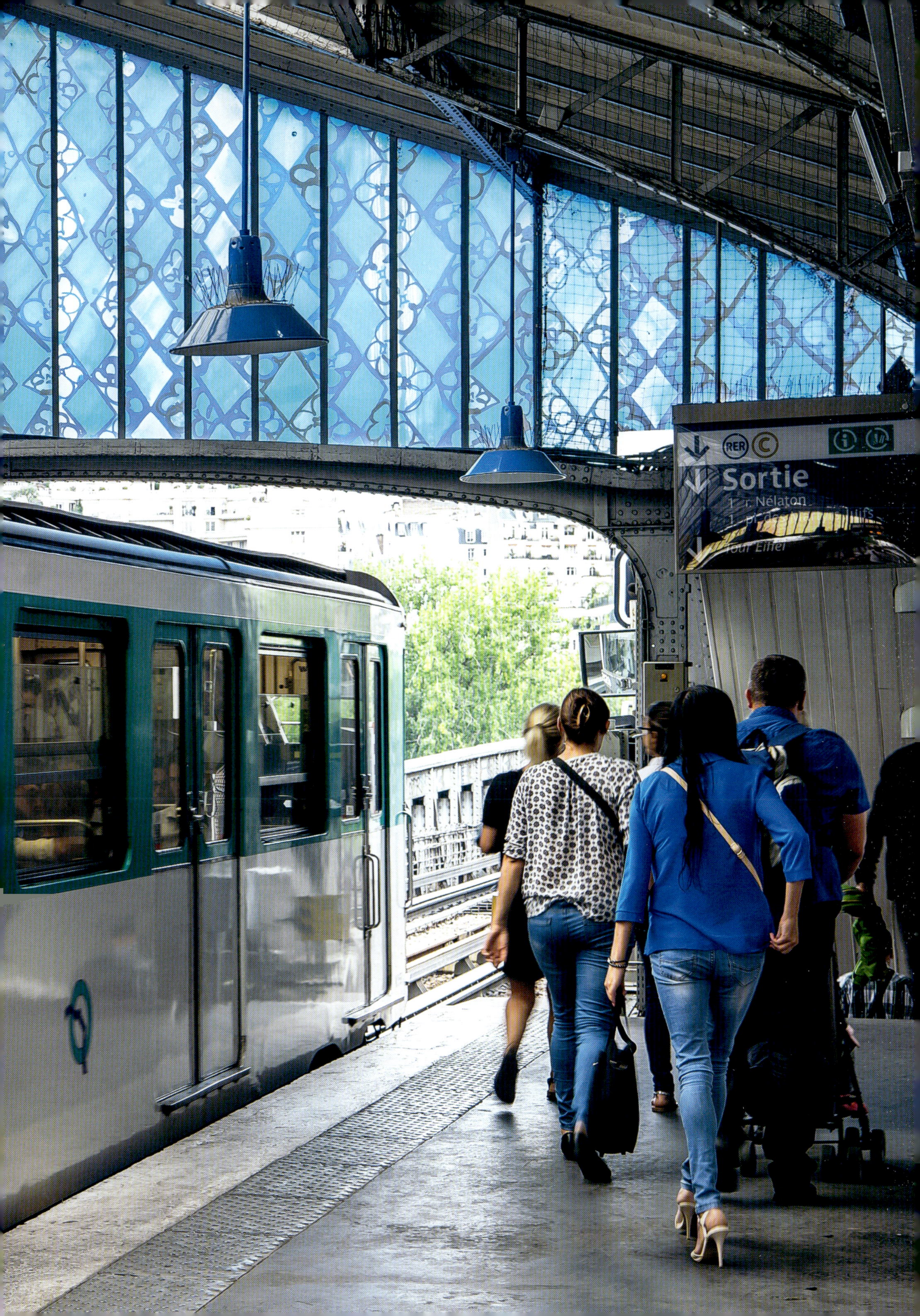
RER C
Sortie
1 r. Nélaton
Tour Eiffel

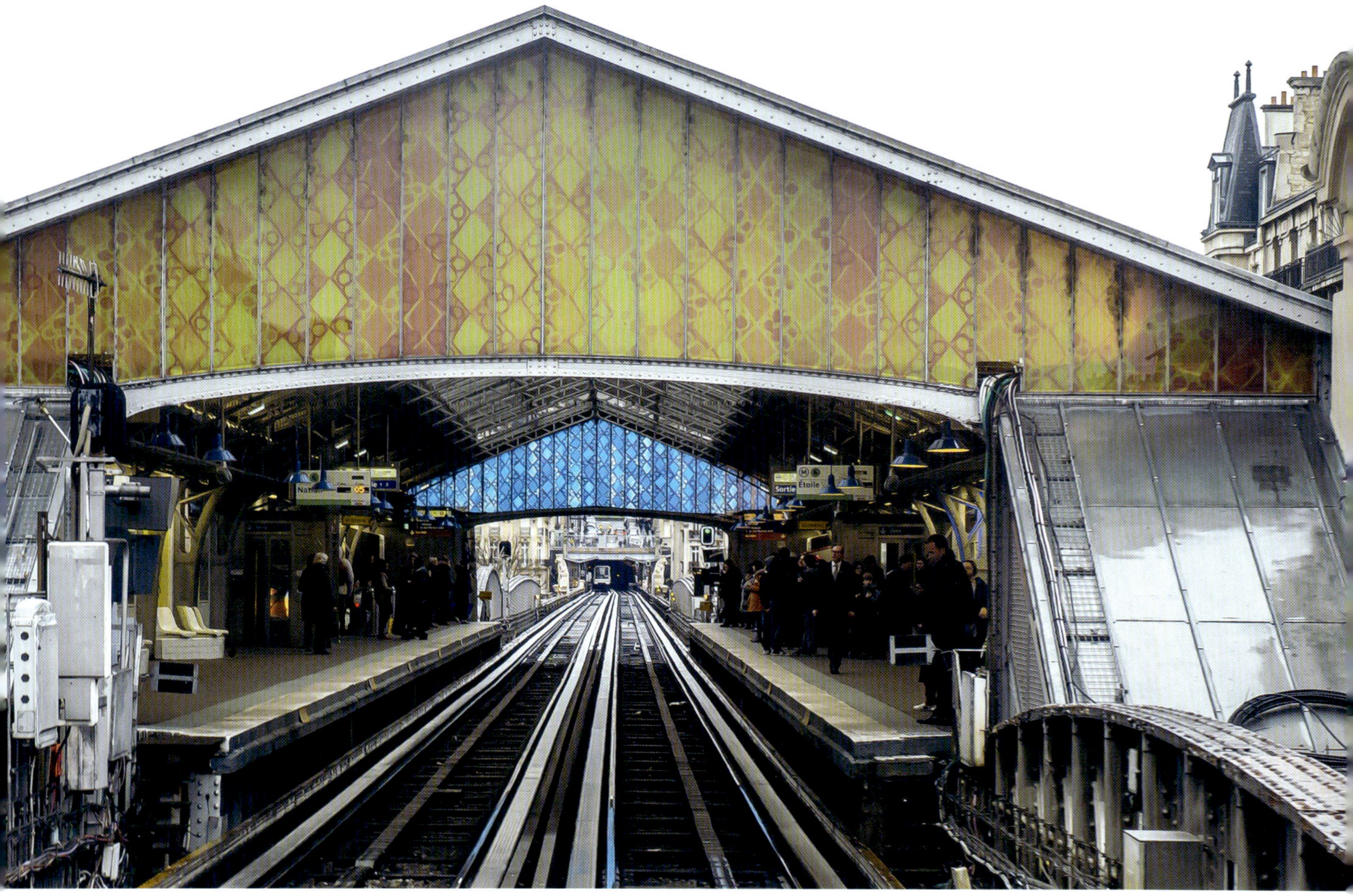

DECORATIVE MOTIFS

The motif? The four-leaf clover, which is, according to Ledgerwood, "a form that I have been using for a long time. It's found in many cultures, from India to the Middle East, and since the Paleolithic period. It also has a decorative aspect and can be linked to the history of modernity." Her paintings are usually large canvases covered with patterns of repeated motifs: sometimes flowers—reminiscent of Andy Warhol's—or simple geometric shapes. In the two large triangles of Bir-Hakeim station, the alternance of lozenges and quatrefoils enlivens the surface of *Night and Day* and gives it an added dimensions when the eye lingers, making it more intimist, like a fabric with vernacular patterns.

PARIS-CHICAGO, ROUND TRIP

Night and Day was created within the framework of cultural exchanges between the RATP and various cities around the world. In the past they simply purchased a Hector Guimard metro entrance, now they could get one in exchange for an artwork. In 2001 a Guimard entrance was installed at Van Buren Street station, near Millennium Park; the story continued in 2008, when Chicago gave the Judy Ledgerwood work to Paris. Bir-Hakeim station, which was about to be renovated, was chosen for its proximity to the Eiffel Tower, which can be seen if you take a few steps along the bank of the Seine. The station is also famous among cinephiles because Bernardo Bertolucci shot one of the best-known scenes of his 1972 film *Last Tango in Paris* there. Ledgerwood says she designed her work with thoughts of travelers in a hurry. "I have a very bad sense of direction. I thought that, with night on one side and day on the other, travelers could easily find their way back."

Night and Day, 2008
64 painted glass panels
Varying dimensions

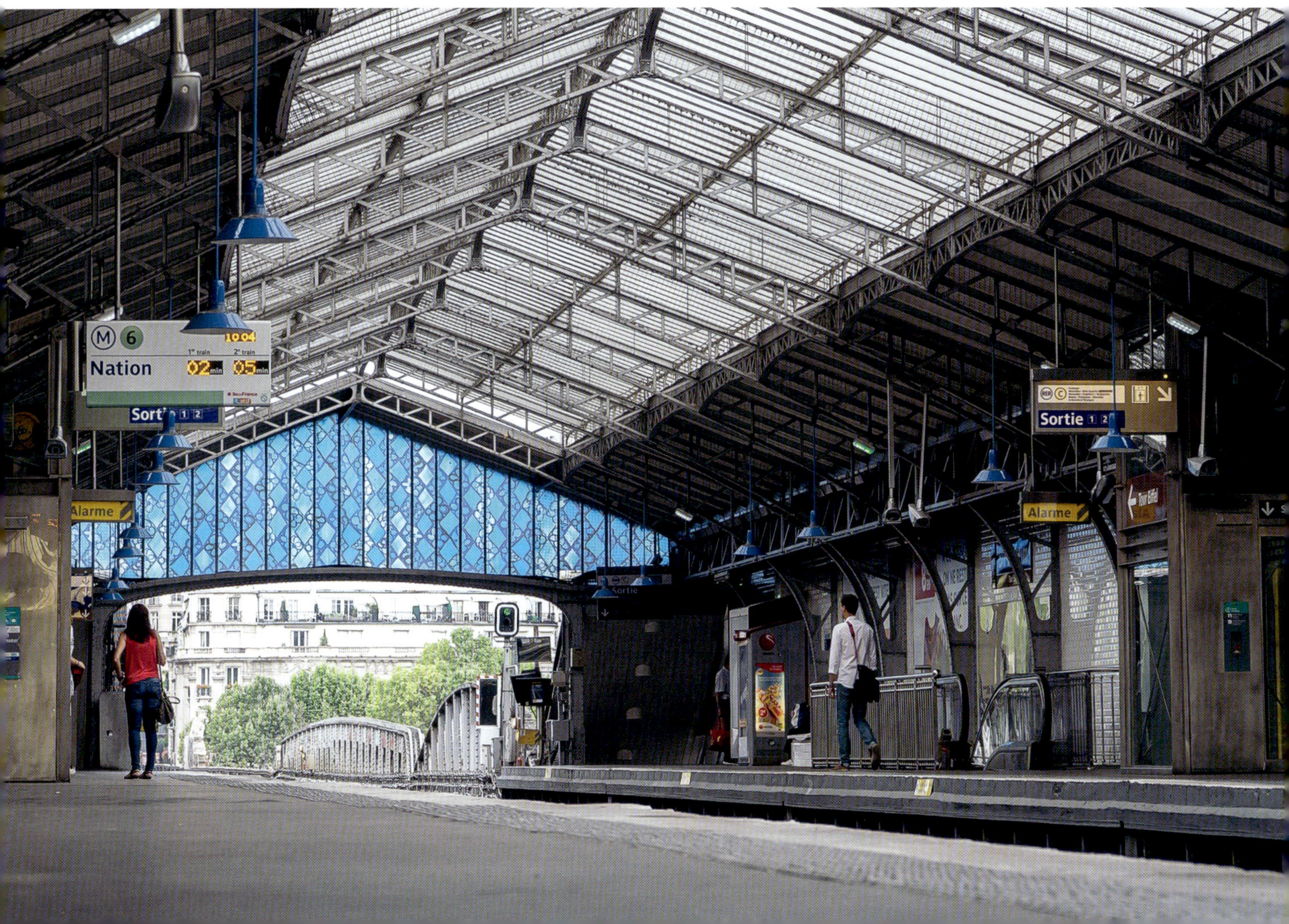

CHAMPS-ÉLYSÉES–CLEMENCEAU METRO STATION WAS DECORATED BY THE PORTUGUESE ARTIST MANUEL CARGALEIRO IN 1994. THE WORK WAS EXTENDED WHEN A NEW ENTRANCE WAS ADDED TO THE STATION IN 2019. THE WORK IS MEANT TO BRIGHTEN PASSENGERS' DAYS.

MANUEL CARGALEIRO

/ *Azulejo géométrique*

COLORFUL HORIZONS

"I want to make people happy, as if I was giving them flowers," said Manuel Cargaleiro, in 2019, during the inauguration of a new entrance to Champs-Élysées–Clemenceau metro station. And people are happy, they are stopped in their tracks by the joy that emanates from his brightly colored compositions. In different formats, they punctuate the corridors like a hanging of paintings. They seem abstract at first glance, but one is also tempted to make out shapes like the towers of a city. Their geometrical frames are also made of azulejos decorated with circles and squares in relief—green, yellow, and blue—a dialogue between Portuguese traditions and the historical metro tiles. In 1994 RATP entrusted the redecoration of Champs-Élysées–Clemenceau metro station to Manuel Cargaleiro. And for the first time in its history, it has renewed this link, as a sign of artistic loyalty, by calling on him again almost a quarter of a century later for the new entrance serving the Grand Palais and the Palais de la Découverte.

A SELF-TAUGHT ARTIST AMONG THE AVANT-GARDE

Born in a village in central Portugal in 1927, Manuel Cargaleiro trained as a painter and was a self-taught azulejo artist. The Arabs brought the ceramic technique to the Iberian peninsula during the Middle Ages, and it later spread from what is now southern Spain to Portugal. In his youth, Cargaleiro made his entrance on the Lisbon avant-garde scene as a regular at the Café A Brasileira, which the poet Fernando Pessoa had frequented. After several sojourns in Rome and Florence, he decided to move to Paris in 1957. At the time, he was represented by Galerie Albert Loeb, one of the best in town and a stone's throw from the École des Beaux-Arts. His studio was also in the neighborhood, 19 quai des Grands-Augustins. Cargaleiro then forged links with the second Paris school of gestural abstract painters, making friends with his compatriot Maria Helena Vieira da Silva and the Russians Mikhail Larionov and Natalya Goncharova, whose colorful forms inspired by the natural world left a lasting mark on his art.

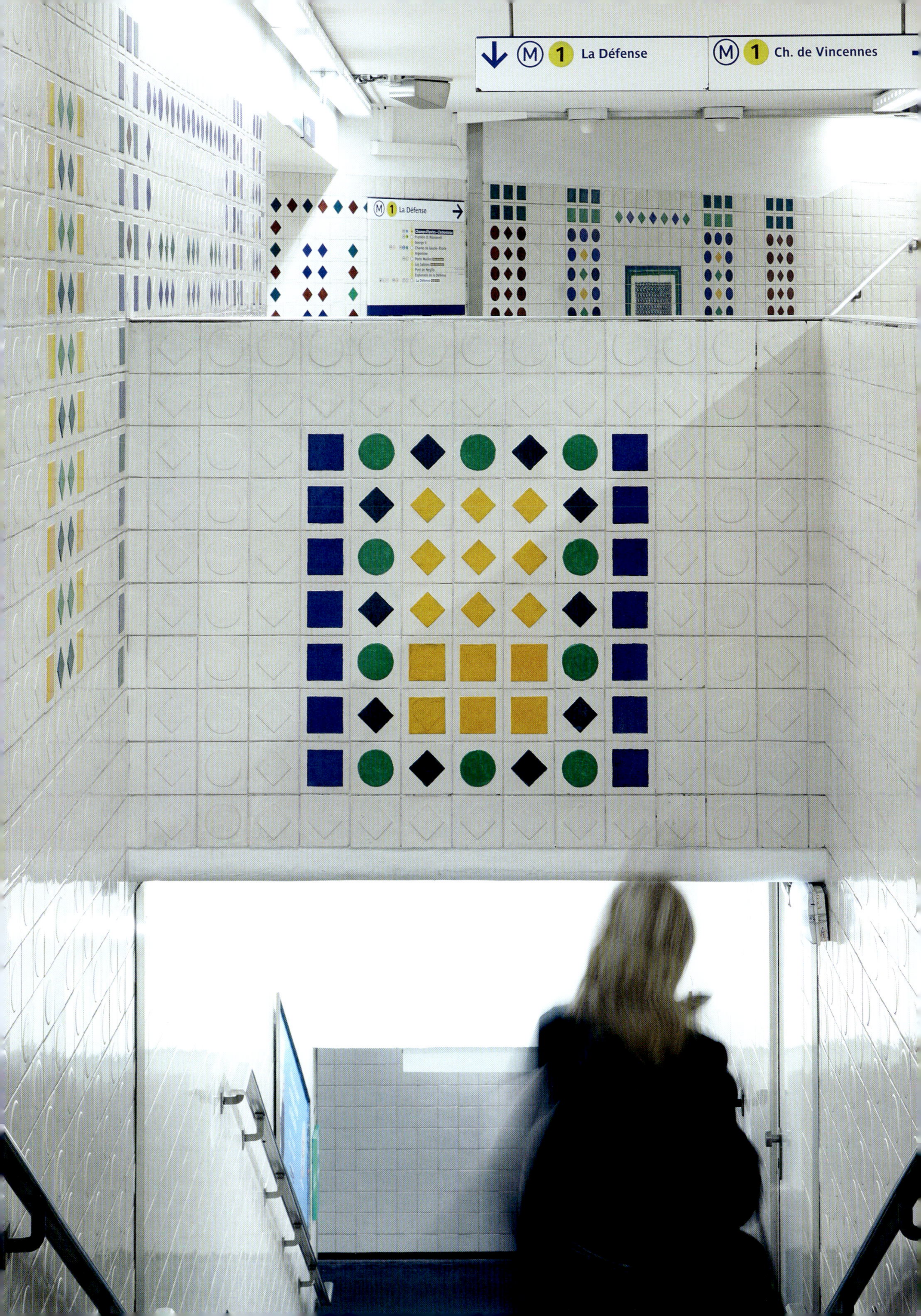

M 1 La Défense
M 1 Ch. de Vincennes
M 1 La Défense

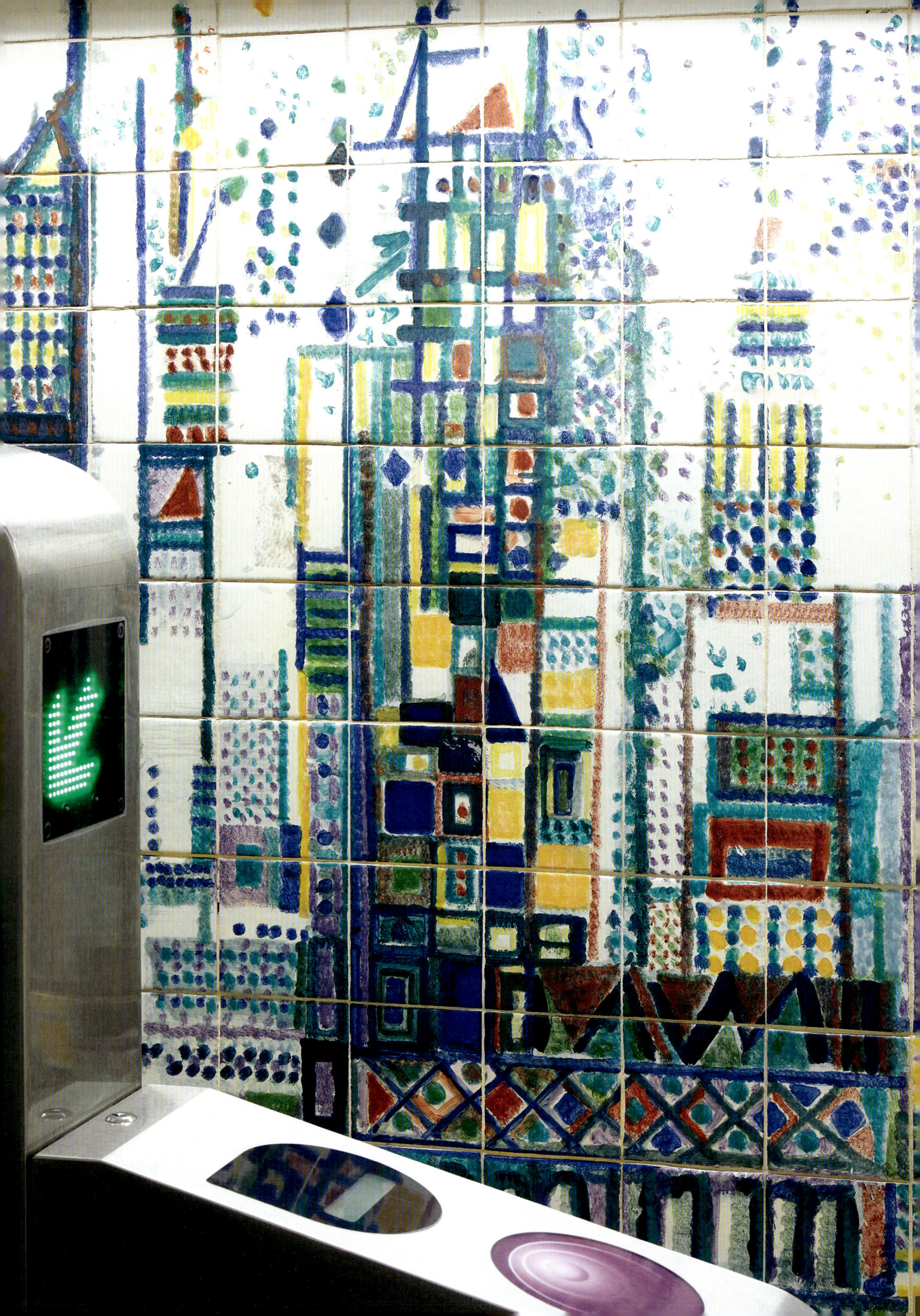

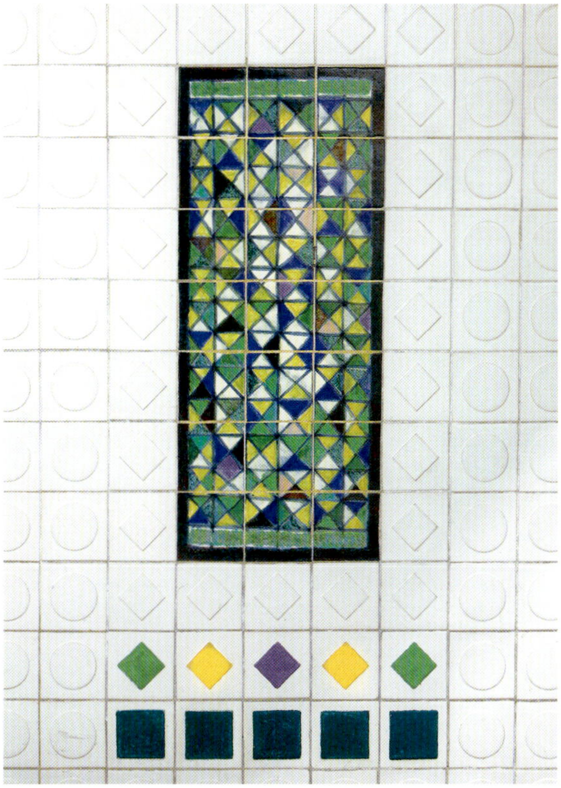

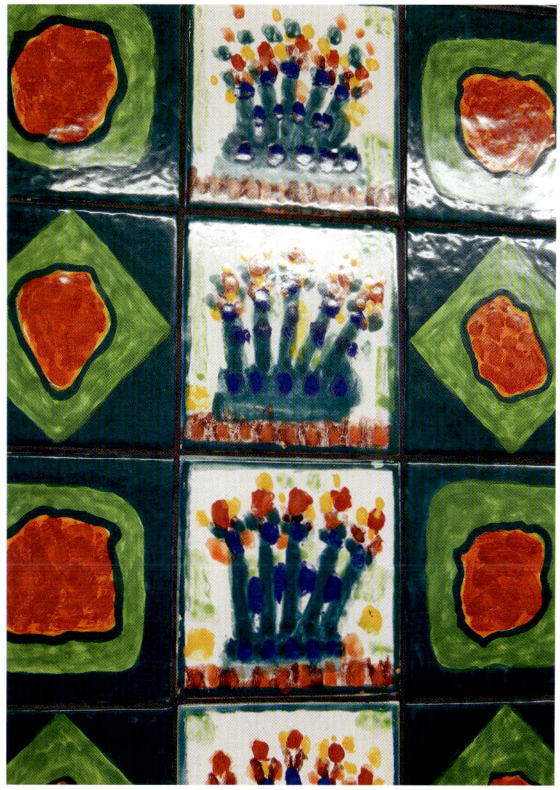

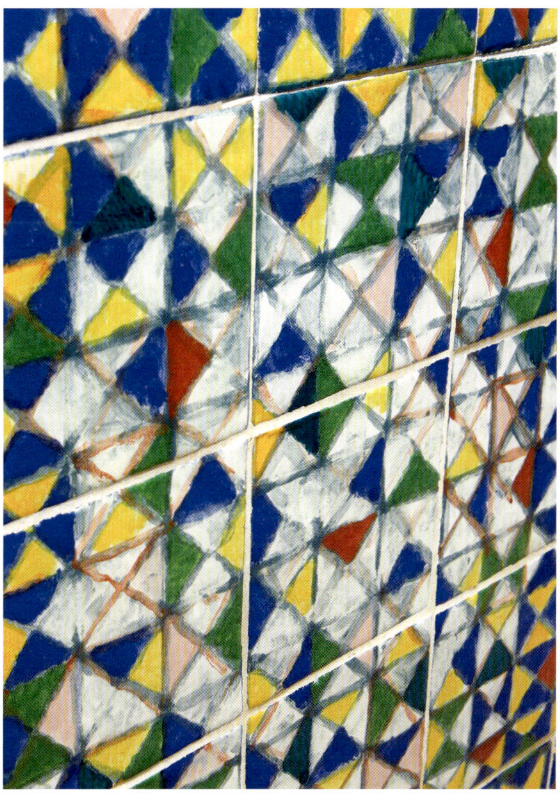

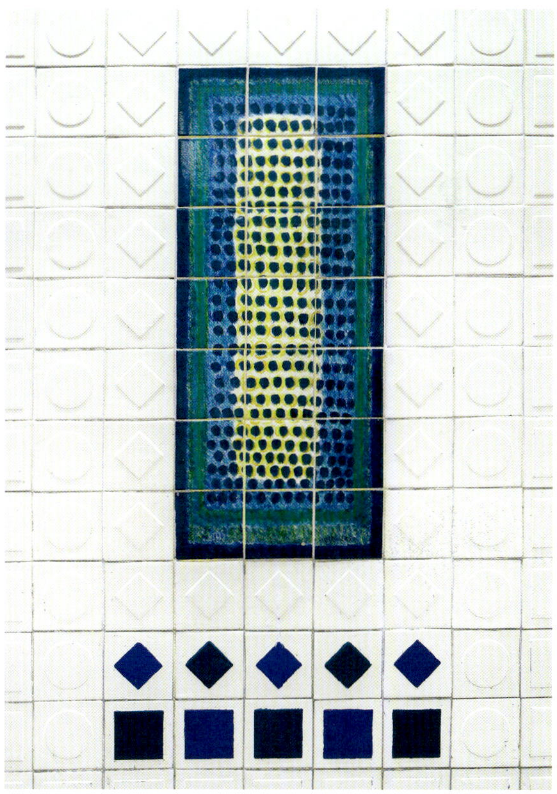

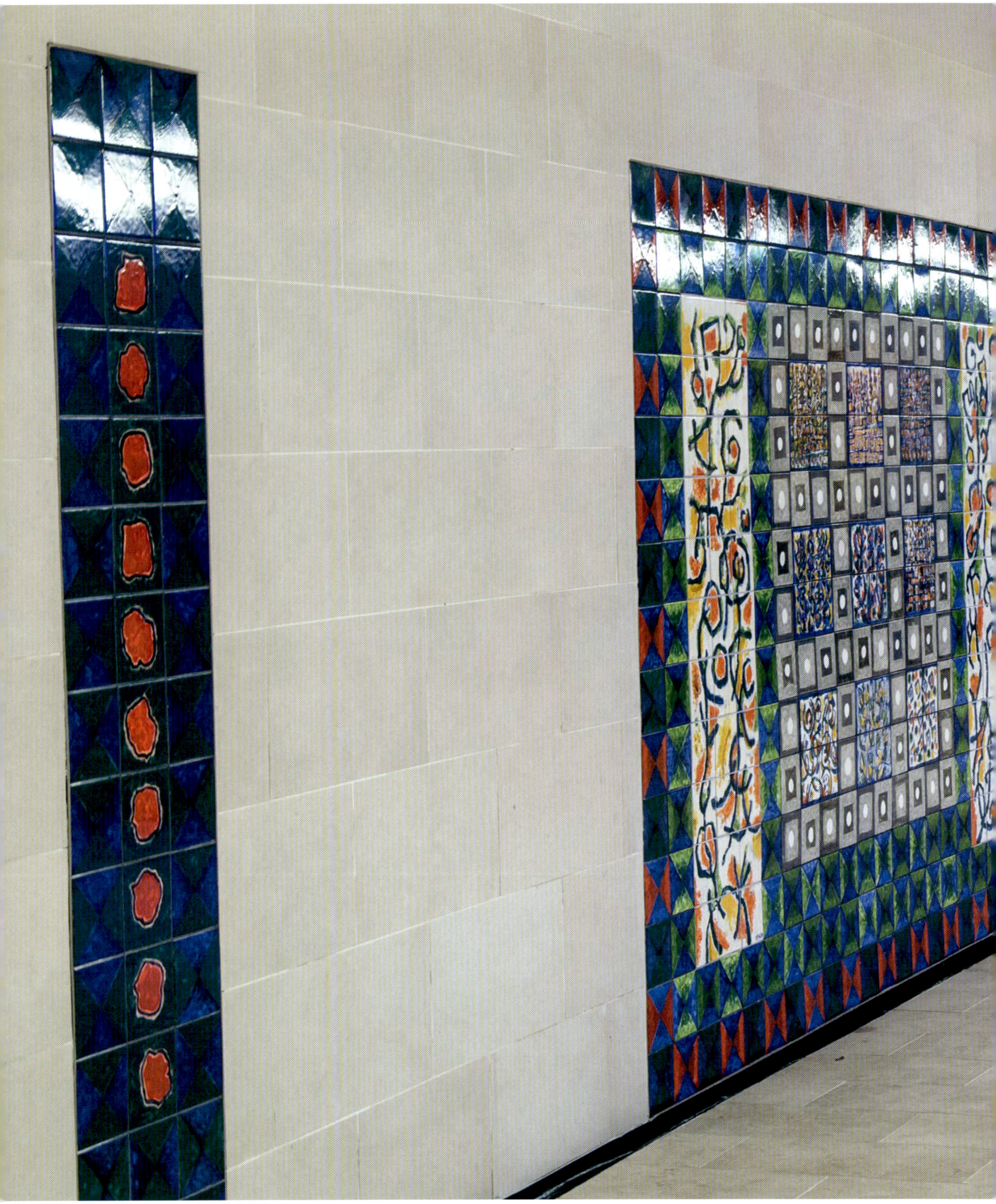

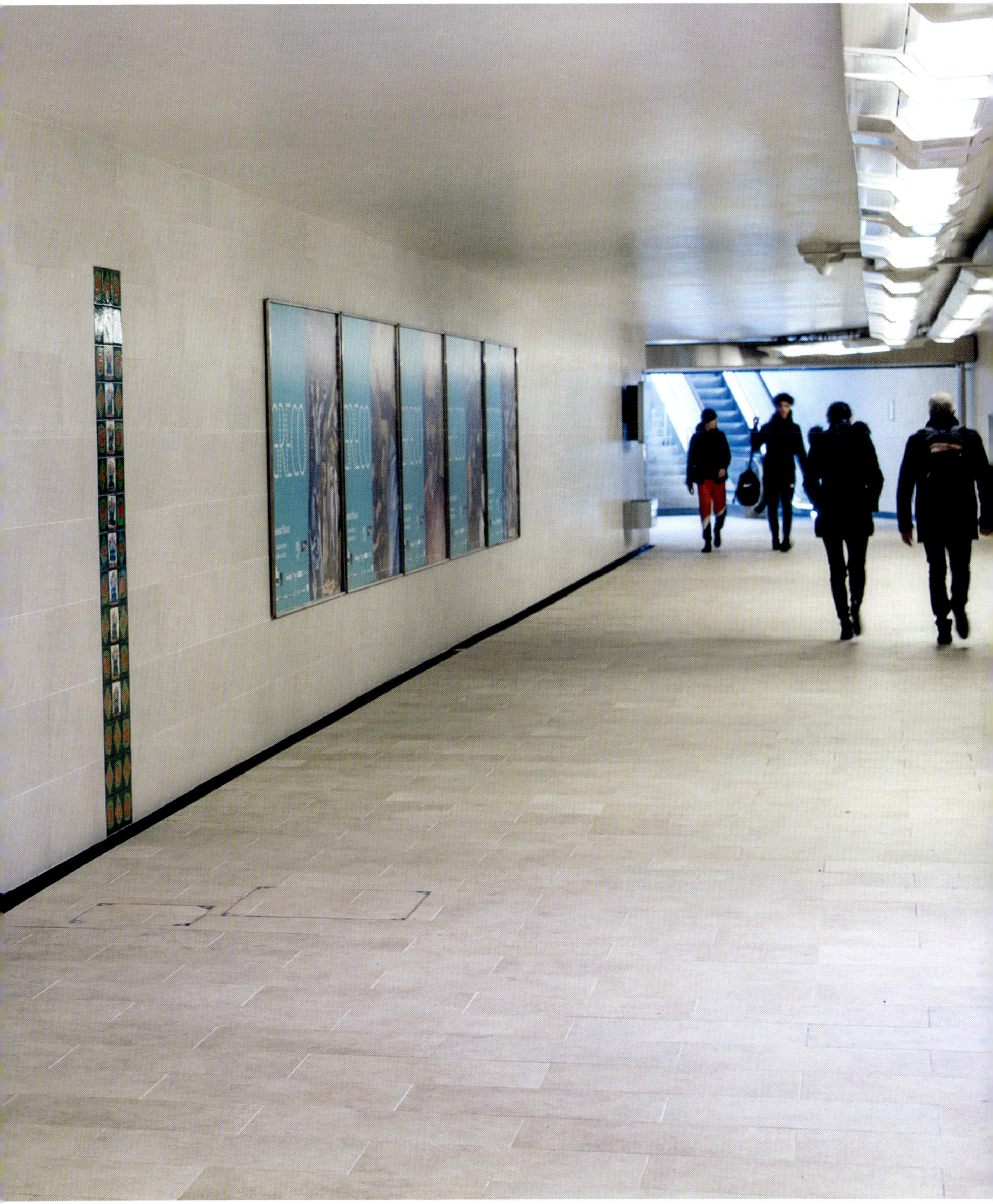
GRECO

A PROFOUND INTEREST IN THE PUBLIC SPACE

Throughout his life Manuel Cargaleiro has continued to experiment in the fields of tapestry and ceramics, and continues to demonstrate a profound interest in the public space. His works include the facade of the Institut Français du Portugal and Colégio Militar/Luz metro station in Lisbon. In 1990 the Fundação Manuel Cargaleiro opened its doors in Castelo Branco, near the village where he was born. He also has a studio in Italy, which moved from Vietri Sul Mare to Ravello on the Amalfi coast, where he spends part of the year. *Azulejo géométrique* (Geometrical Azulejo) is part of the 1994 cultural exchange between the RATP and the Metropolitano de Lisboa (ML): a Guimard entrance was installed at Picoas metro station, not far from Parque Eduardo VII and the ML headquarters. It adds a touch of exoticism.

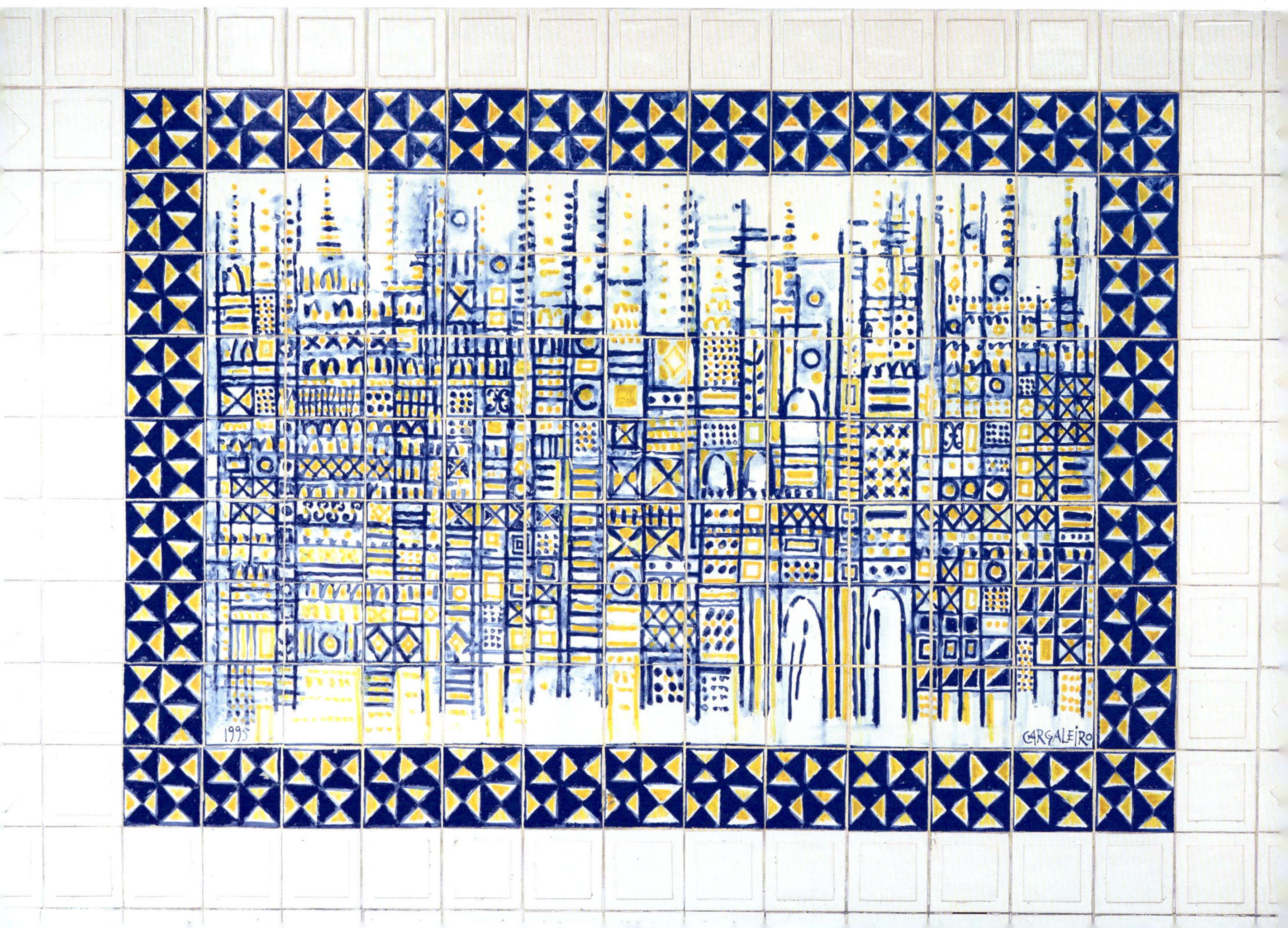

***Azulejo géométrique*, 1995 and 2019**

Faience

About 100 m^2, initial work

11.4 m^2, new entrance

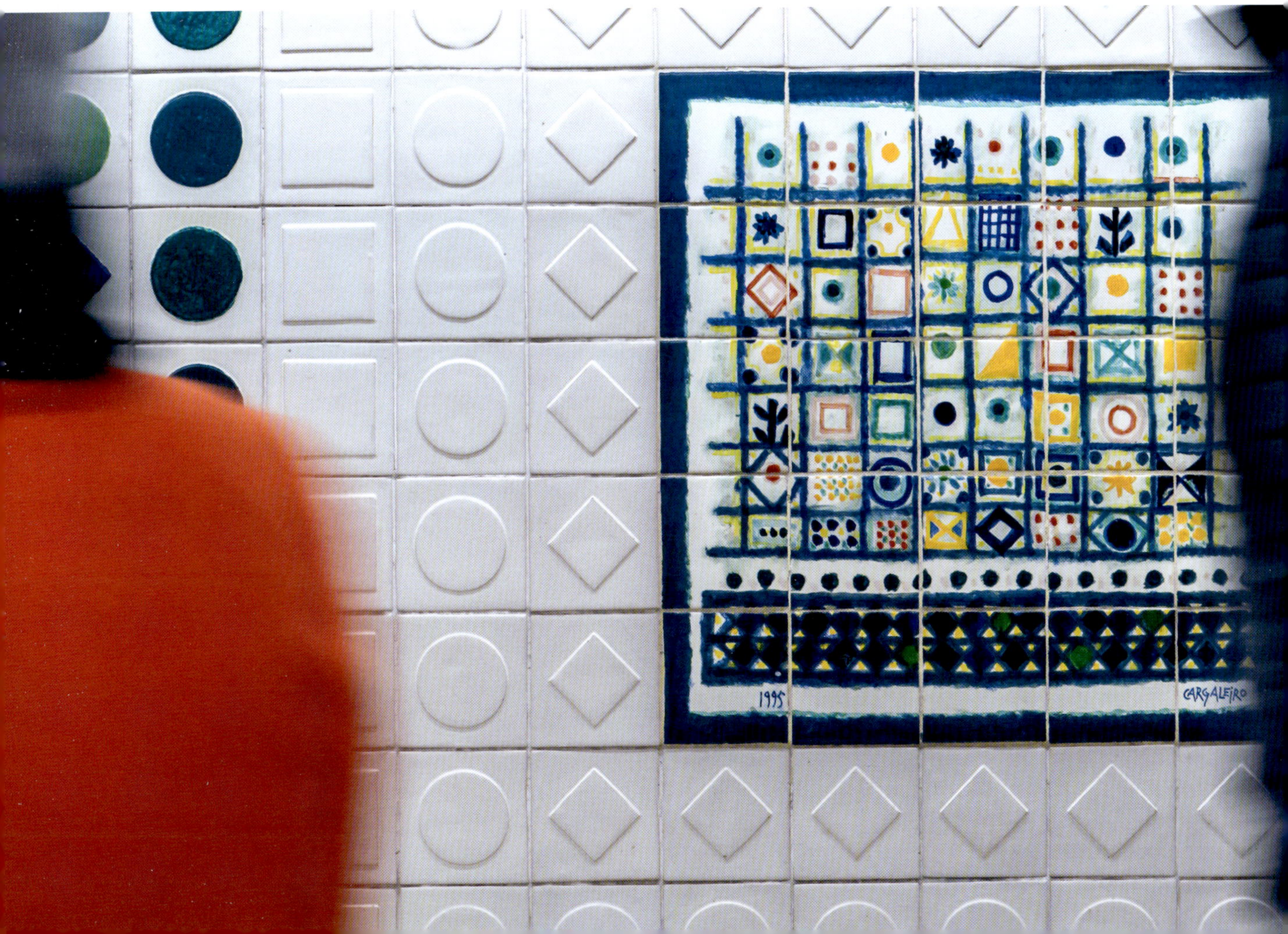

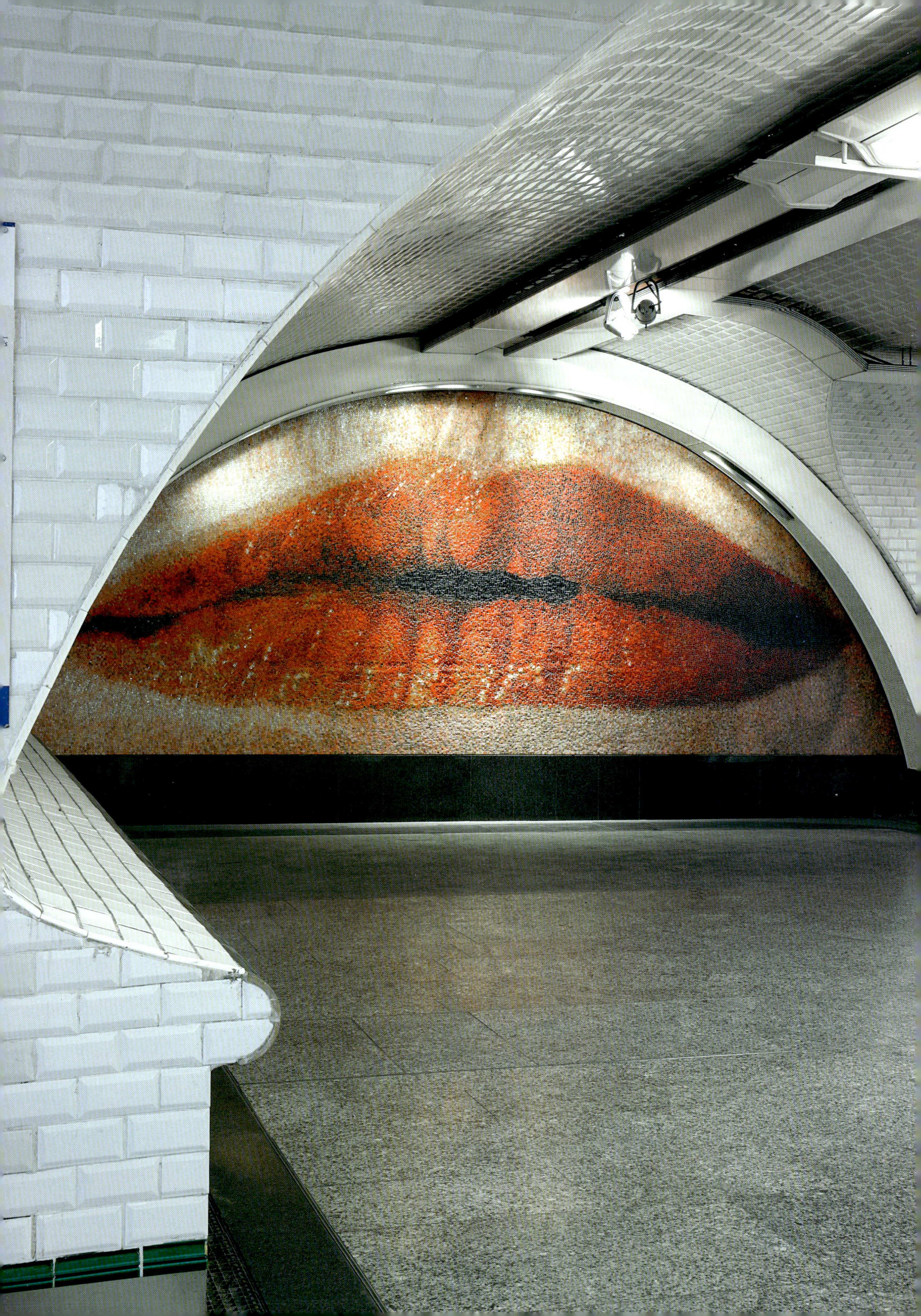

GENEVIÈVE CADIEUX

/ *La Voix lactée*

FROM THE END OF THE CORRIDOR, WE SEE A PHOTOGRAPH OF A WOMAN'S MOUTH. AND AS WE MOVE NEARER, A SHIMMER OF BRIGHT COLORS. LISTEN CAREFULLY, SHE MIGHT WHISPER SOME WORDS, THE ONES THAT MAY BE READ IN THE SURROUNDING CORRIDOR, WORDS FROM A POEM BY ANNE HÉBERT.

A CULTURAL EXCHANGE BETWEEN PARIS AND MONTREAL

The story begins in 1967, when the RATP loaned the Société de Transport de Montréal (STM) an original Hector Guimard metro entrance, the only one outside France. It was removed from Étoile station in Paris, then installed at Square-Victoria station in Montreal. Then in 2003, during the renovation of what is now Square-Victoria–OACI station, the RATP made a permanent gift of the Guimard entrance to the STM, which decided to reciprocate by giving an artwork to the Parisian organization. A competition was launched, with the French language as its theme. "So I tried my luck," says Geneviève Cadieux, one of the best-known Quebec artists of her generation.

Born in Montreal in 1955, Cadieux represented Canada at the Venice Biennale in 1990. The Paris location of the artwork was already chosen: the corridor connecting Saint-Augustin metro station on line 9 to the brand-new Saint-Lazare station on line 14, which opened in 2003. Cadieux made the best of the location with an artwork that may be read two ways—from very far away like a photograph with precise lines, and from up close like an image on the verge of abstraction. The inauguration took place on August 4, 2011.

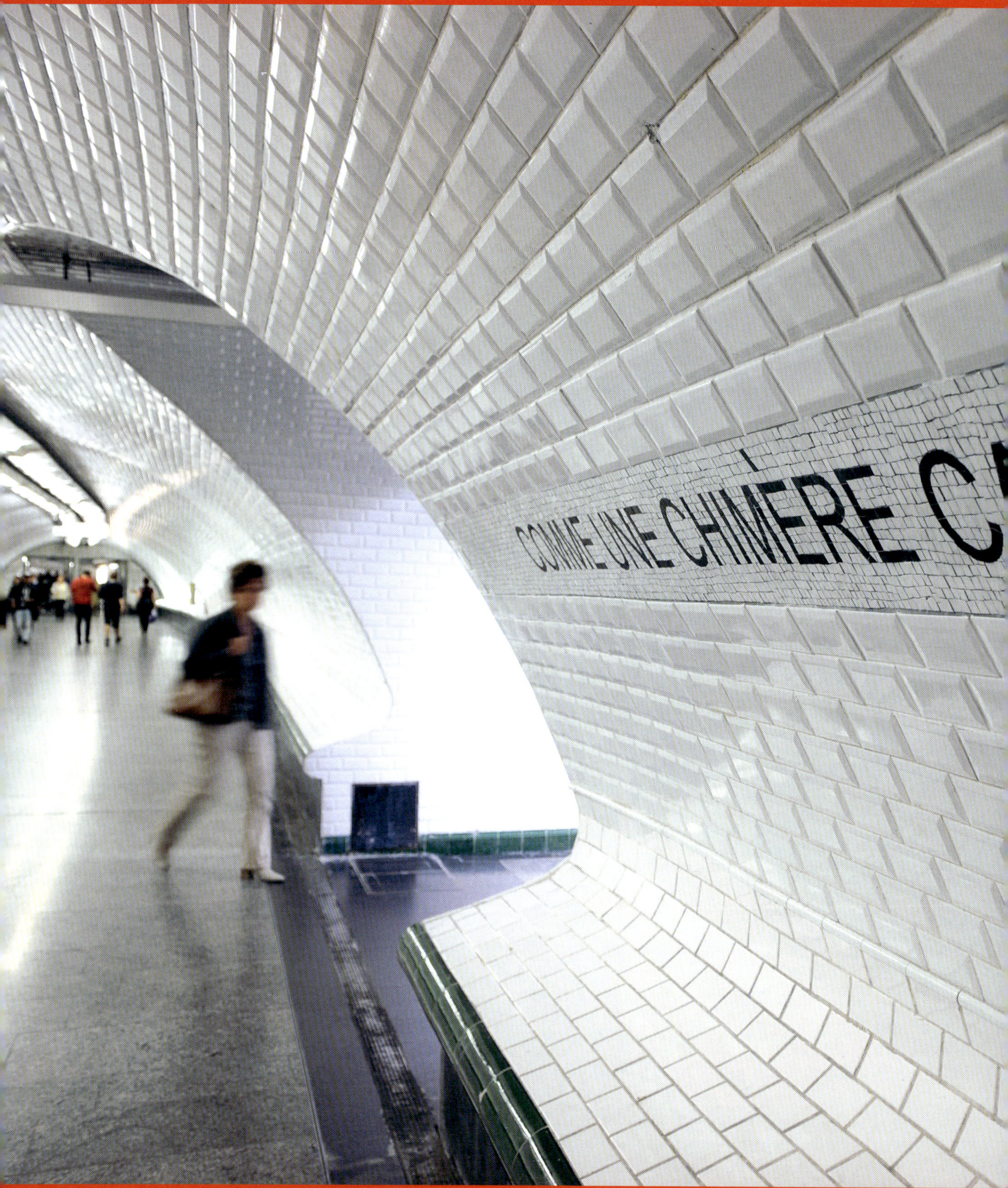
COMME UNE CHIMÈRE C

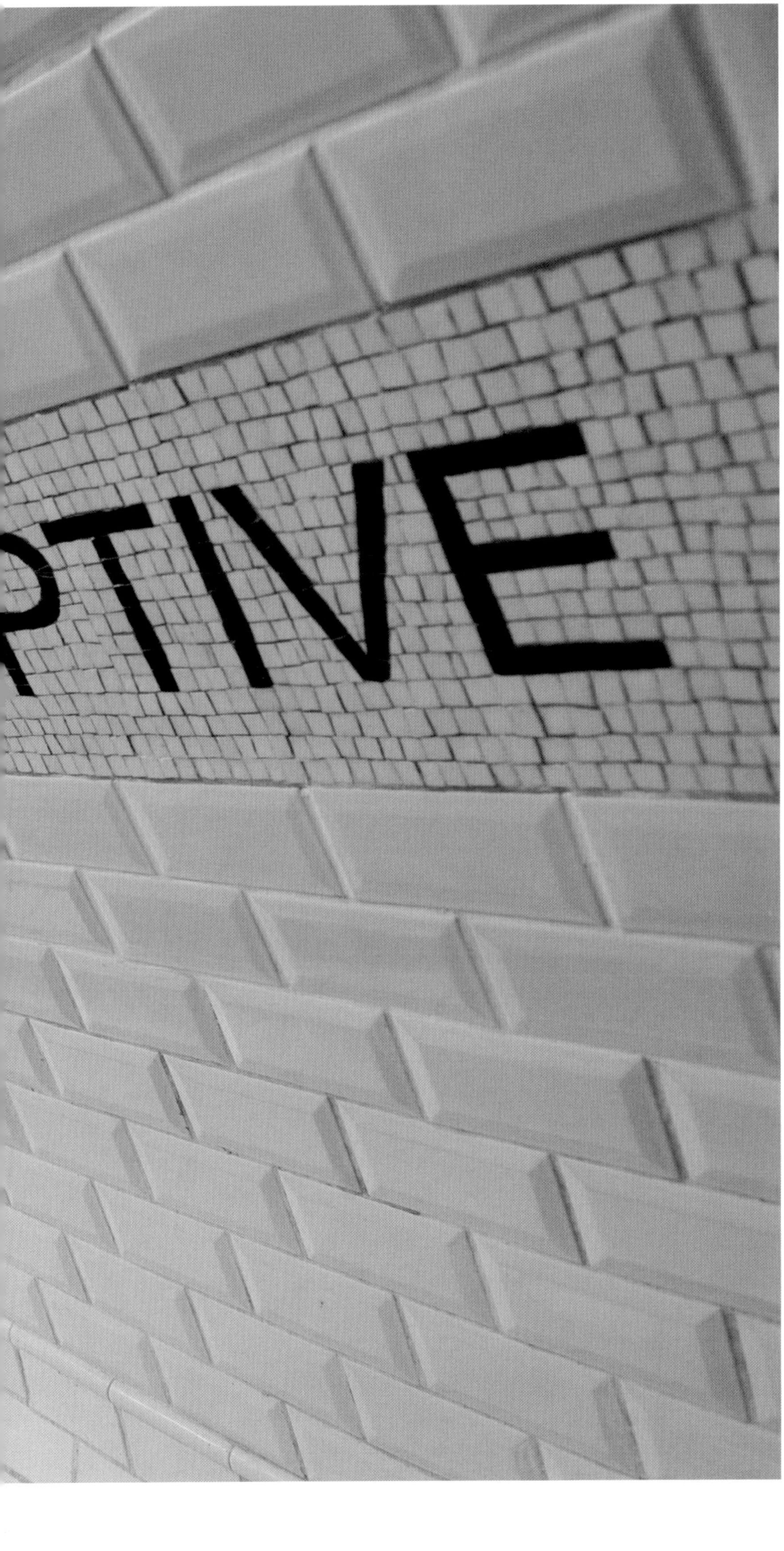
RTIVE

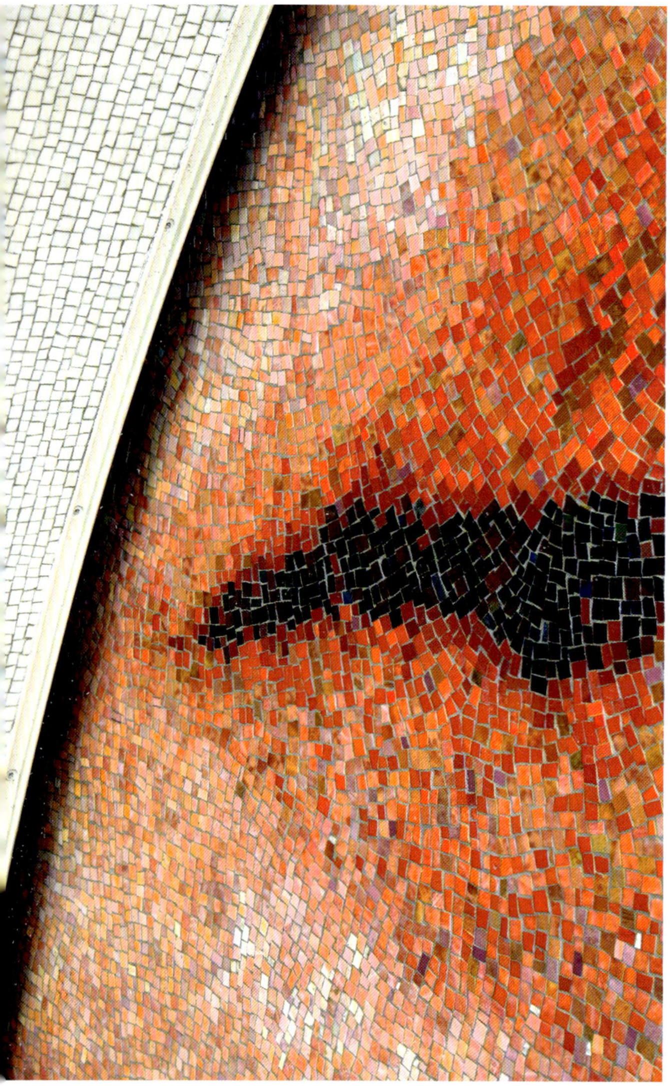

FROM *LA VOIE LACTÉE* TO *LA VOIX LACTÉE*

A photographer by training, Geneviève Cadieux has long been interested in transcribing the medium into other forms, especially in durable materials. That is why she proposed transposing her work *La Voie lactée*, a monumental photograph that was installed on the roof of the Musée d'Art Contemporain de Montréal in 1992, to the Paris metro in mosaic form. "It was not only a way of playing with the pixels that make up an image, but also of passing from sky to earth," she explains.

In her work, the human body occupies a primordial place, and it is often represented on a monumental scale, like a landscape. The bodies she chooses are often those of her friends or family. This work features her mother's mouth. Perhaps that is why it is intimate and reassuring—and could be said to emanate solicitude.

Cadieux recounts how she chose to respond to the theme of the French language, Quebec French: "I did a lot of reading, and chose to use this verse from a poem by Anne Hébert [1916–2000] for the project by inscribing it on the ceramic tiles of the corridor adjacent to the mosaic: 'Bien avant les images et les couleurs / La source du chant s'imaginait / À bouche fermée / Comme une chimère captive.' [Long before images and colors / The source of the song pictured itself / With a closed mouth / Like a captive chimera.] In this new context, I decided that *La Voie lactée* would become *La Voix lactée*."

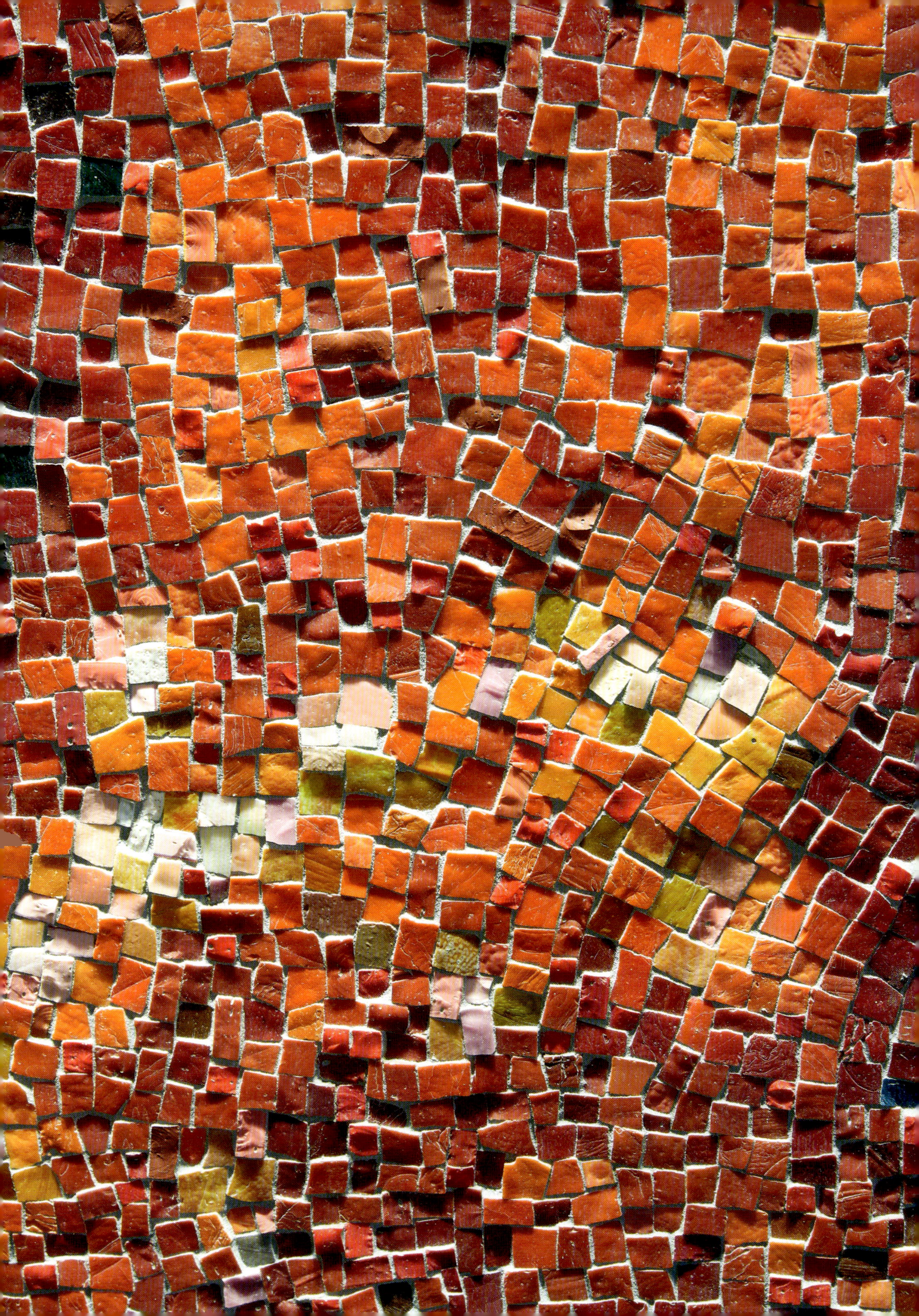

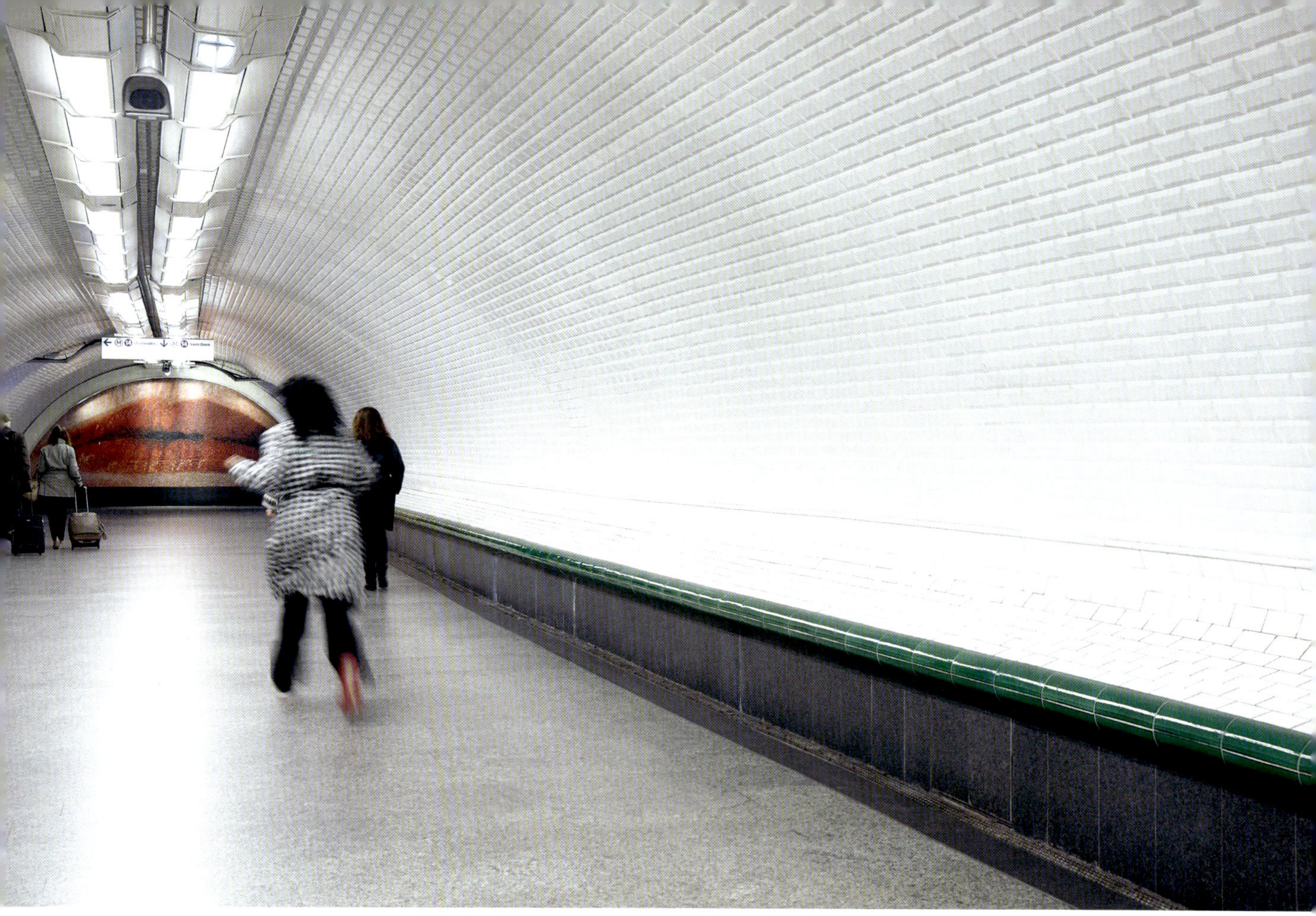

THE LIFE OF A WORK

The project was executed by Franz Mayer of Munich, a German stained-glass and mosaic firm founded in 1847 that has worked with many museums and churches around the world, from Los Angeles to Amman, Jordan. Geneviève Cadieux personally oversaw the execution, transportation, and Paris installation of the panels. She observes: "The work of public art has a very independent life, and then it belongs to the citizens. They adopt or refuse such works; it's very democratic. Passengers seem to have taken to *La Voix lactée*." The artwork has also entered cinematic history by making an appearance in François Ozon's 2013 film, *Jeune & Jolie* (*Young & Beautiful*).

La Voix lactée, 2011
Glass mosaic
2.5 × 4 m

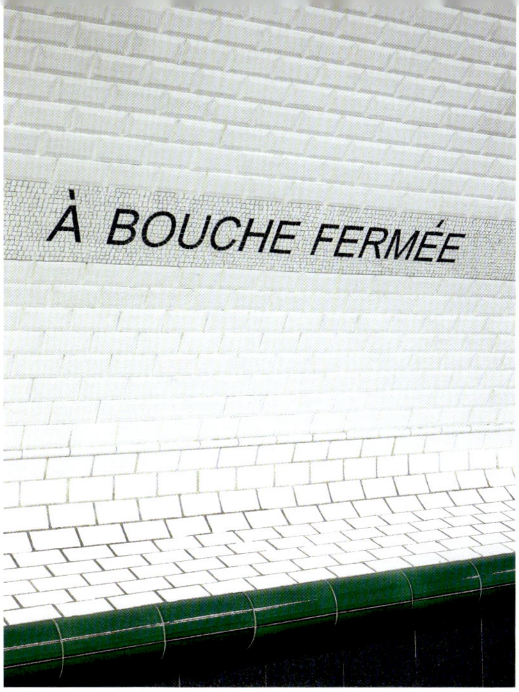
À BOUCHE FERMÉE

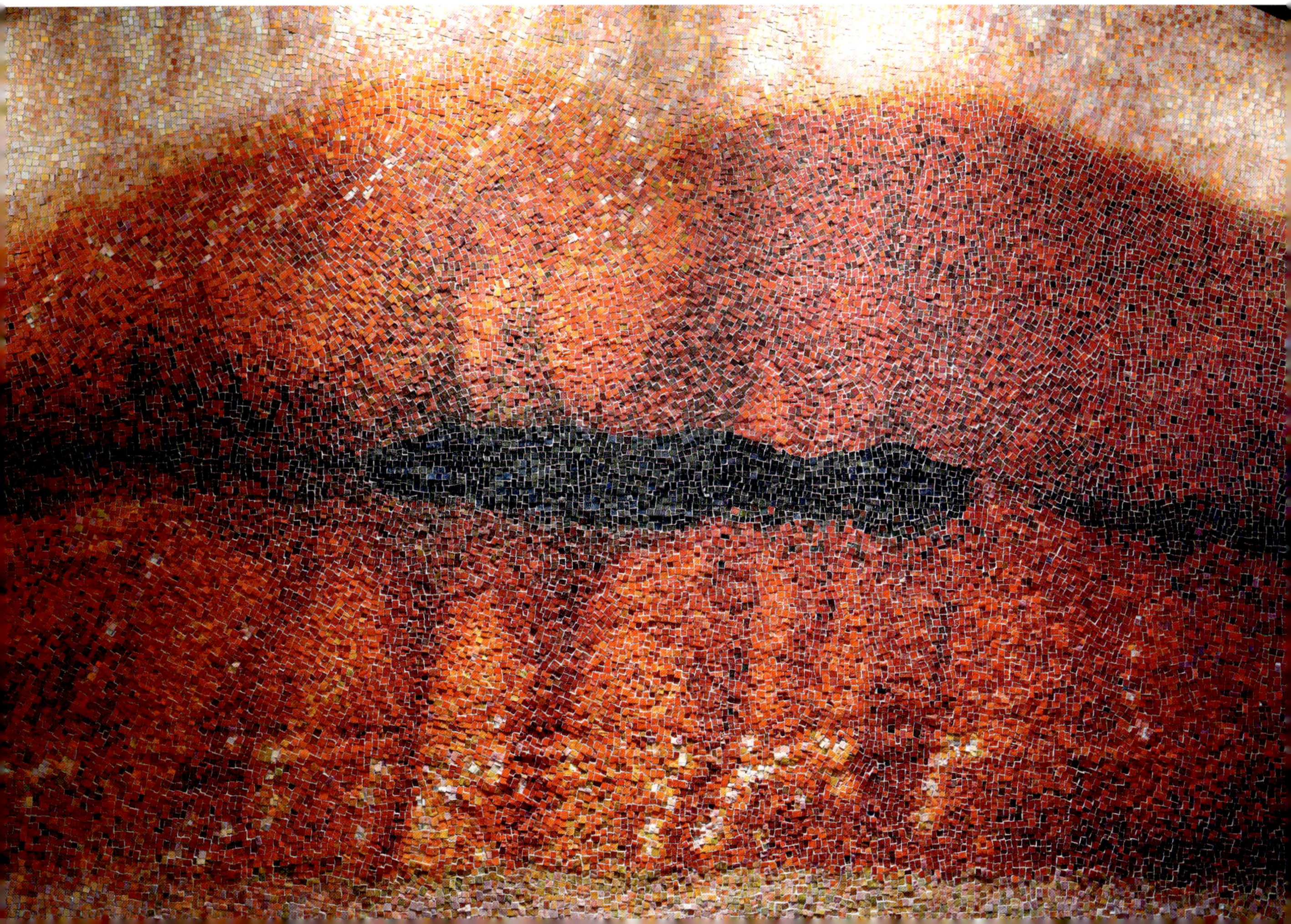

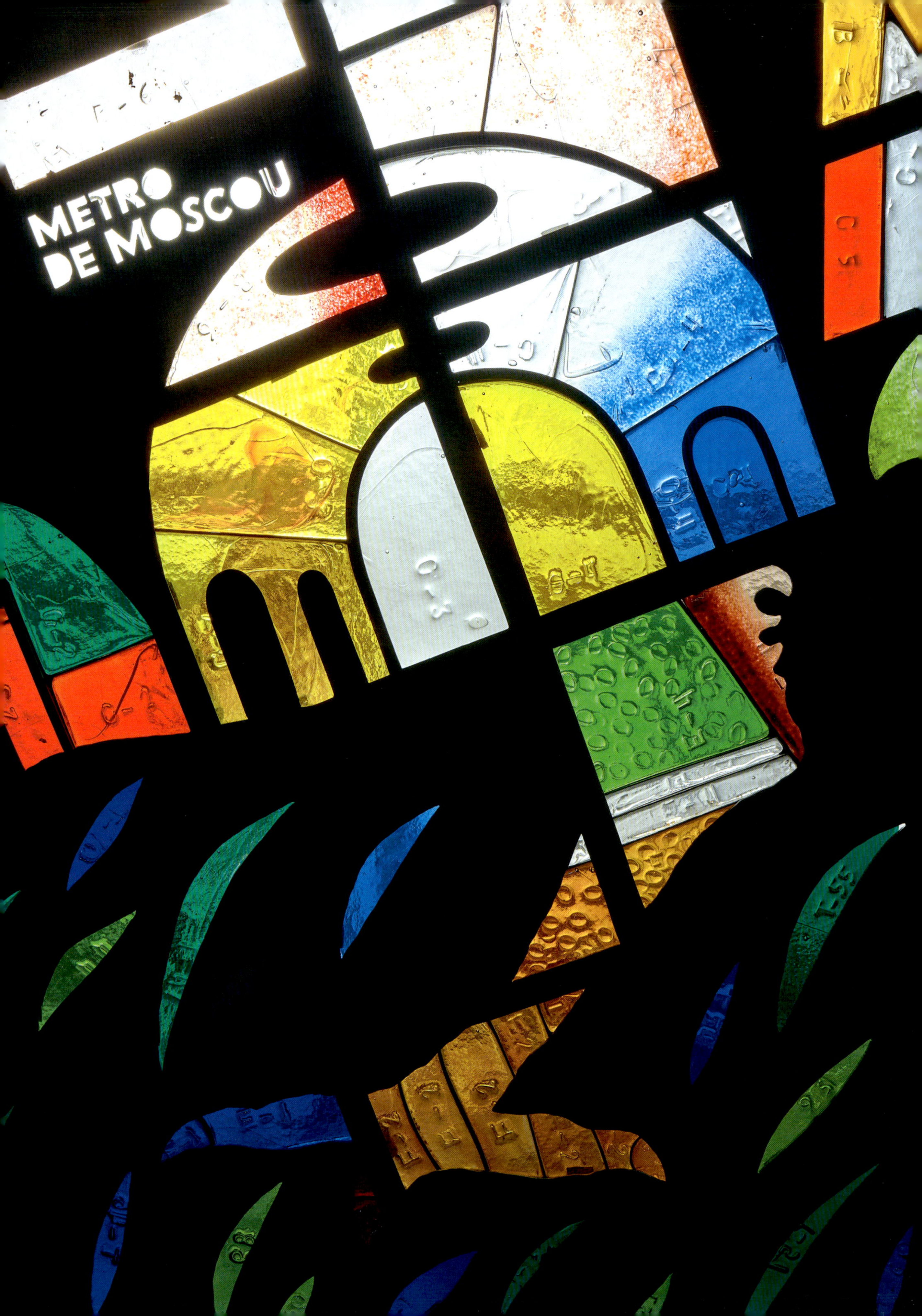
METRO
DE MOSCOU

IVAN LUBENNIKOV

/ Ryaba la Poule

ON THE MEZZANINE OF THE LINE 14 PLATFORM IS A MONUMENTAL HEN WITH BRIGHTLY COLORED FEATHERS PECKING AT THE GROUND IN FRONT OF A STARRY SKY. AT ITS FEET, FALLEN IN THE GRASS, IS A GOLDEN EGG, WHICH IS THOUGHT TO BRING GOOD LUCK.

CHICKEN AND EGG

Ryaba the hen is the heroine of a Russian nursery rhyme whose text is reproduced in French and Russian on either side of Ivan Lubennikov's artwork: a chicken lays a golden egg, which breaks immediately. Ryaba tries to comfort the old peasant couple: "Don't cry grandpa, don't cry grandma. I'll lay a new egg for you, but not a golden one." The moral of the story resembles that of the fables of Aesop and Jean de La Fontaine. In La Fontaine's version, the farmer wants to see the insides of his chicken, which lays precious eggs, and ends up killing it: "How often does one see / Men made as poor as he / By force of getting rich too soon?" Something to ponder during a long metro journey.

AN IMAGE OF RUSSIA

Ivan Lubennikov's artwork also allows passersby to immerse themselves in Russian culture. The artist was inspired by age-old tales, and his hen's body features a series of images evoking Russia from the time of the czars to the USSR: golden onion domes, an eagle, Orthodox crosses, red stars, hammers and sickles, and the Kremlin clock on Spassakaya (Savior) Tower. The stained-glass window, made up of 20 panels, covers 30 square meters. The pieces of inlaid glass were produced by Gus Crystal, one of the oldest glassworks in Russia; founded in 1756, the firm continues a legacy of traditional craftsmanship and savoir-faire. Like other artworks installed in the Paris network, *Ryaba la Poule* was part of a cultural exchange between the RATP and metro of Moscow, where a Hector Guimard entrance was installed at Kievskaya station in 2008.

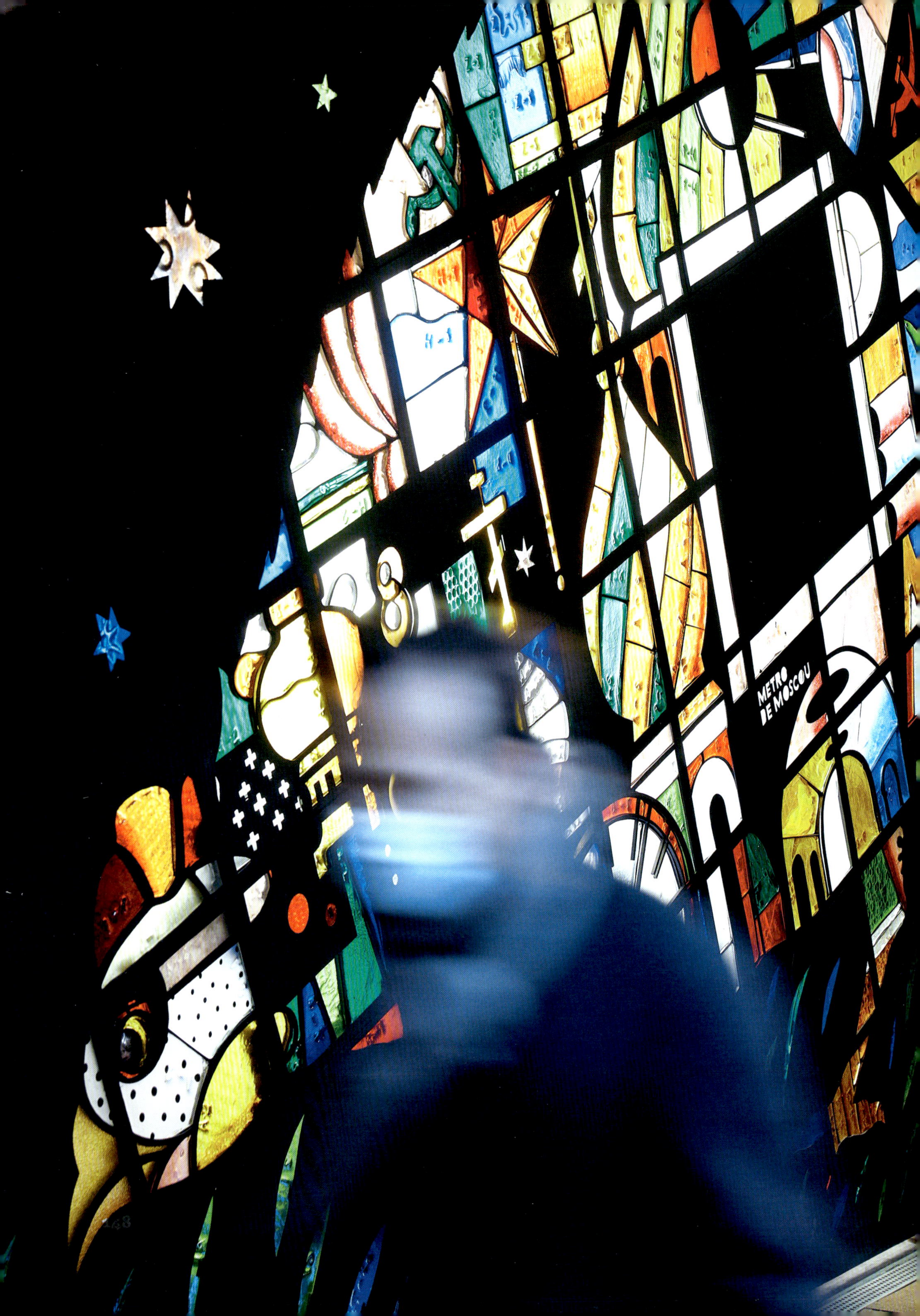

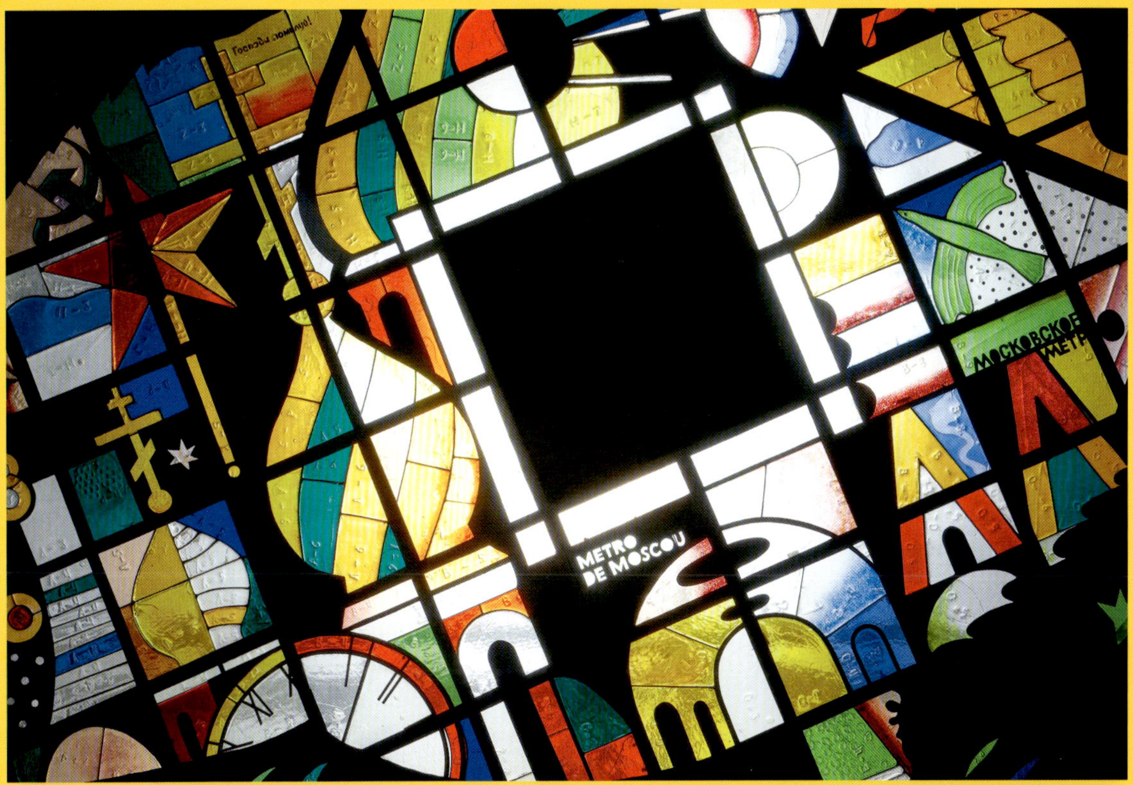
МОСКОВСКОЕ
METRO
DE MOSCOU

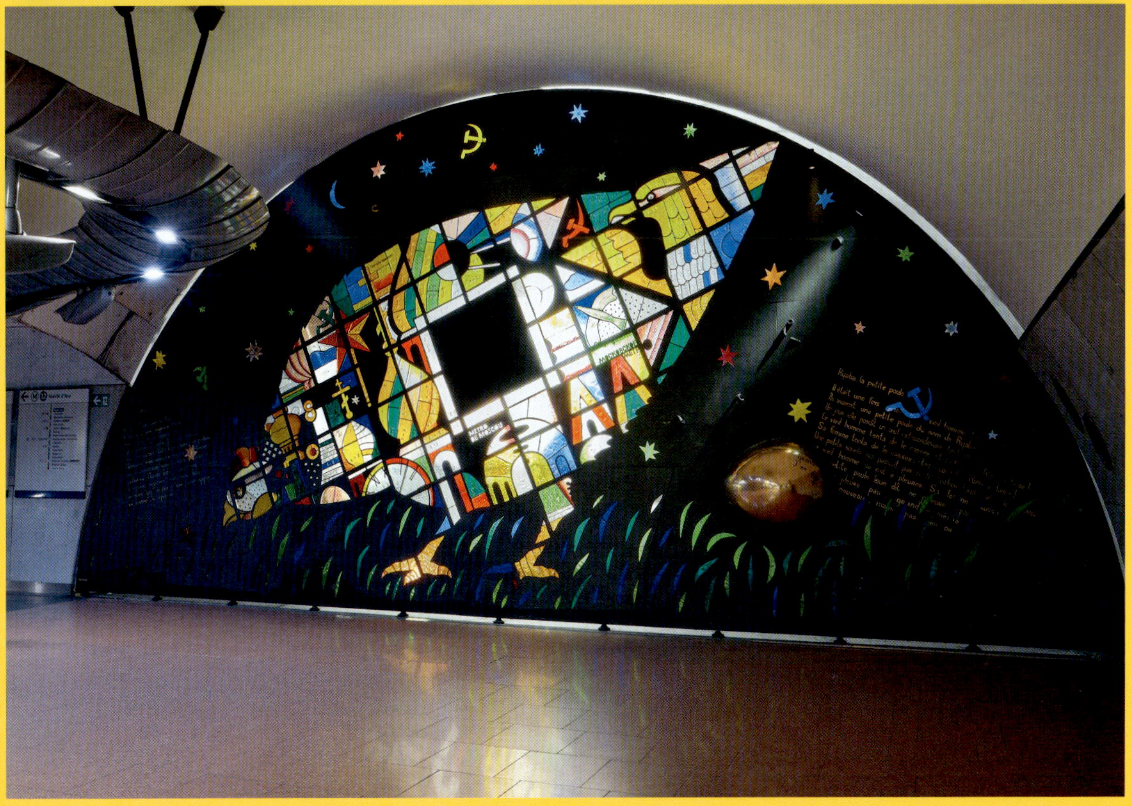

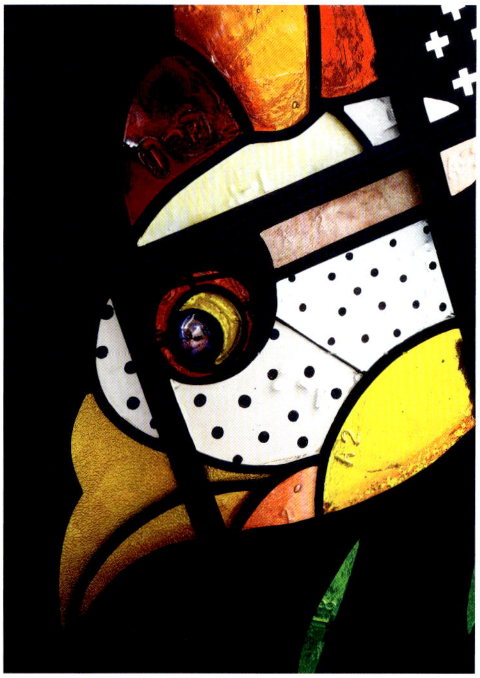

A PAINTER AND ARCHITECT

Born in Minsk, Belorussia, in 1951, Ivan Lubennikov had a childhood in Siberia surrounded by nature, fishing, and hunting. Numerous monuments and architectural achievements mark his career as an artist, including the memorial in the Russian section of the Auschwitz-Birkenau State Museum (1985); the design of the museum dedicated to the poet Vladimir Mayakovsky (1991); and the decoration of three Muscovite metro stations: Mayakovskaya, Sretensky Bulvar, and Slavyansky Bulvar (2005–08). Many of his works were destroyed during the final years of the Soviet regime. His paintings are generally very structured––not surprising given his architectural sensibility. They feature stylized, sensual depictions of the Russian countryside, such as those of his great modernist predecessors Kazimir Malevich and Wassily Kandinsky. Lubennikov is now a renowned artist in Russia, and his work is collected by the world's great museums.

Ryaba la Poule, 2009
Glass and metal
5 × 6 m

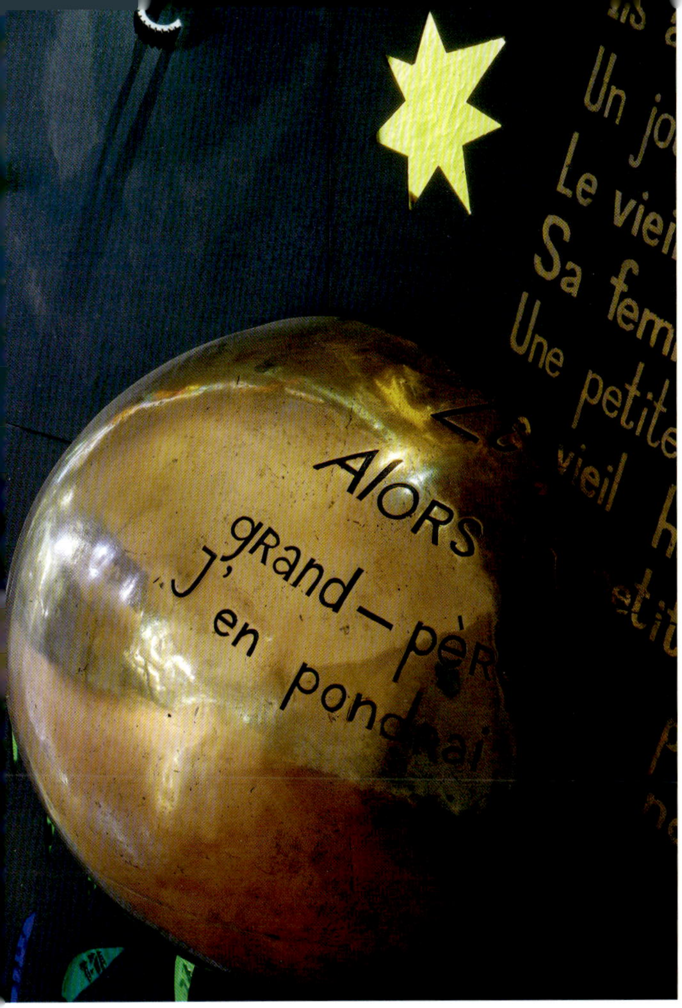
Un jo
Le vieil
Sa fem
Une petite
vieil
Alors
grand-pèr
J'en
en
pond

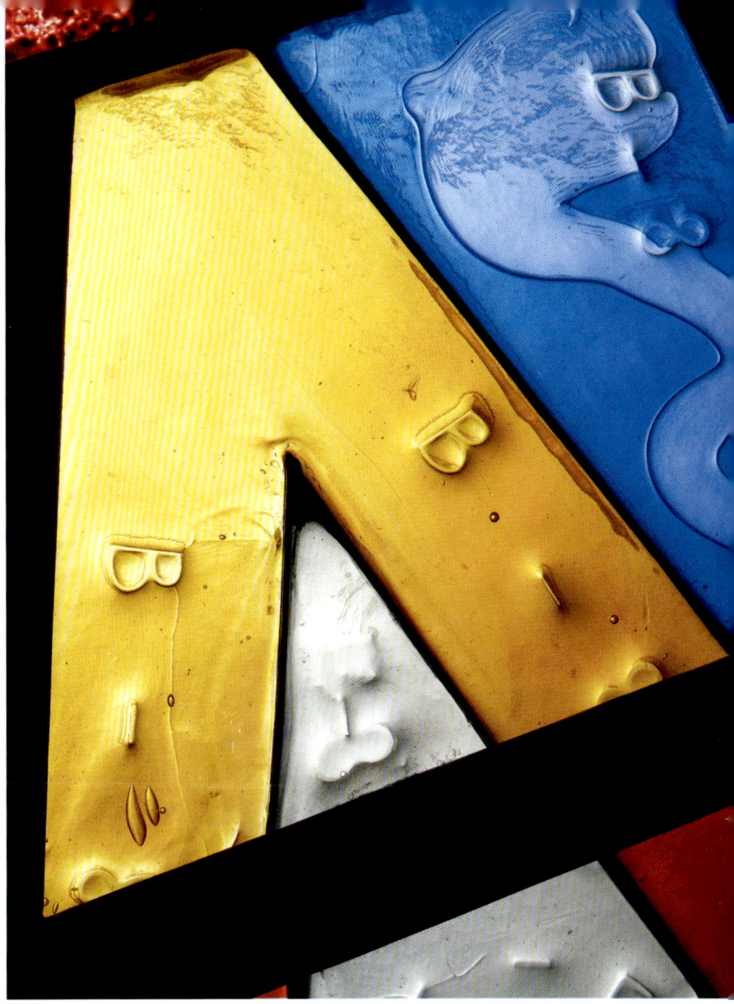

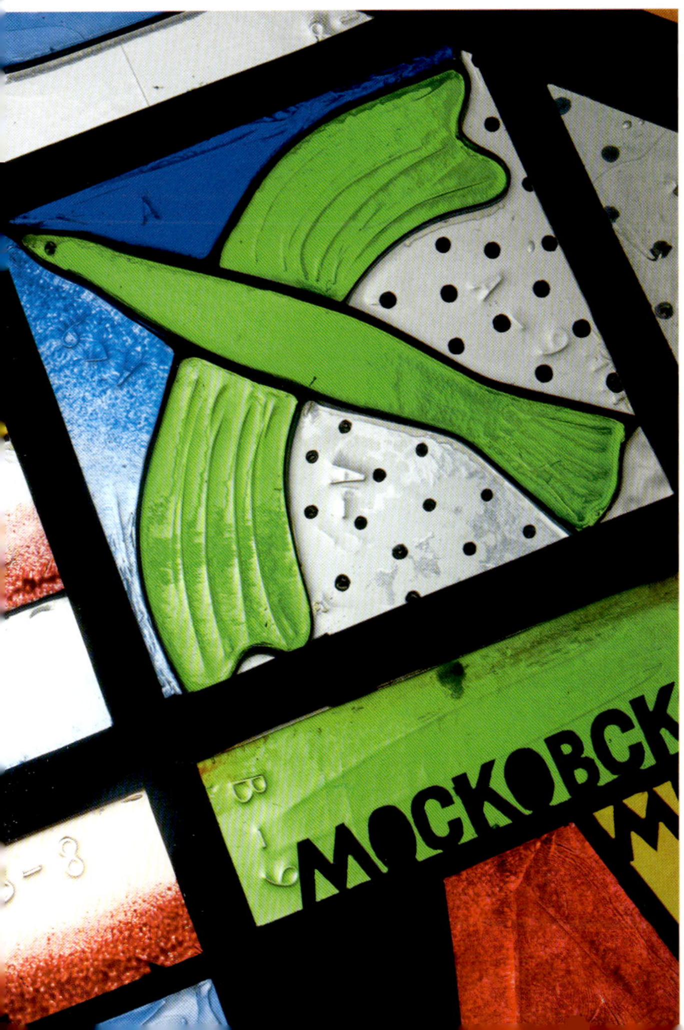
МОСКОВСК

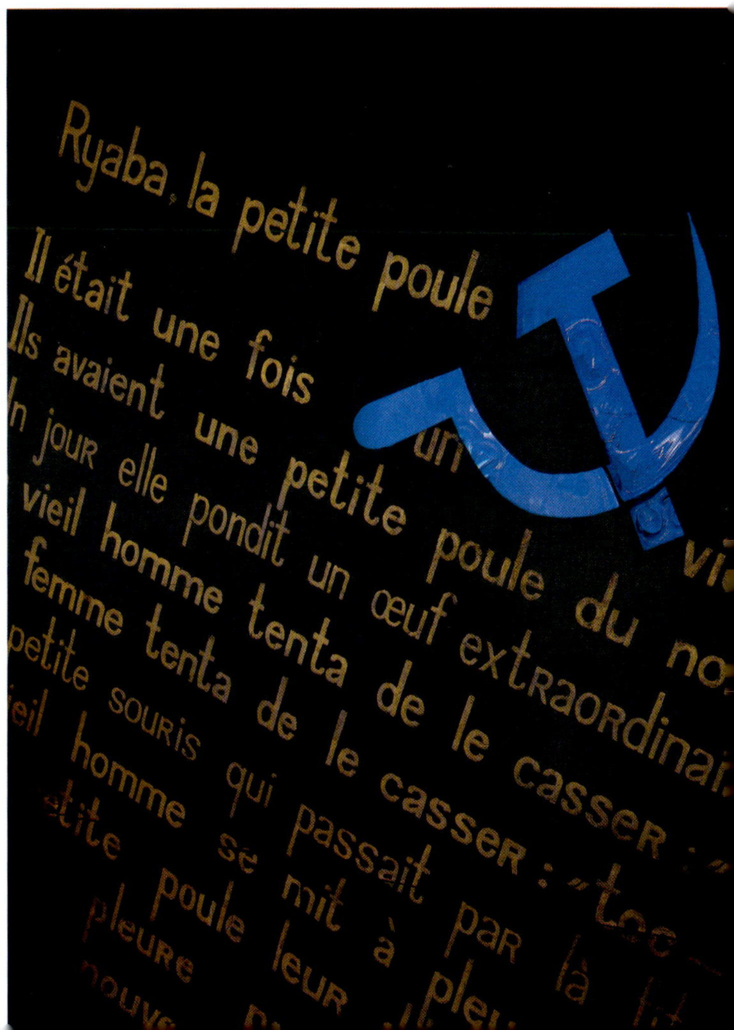
Ryaba, la petite poule
Il était une fois
Ils avaient une petite poule du no
jour elle pondit un œuf extraordinai
vieil homme tenta de le casser
femme tenta de le casser
petite souris qui passait par la

A

Pierre Alferi and Olivier Cadiot
Barricades, 2013, eastern stops (Porte de La Chapelle–Porte d'Ivry), tramway line T3

David d'Angers
Bust of Victor Hugo, 1985, Victor Hugo metro station

B

Jean-Christophe Bailly and Antoine Grumbach
La Pluie de citations, 1998, Bibliothèque François Mitterrand metro station

Philippe Baudelocque
Du corps au fruit, du fruit au corps, 2018, Châtelet–Les Halles RER station

Jean Bazaine
Ailes et Flammes, 1988, Cluny–La Sorbonne metro station

Liliane Bélembert and Odile Jacquot
Fresco, 1989, Bastille metro station

Nikki Bell and Ben Langlands
Call & Response, 2012 Porte de Vincennes station

Mai-Li Bernard
Decorations, 2018, stops from Porte de la Chapelle to Porte d'Asnières, tramway line T3b (north)

Gualtiero Busato
Les Messagers, 1983, Saint-Germain-des-Prés metro station

C

Geneviève Cadieux
La Voix lactée, 2011, Saint-Lazare metro station

Olivier Cadiot and Pierre Alferi
Barricades, 2013, eastern stops (Porte de La Chapelle–Porte d'Ivry), tramway line T3

Manuel Cargaleiro
Azulejo géométrique, 1995 and 2019, Champs-Élysées–Clemenceau metro station

Jean-Paul Chambas
La Fayette et la Révolution, 1991, Chaussée d'Antin–La Fayette metro station

Patrick Corillon
Fables urbaines, les fleurs des Maréchaux, 2006, all stops from Porte de Vincennes to Pont du Garigliano, tramway line T3a (south)
Untitled, 2012, Liège metro station

D

Michel Deverne
Reflets ou Rythmes, 1970, Grande Arche de La Défense RER station

Jacques-Antoine Ducatez
La Bastille à Jaurès, 1989, Jaurès metro station

F

Philippe Favier
P.I.L.I., 2000, Pyramides metro station

Albert Féraud
Reliefs, 1972, Saint-Germain-en-Laye RER station
Relief, 1990, Bagneux RER station

G. Foliot
Wrought-iron railing, 1983, Saint-Germain-des-Prés metro station

G

Thierry Grave
Articulations, 1990, Ourcq metro station

Antoine Grumbach
L'Escalier de signes et de nombres, 1998, Bibliothèque François Mitterrand metro station

Antoine Grumbach and Jean-Christophe Bailly
La Pluie de citations, 1998, Bibliothèque François Mitterrand metro station

Hector Guimard
Metro entrance structures, early twentieth century

H

Daniel Hicter and Marie-Claire Van Vuchelen
Mosaics, 1982, Liège metro station

I

Itsok
Les Secrets de l'Opéra, 2021, An original composition by Victor Nebbiolo di Castri and Valeria Zane Opéra metro station

J

Odile Jacquot and Liliane Bélembert
Fresco, 1989, Bastille metro station

Reynald Jenneret
Bust of Danton, 1992, Odéon metro station

L

Ben Langlands and Nikki Bell
Call & Response, 2012, Porte de Vincennes station

Judy Ledgerwood
Night and Day, 2008, Bir-Hakeim metro station

Jean-Rémy Locret
Frescoes, 1977, Gare de Lyon
1980, Boulogne–Jean Jaurès metro station
1981, La Chapelle metro station
1987, La Courneuve metro station
Untitled, 1986, Nanterre Préfecture RER station

Ivan Lubennikov
Ryaba la Poule, 2009, Madeleine metro station

M

Nino Maiello
La Colombe de Picasso, 1985, Bobigny–Pablo Picasso metro station

Claude Maréchal
Corridor mosaic, 1988, Cluny–La Sorbonne metro station

Hervé Mathieu-Bachelot
Untitled, 1977, Châtelet–Les Halles RER station
Couleur en masses, 1982, Temple metro station
Lumière en éclat, 1982, Cadet metro station
Neige en prisme, 1982, Marcadet-Poissonniers metro station
Cascade de temps, 1985, Grands Boulevards metro station
Untitled, 1991, Créteil–Université metro station

with André Ropion
Bas-relief, 1970, Grande Arche de La Défense RER station
Traits d'union, 1979, Grande Arche de La Défense RER station
Volutes en gerbe, 1981, Grande Arche de La Défense RER station

Hilton McConnico
La Fayette en Amérique, 1989, Chaussée d'Antin–La Fayette metro station

Anita Molinero
Decoration, 2012–13, Porte de La Villette metro station

M.U.R. (collective)
Featuring works by the artists Ardif, Bault, Noon, Petite Poissone, Ratur, Romain Froquet, Stoul, and Tempo Nok. *Street Art*, 2021, corridor between Opéra metro station and Auber RER station

O

Julian Opie
Passage, 2022, Porte de Clichy metro station

Jean-Michel Othoniel
Le Kiosque des noctambules, 2000, Palais-Royal–Musée du Louvre metro station

Guy Outhier
Untitled, 1987, Charles de Gaulle–Étoile RER station
Untitled, 1987, Châtillon–Montrouge metro station
Hommage au général La Fayette, 1988, Cadet metro station
Fresco, 1991, Porte de Pantin metro station

P

Marta Pan
Balustrades, 1972, Auber RER station

Henri Papin
Ceramic tiles, ca. 1934, Pont de Sèvres metro station

Bernard Potel
Bust of Fulgence Bienvenüe, 1998, Montparnasse-Bienvenüe metro station

R

Tobias Rehberger
Je ne suis jamais allé nulle part, 2021, Pont Cardinet metro station

Hugues Reip
Périple, 2013, Mairie de Montrouge metro station

André Ropion
Gutenberg, 1983, Saint-Germain-des-Prés metro station

with Hervé Mathieu-Bachelot
Bas-relief, 1970, Grande Arche de La Défense RER station
Traits d'union, 1979, Grande Arche de La Défense RER station
Volutes en gerbe, 1981, Grande Arche de La Défense RER station

S

Santiago Santos de la Torre
La Pensée et l'âme huchioles, 1997, Palais-Royal–Musée du Louvre station

Carlo Sarrabezolles
Monument à la mémoire des agents du Métropolitain morts pour la France, 1931, Richelieu-Drouot metro station

Françoise Schein
Concorde, 1989–91, Concorde station

François Schuiten
Nautilus, 1994, Arts et Métiers metro station

Ilio Signori
Point de rencontre, 1977, Châtelet–Les Halles RER station

France et Hugues Siptrott
Les Hommes de la Cité, 1992, Esplanade de La Défense metro station

T

Jacques Tissinier
Tissignalisation n°14, 1997, Pyramides and Madeleine metro stations

Barthélémy Toguo
Célébrations, 2017, Château Rouge metro station

Pierre-Yves Trémois
Énergies, 1977, Châtelet–Les Halles RER station

U

Unknown maker
La Prière (copy of the sculpture by Constantin Brancusi), 2001, Madeleine metro station

V

Marie-Claire Van Vuchelen and Daniel Hicter
Mosaics, 1982, Liège metro station

Claude Viseux
Untitled, 1972, Auber RER station

W

Neil Wood
Et toi là, attrape ton étoile, 2017, Charles de Gaulle–Étoile RER station

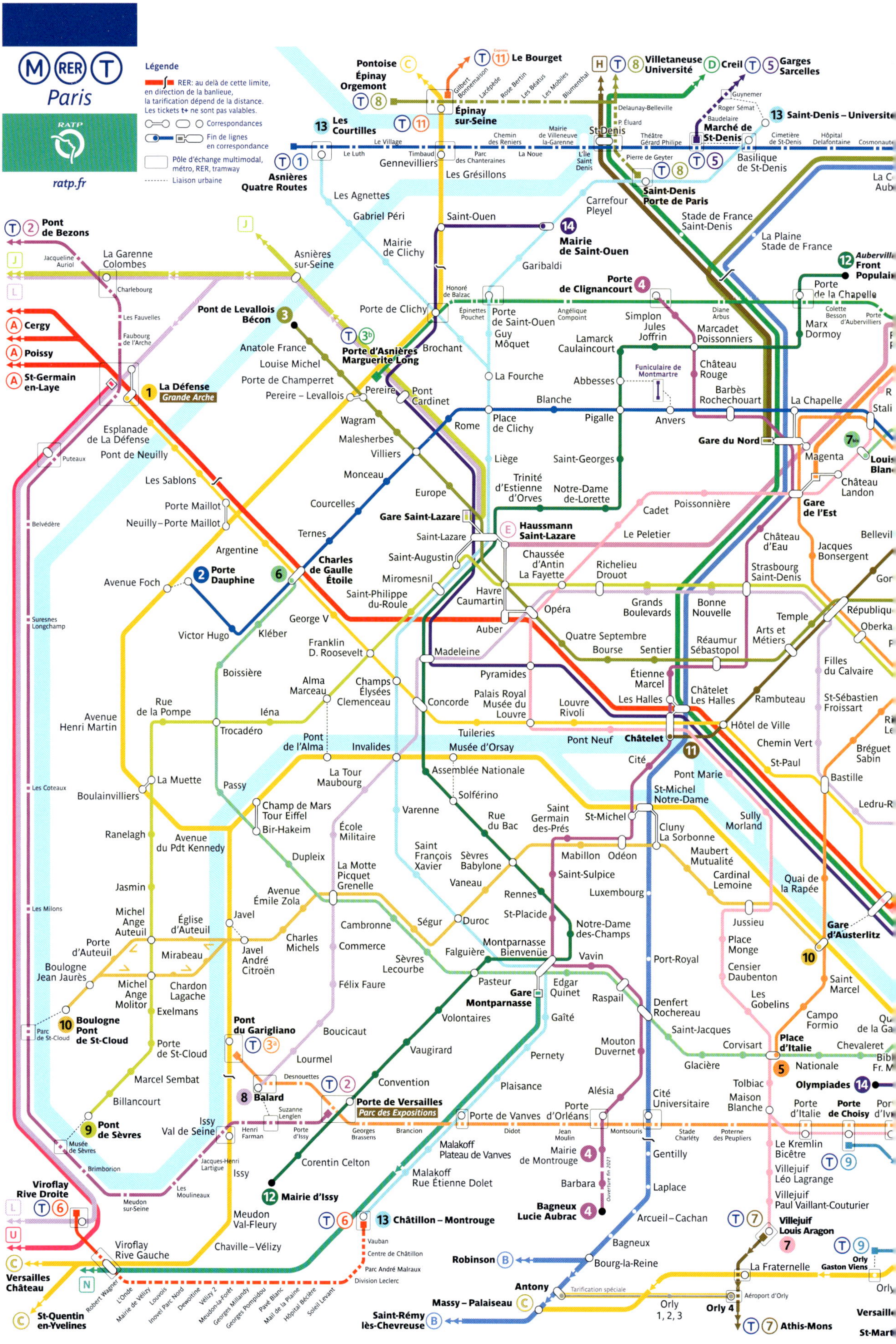

M RER T
Paris
RATP
ratp.fr
Légende
RER: au delà de cette limite, en direction de la banlieue, la tarification dépend de la distance. Les tickets t+ ne sont pas valables.
Correspondances
Fin de lignes en correspondance
Pôle d'échange multimodal, métro, RER, tramway
Liaison urbaine
Pontoise
Épinay
Orgemont
Le Bourget
Gilbert Bonnemaison
Lacépède
Rose Bertin
Les Béatus
Les Mobiles
Blumenthal
Villetaneuse Université
Creil
Garges Sarcelles
Guynemer
Roger Sémat
Baudelaire
Marché de St-Denis
13 Saint-Denis – Université
Delaunay-Belleville
P. Éluard
Théâtre Gérard Philipe
Cimetière de St-Denis
Hôpital Delafontaine
Cosmonautes
Épinay sur-Seine
13 Les Courtilles
Le Village
Le Luth
Timbaud
Chemin des Reniers
Parc des Chanteraines
Mairie de Villeneuve la-Garenne
La Noue
L'Ile Saint Denis
St-Denis
Pierre de Geyter
Basilique de St-Denis
Asnières Quatre Routes
Gennevilliers
Les Grésillons
Saint-Denis Porte de Paris
Carrefour Pleyel
Stade de France Saint-Denis
La Plaine Stade de France
Les Agnettes
Gabriel Péri
Saint-Ouen
14 Mairie de Saint-Ouen
Mairie de Clichy
Garibaldi
12 Aubervilliers Front Populaire
Pont de Bezons
La Garenne Colombes
Jacqueline Auriol
Charlebourg
Asnières sur-Seine
Porte de Clignancourt
Porte de la Chapelle
Les Fauvelles
Faubourg de l'Arche
Pont de Levallois Bécon
Porte de Clichy
Honoré de Balzac
Épinettes Pouchet
Porte de Saint-Ouen
Angélique Compoint
Simplon
Jules Joffrin
Diane Arbus
Colette Besson
Porte d'Aubervilliers
Marx Dormoy
Marcadet Poissonniers
Cergy
Poissy
St-Germain en-Laye
Anatole France
Louise Michel
Porte de Champerret
Pereire – Levallois
Porte d'Asnières Marguerite Long
Brochant
Guy Môquet
Lamarck Caulaincourt
Château Rouge
Funiculaire de Montmartre
Abbesses
La Fourche
La Défense Grande Arche
Pereire
Pont Cardinet
Barbès Rochechouart
La Chapelle
Blanche
Anvers
Pigalle
Place de Clichy
Rome
Wagram
Esplanade de La Défense
Puteaux
Malesherbes
Villiers
Pont de Neuilly
Gare du Nord
Magenta
Liège
Saint-Georges
Monceau
Europe
Trinité d'Estienne d'Orves
Notre-Dame de-Lorette
Les Sablons
Courcelles
Gare Saint-Lazare
Château Landon
Gare de l'Est
Porte Maillot
Cadet
Poissonnière
Neuilly – Porte Maillot
Belvédère
Ternes
Saint-Lazare
Haussmann Saint-Lazare
Le Peletier
Château d'Eau
Jacques Bonsergent
Argentine
Charles de Gaulle Étoile
Saint-Augustin
Chaussée d'Antin La Fayette
Richelieu Drouot
Strasbourg Saint-Denis
Porte Dauphine
Miromesnil
Avenue Foch
Havre Caumartin
Saint-Philippe du-Roule
Opéra
Grands Boulevards
Bonne Nouvelle
Temple
République
Oberkampf
George V
Auber
Arts et Métiers
Suresnes Longchamp
Victor Hugo
Kléber
Franklin D. Roosevelt
Quatre Septembre
Réaumur Sébastopol
Bourse
Sentier
Madeleine
Filles du Calvaire
Boissière
Pyramides
Étienne Marcel
Alma Marceau
Champs Élysées Clemenceau
Palais Royal Musée du Louvre
Louvre Rivoli
Châtelet Les Halles
Les Halles
Rambuteau
St-Sébastien Froissart
Rue de la Pompe
Concorde
Avenue Henri Martin
Iéna
Trocadéro
Hôtel de Ville
Tuileries
Pont de l'Alma
Invalides
Musée d'Orsay
Pont Neuf
Châtelet
Chemin Vert
Bréguet Sabin
Cité
St-Paul
La Tour Maubourg
Assemblée Nationale
Pont Marie
La Muette
Passy
Bastille
St-Michel Notre-Dame
Les Coteaux
Boulainvilliers
Solférino
Champ de Mars Tour Eiffel
Bir-Hakeim
Varenne
Saint Germain des-Prés
Rue du Bac
St-Michel
Sully Morland
Ledru-Rollin
Ranelagh
Avenue du Pdt Kennedy
École Militaire
Cluny La Sorbonne
Saint François Xavier
Sèvres Babylone
Mabillon
Odéon
Maubert Mutualité
Dupleix
La Motte Picquet Grenelle
Saint-Sulpice
Cardinal Lemoine
Quai de la Rapée
Jasmin
Vaneau
Avenue Émile Zola
Rennes
Luxembourg
Les Milons
Michel Ange Auteuil
Église d'Auteuil
Javel
Ségur
Duroc
St-Placide
Jussieu
Porte d'Auteuil
Cambronne
Notre-Dame des-Champs
Place Monge
Gare d'Austerlitz
Charles Michels
Javel André Citroën
Commerce
Montparnasse Bienvenüe
Mirabeau
Falguière
Vavin
Port-Royal
Censier Daubenton
Boulogne Jean Jaurès
Sèvres Lecourbe
Pasteur
Edgar Quinet
Saint Marcel
Michel Ange Molitor
Chardon Lagache
Félix Faure
Gare Montparnasse
Raspail
Denfert Rochereau
Les Gobelins
Exelmans
Campo Formio
Boulogne Pont de St-Cloud
Parc de St-Cloud
Volontaires
Gaîté
Saint-Jacques
Place d'Italie
Pont du Garigliano
Boucicaut
Corvisart
Chevaleret
Porte de St-Cloud
Vaugirard
Mouton Duvernet
Glacière
Nationale
Lourmel
Pernety
Marcel Sembat
Desnouettes
Convention
Plaisance
Alésia
Tolbiac
Olympiades
Billancourt
8 Balard
Porte de Versailles Parc des Expositions
Cité Universitaire
Maison Blanche
Suzanne Lenglen
Porte d'Orléans
Porte d'Italie
Porte de Choisy
Porte d'Ivry
Pont de Sèvres
Issy Val de Seine
Henri Farman
Porte d'Issy
Georges Brassens
Brancion
Porte de Vanves
Didot
Jean Moulin
Montsouris
Stade Charléty
Poterne des Peupliers
Musée de Sèvres
Brimborion
Jacques-Henri Lartigue
Issy
Corentin Celton
Malakoff Plateau de Vanves
Mairie de Montrouge
Gentilly
Le Kremlin Bicêtre
Villejuif Léo Lagrange
Viroflay Rive Droite
Les Moulineaux
Meudon sur-Seine
Malakoff Rue Étienne Dolet
Barbara
Laplace
Villejuif Paul Vaillant-Couturier
12 Mairie d'Issy
Ouverture fin 2021
Meudon Val-Fleury
13 Châtillon – Montrouge
Bagneux Lucie Aubrac
Arcueil – Cachan
Villejuif Louis Aragon
Vauban
Centre de Châtillon
Parc André Malraux
Division Leclerc
Viroflay Rive Gauche
Chaville – Vélizy
Bagneux
Robinson
Bourg-la-Reine
La Fraternelle
Gaston Viens
Orly
Versailles Château
Robert Wagner
L'Onde
Mairie de Vélizy
Louvois
Inovel Parc Nord
Dewoitine
Vélizy 2
Meudon-la-Forêt
Georges Millandy
Georges Pompidou
Pavé Blanc
Mail de la Plaine
Hôpital Béclère
Soleil Levant
Antony
Tarification spéciale
Aéroport d'Orly
Massy – Palaiseau
Orly 1, 2, 3
Orly 4
Saint-Rémy lès-Chevreuse
Athis-Mons
St-Quentin en-Yvelines
Versailles

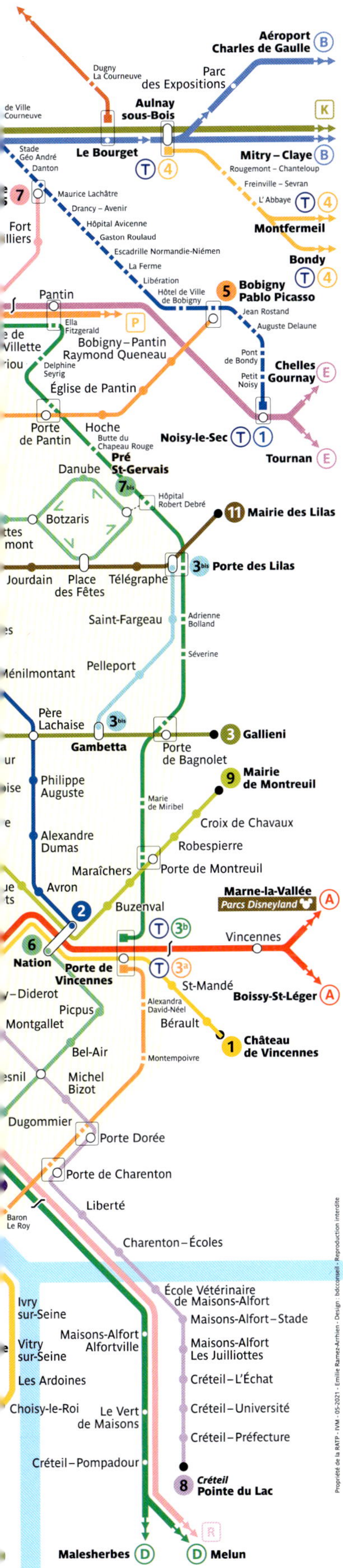
Aéroport
Charles de Gaulle
Dugny
La Courneuve
Parc
des Expositions
Aulnay
sous-Bois
Stade
Géo André
Le Bourget
Mitry – Claye
Rougemont – Chanteloup
Freinville – Sevran
L'Abbaye
Danton
Maurice Lachâtre
Drancy – Avenir
Hôpital Avicenne
Gaston Roulaud
Escadrille Normandie-Niémen
La Ferme
Libération
Hôtel de Ville
de Bobigny
Montfermeil
Bondy
Bobigny
Pablo Picasso
Jean Rostand
Auguste Delaune
Pantin
Ella
Fitzgerald
Bobigny – Pantin
Raymond Queneau
Delphine
Seyrig
Église de Pantin
Pont
de Bondy
Petit
Noisy
Chelles
Gournay
Porte
de Pantin
Hoche
Butte du
Chapeau Rouge
Noisy-le-Sec
Tournan
Pré
St-Gervais
Danube
Hôpital
Robert Debré
Mairie des Lilas
Botzaris
Jourdain
Place
des Fêtes
Télégraphe
Porte des Lilas
Saint-Fargeau
Adrienne
Bolland
Séverine
Ménilmontant
Pelleport
Père
Lachaise
Gambetta
Gallieni
Porte
de Bagnolet
Philippe
Auguste
Mairie
de Montreuil
Marie
de Miribel
Croix de Chavaux
Alexandre
Dumas
Robespierre
Maraîchers
Porte de Montreuil
Avron
Marne-la-Vallée
Parcs Disneyland
Buzenval
Vincennes
Nation
Porte de
Vincennes
St-Mandé
Boissy-St-Léger
Alexandra
David-Néel
Bérault
Picpus
Château
de Vincennes
Montgallet
Bel-Air
Montempoivre
Michel
Bizot
Dugommier
Porte Dorée
Porte de Charenton
Liberté
Baron
Le Roy
Charenton – Écoles
École Vétérinaire
de Maisons-Alfort
Ivry
sur-Seine
Maisons-Alfort – Stade
Maisons-Alfort
Alfortville
Vitry
sur-Seine
Maisons-Alfort
Les Juilliottes
Les Ardoines
Créteil – L'Échat
Choisy-le-Roi
Le Vert
de Maisons
Créteil – Université
Créteil – Préfecture
Créteil – Pompadour
Créteil
Pointe du Lac
Malesherbes
Melun

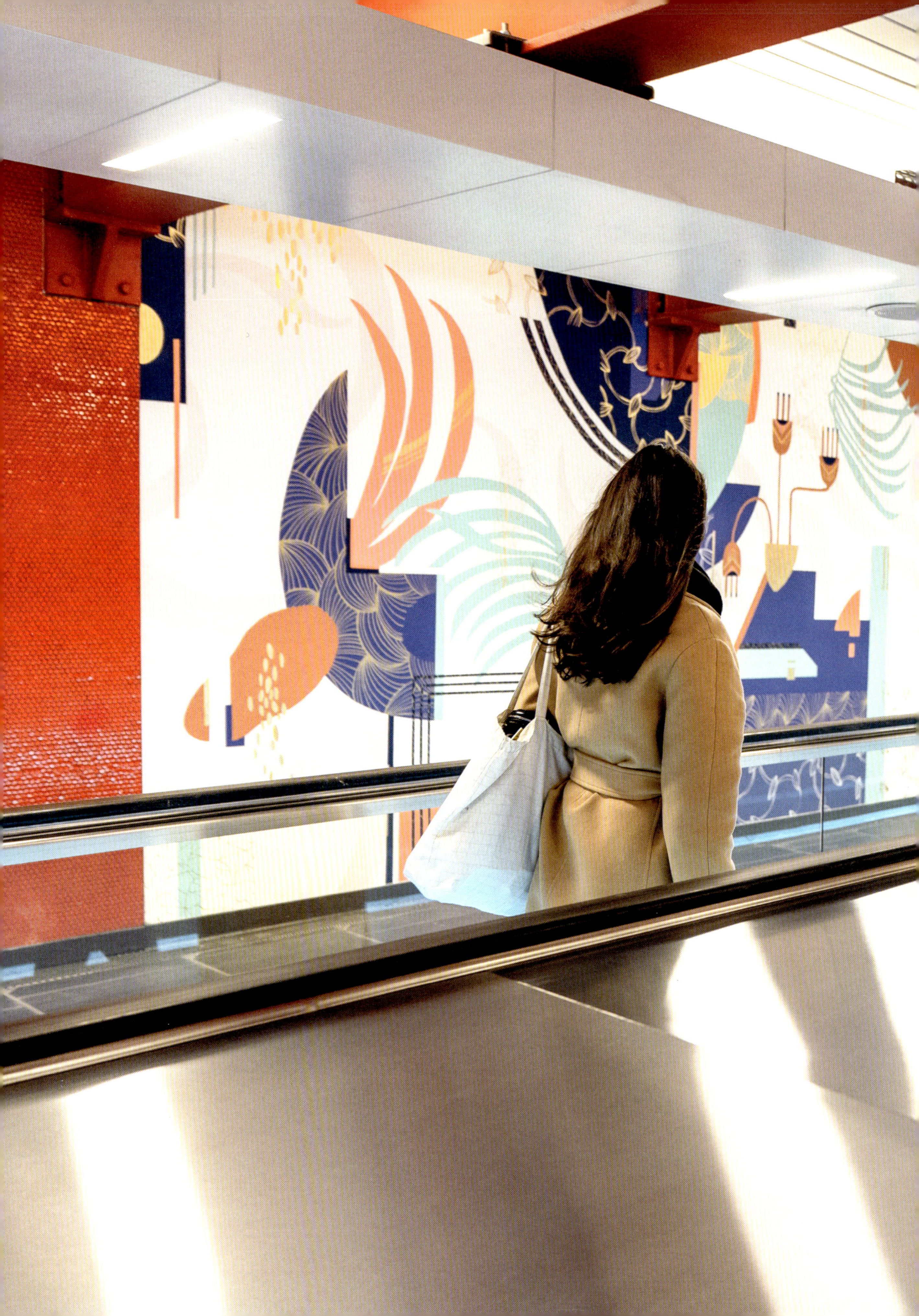

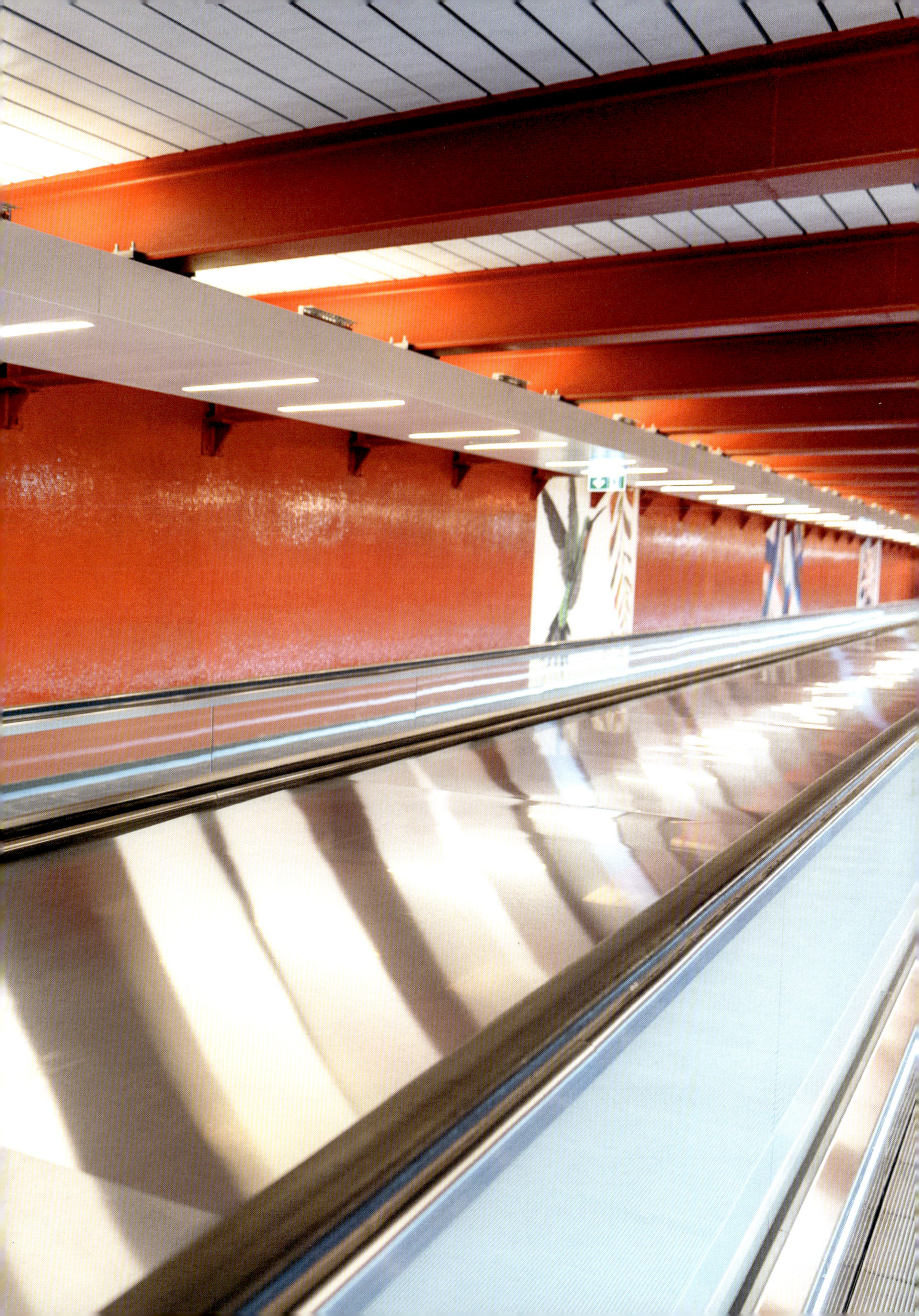

Acknowledgments

This book was produced on the initiative of the RATP and under its supervision.

Éditions de La Martinière would warmly like to thank Anaïs Lançon, director of Group communications, commitment, and brand strategy, for her trust and support; Mariah Camargo de Staal and Émilie Potonet-Stec, who oversaw the editorial process; and all those at the RATP who contributed to the production of this volume, particularly Didier Bernard, Olivier Coudert, Xavier Gastineau, Yo Kaminagai, Jean-Michel Leblanc, Laurence Loy, and Estelle Revesche-Pucharski.

The publisher and the RATP would both like to thank the Byart agency for its support in the creation of this book.

Anaël Pigeat would like to express her gratitude to the artists for the conversations she had with them during the preparation of this book. She also extends her warmest thanks to Corinne Schmidt, Charlotte Court, and the Éditions de La Martinière team, as well as to Nathalie Cogis and Vadim Grigoryan de Grainville for the fruitful exchanges that took place throughout the elaboration of the project.

A big thank you to Nathalie Mayevski for being such a wonderful editor, as well as to Claire Lemoine and Virginie Mahieux. This book would not exist without the valuable support of the RATP team, Mariah Camargo de Staal, Émilie Potonet-Stec and Yo Kaminagai.

Photographic Credits

All photographs by Philippe Garcia, except

page 8: © RATP—RATP Collection
page 9: © Bruno Marguerite RATP / "La RATP Invite l'artiste JR"
pages 10 top, 156–57: © RATP—Xavier Chibout
page 10 bottom: © RATP—Noam Cilirie
page 11 top: © Hamdi Chref RATP / "La RATP Invite Sebastião Salgado—Amazônia"
pages 12–13, 55, 97, 100, 126–27, 128, 129, 134–35, 137, 140–41: © RATP—Bruno Marguerite
page 35 top: © Hamdi Chref
page 65: © RATP—Antoine Jallas
pages 58, 96: © RATP—Jean-François Mauboussin
page 121: © Julian Opie Studio

Plan (pages 154–55): © RATP All rights reserved—Courtesy RATP

Artists' Rights

page 9: © JR / pages 10 top, 156–57: LE M.U.R.

page 11: © Sebastião Salgado, photographs from the exhibition "Salgado Amazônia," Philharmonie de Paris

pages 12–13: Arte Charpentier, Abbès Tahir with thanks to Paul de la Forêt Divonne

pages 30, 32–33, 34: © Biecher Architectes and MAD Architects

© Adagp, Paris 2021 for the artworks by Jean-Michel Othoniel, Langlands & Bell, Barthélémy Toguo, Jean Bazaine, Françoise Schein, Philippe Favier, Carlo Sarrabezolles, Philippe Baudelocque, Pierre-Yves Trémois, Hugues Reip, Jacques Tissinier, and Manuel Cargaleiro

© Courtesy Julian Opie Studio / Adagp, Paris 2021

Editorial consultants
Nathalie Cogis and Vadim Grigoryan de Grainville, Byart

Coordinating editor
Nathalie Mayevski

Graphic design
Laurence Maillet

Translation from the French
(except for the Julian Opie interview)
Chrisoula Petridis

Photoengraving
Escourbiac

Distributed in 2022 by Abrams, an imprint of ABRAMS

Printed and bound in France by Escourbiac in October 2021
ISBN: 9781419761041
Dépôt légal: October 2021
Abrams® is a registered trademark of Harry N. Abrams, Inc.

ABRAMS
The Art of Books

195 Broadway
New York, NY 10007
abramsbooks.com